# Guide to Reference and Information Sources in Plant Biology

**Recent Titles in Reference Sources in Science and Technology**
*Judy Matthews, Series Editor*

American Military History: A Guide to Reference and Information Sources
*Daniel K. Blewett*

Education: A Guide to Reference and Information Sources
*Nancy Patricia O'Brien*

Northern Africa: A Guide to Reference and Information Sources
*Paula Youngman Skreslet*

Zoological Sciences: A Guide to Reference and Information Sources
*Diane Schmidt*

Guide to Information Sources in Mathematics and Statistics
*Martha A. Tucker and Nancy D. Anderson*

Computer Science and Computing: A Guide to the Literature
*Michael Knee*

# Guide to Reference and Information Sources in Plant Biology

## Third Edition

Diane Schmidt, Melody M. Allison, Kathleen A. Clark, Pamela F. Jacobs, and Maria A. Porta

Reference Sources in Science and Technology
*Judith Matthews, Series Editor*

LIBRARIES
UNLIMITED
A Member of the Greenwood Publishing Group

Westport, Connecticut • London

**Library of Congress Cataloging-in-Publication Data**

Guide to reference and information sources in plant biology /
by Diane Schmidt . . . [et al]. —3rd ed.
    p. cm.—(Reference sources in science and technology)
  Includes bibliographical references and indexes.
  ISBN 1-56308-968-8 (alk. paper)
 1. Botany—Bibliography.  2. Botany—Reference books—Bibliography.
3. Botany—Information services—Directories.  4. Botany—Databases
—Directories.  I. Schmidt, Diane, 1956—  II. Title.  III. Series: Reference
sources in science and technology series.
Z5351.G85 2006
[QK45.2]
016.58—dc22     2005030837

British Library Cataloguing in Publication Data is available.

Library of Congress Catalog Card Number: 2005030837
ISBN: 1–56308–968–8

First published in 2006

Libraries Unlimited, 88 Post Road West, Westport, CT 06881
A Member of the Greenwood Publishing Group, Inc.
www.lu.com

Printed in the United States of America

The paper used in this book complies with the
Permanent Paper Standard issued by the National
Information Standards Organization (Z39.48–1984).

10 9 8 7 6 5 4 3 2 1

# CONTENTS

**V**

# PREFACE TO THE THIRD EDITION

This guide is the third edition of *Guide to Information Sources in the Botanical Sciences*\*, by Elisabeth B. Davis and Diane Schmidt. This edition is arranged by topic rather than by material type (bibliographic sources, handbooks, etc.) as in the first and second editions. Also, the second edition was written just as the first Web browser became available and at a time when very few electronic resources had been published, so the third edition includes greatly expanded coverage of major Web resources for plant biology. Like its predecessor, *Guide to Reference and Information Sources in Plant Biology* focuses on core materials for plant biologists and excludes agriculture and gardening resources. The emphasis is on authoritative Web sites and recent books and journals that are in print. Important classic resources are included even if they are no longer in print.

The authors wish to acknowledge the Research and Publication Committee of the University of Illinois at Urbana-Champaign Library, which provided support for the completion of this guide, and Alison M. Scott for her editorial assistance.

\* Elisabeth B. Davis is the sole author of the first edition, and Elisabeth Davis and Diane Schmidt are the authors of the second edition.

# 1
# Introduction to the Literature of Plant Biology

## The Study of Plants

Botany, the study of plants, has been of great importance and a major influence on humans ever since the first stirrings of intelligent life. The botanical sciences encompass areas from the applied to the theoretical, the descriptive to the functional, the ancient to the modern, the tiny algae to the giant redwoods. In the early centuries, human life was sustained by plants, which were used for food, drink, shelter, and weapons, and indirectly, for clothing. The domestication of plants and the origins of agriculture marked the beginnings of civilization.

In the sixth edition of *Biology of Plants* (Raven, Evert, and Eichhorn, 1999), botany is defined as that part of biology that deals with plants and, by tradition, with prokaryotes, viruses, fungi, and algae. In this book, however, only fungi, algae, and "true" plants will be covered. Only a few kinds of organisms (plants, algae, and some bacteria) obtain their food by photosynthesis, that is, make their own food from the raw materials of carbon dioxide and water using light as an energy source. Photosynthesis converts energy to food and produces oxygen as a by-product. Because plants are producers of food and oxygen, they are indispensable for life on Earth.

Classification of plant life has been important ever since ancient philosophers began organizing observations and facts into a knowledge framework. Plants almost always have been recognized as a distinct entity, quite different from animals or minerals. For much of history, life had been divided into two kingdoms: the Plant Kingdom and the Animal Kingdom. Various refinements have evolved leading to models containing four to six kingdoms, depending on the criteria used. Until recently the most commonly used system was the Five

**1**

Kingdom model, including Prokaryotae, Protoctista, Fungi, Plantae, and Animalia, but since the late 1990s the Three Domain system has gained general acceptance. This system consists of three large domains above the kingdom level: the Archaebacteria, Eubacteria, and Eukaryota. Plants, fungi, and animals all fall under the Eukaryota domain. Within the Eukaryota, plants are in the Kingdom Plantae, which does not include bacteria, algae, or fungi.

The scope of plant biology is exceedingly broad. The major botanical subdivisions of morphology, physiology, ecology, and taxonomy (also called classification or systematics) may be further broken down into plant anatomy, cytology, histology, development, biochemistry, biophysics, bacteriology, genetics, mycology, paleobotany, pathology, pharmacognosy, ethnobotany, and other more esoteric specialties. Botany impacts the arts of weaving, painting, and decoration; scientific disciplines, including medicine, pharmacology, and organic chemistry; and applied work in agriculture, horticulture, and forestry. Important tools used in the study of botany range from microscopy, staining techniques, gas and paper chromatography, electrophoresis, spectroscopy, molecular and tissue analysis, field data, carbon 14 dating, and bioinformatics to organized research centers such as the Genomics Institute, the herbarium, the botanical garden, and the library.

Although the Greek and Roman philosophers laid the early foundations for the science of botany (Morton, 1981), its economic and medicinal usefulness was established even earlier by the Assyrians, Chinese, Egyptians, and Hindus, who had knowledge of plant cultivation, the medicinal and hallucinatory properties of plants, and production methods for food, beverages, and spices. Aristotle was one of the first Western philosophers who wrote about plants, but Theophrastus, Dioscorides, and Pliny the Elder were the main botanical writers of antiquity. Theophrastus is generally given credit for being the founder of botany; Dioscorides wrote one of the earliest herbals describing and illustrating medicinal plants; Pliny the Elder produced the 37-volume *Historia Naturalis*, including 16 volumes on botany. Although various Roman philosophers also wrote on botanical subjects, their emphasis was on farming, not scientific inquiry.

During the Dark Ages, scientific observation of all kinds declined, and it was not until the fifteenth and sixteenth centuries that the study of botany again flourished with the production of handbooks and catalogs by such naturalists as Otto Brunfels, Hieronymus Bosch, Leonard Fuchs, William Turner, and John Gerard, to name a few of the early herbalists. The seventeenth and eighteenth centuries were the age of collectors and classifiers, and descriptive botany thrived in this atmosphere. During the eighteenth century, botany was established as a pure science, with experimenters and classifiers such as Gaspard Bauhin, Joseph Priestley, Jan Ingen-Housz, John Ray, and Carolus Linnaeus making great contributions to plant anatomy, plant physiology, plant chemistry, and taxonomy.

Linnaeus's career marked a watershed in the history of botany. He was a teacher, a writer, a collector, a proselytizer with hundreds of correspondents and disciples, and an inventor of a system of binomial nomenclature that is still used today by modern plant taxonomists. His *Species Plantarum* (1753) together with his *Genera Plantarum* (5th ed., 1754) has been accepted by international agreement among botanists as the starting point for the nomenclature of plants in general. Linnaeus was not an experimentalist; in his view, the foundations of botany were twofold: classification and nomenclature. He exemplified this spirit with enthusiasm. Linnaeus not only marked the end of an era; he also heralded the beginning of modern botany.

If great men marked the earlier epochs, it is fair to say that after 1860, botany was marked by great ideas. Charles Darwin's theory of evolution by natural selection and Gregor Mendel's laws of heredity both had great impact on botany. From that time on there was a gradual linking of the divisions of descriptive, morphological, and functional botany. This greater emphasis on the physiological aspects led to a devaluation of systematics to the point that the great plant taxonomist J. D. Hooker felt the need to defend the value of taxonomy as far back as the 1860s (Browne, 2001), a need that many modern taxonomists also echo.

The rise of plant cytology, ecology, genetics, biochemistry, and other inter-related and interdependent botanical sciences began in the twentieth century, nurtured by the revolutions in biological thinking and encouraged by the success of federal funding, team research, and a myriad of new biotechnological techniques. Somerville (2000), for instance, observed that most of the major advances in plant biology in the twentieth century could be explained by advances in instrumentation and techniques, advances in cell and molecular biology, and the discovery of the similarity between plant and nonplant genes. Raikhel (2001) observed that the speed of advancement in plant biology has accelerated in the previous 25 years due to three major advances: the development of molecular biology, the development of transgenic techniques, and the adoption of *Arabidopsis* as a model organism. All these tendencies are expected to continue into the future, although, as Bazzaz (2001) stated, there will be a need to modify the training of plant biologists to emphasize these techniques.

Despite the obvious health of plant biology research and our recent gains in understanding and utilizing plants, plant biologists feel under siege to some extent. Systematic botanists, like their counterparts for microbial and animal taxonomy, find that funding has shifted away from classical taxonomy. Prather et al. (2004a), for instance, reported data showing that the rate of local plant collecting has declined significantly over the past 40 years in more than two-thirds of all North American herbaria, even the largest ones. In a subsequent commentary on their findings (Prather et al., 2004b), the authors described a number of reasons why this decline is such a problem. Despite the general impression that we know all there is to know about the flora of North America, it is changing rapidly for a number of reasons, and many regions have not been extensively studied for a long time. The authors attributed the decline to changing priorities within systematics away from collecting toward phylogenetics; a change in emphasis from collecting in temperate regions to poorly studied tropical regions; and shifting priorities and limited funding at the herbaria themselves.

Plant biology, as a distinct department or field, may also be in trouble. Sundberg (2004) reported on a survey of botany departments across the United States. He found that plant biology departments were increasingly subsumed into other departments or units; distinct plant biology departments were fewer in number and restricted to large research universities. Plant biology courses were being offered at fewer comprehensive universities and liberal arts colleges as well, and enrollment was generally down.

# The Literature of Plant Biology

Botanical literature mirrors the development of the literature of other biological disciplines, which, in turn, mirrors the growth of the literature of science as a whole. The growth of scientific literature shows a gradual progression from the time of the ancients, through the Dark Ages, to the invention of the printing press by Gutenberg in the fifteenth century. Until that time scientific botanical literature, composed mostly of herbals and descriptive writing, was not widely available. After the invention of the printing press the printed word spread rapidly, with the first English language journal serving scientists, *Philosophical Transactions of the Royal Society of London*, established in 1665 (the French *Journal des Scavans* had debuted a couple of months earlier). By 1800 there were 100 scientific journals, a number that had grown to an incredible 10,000 by 1900 and included such important botanical abstracting and indexing publications as *Botanisches Centralblatt*, *Justs's Botanischer Jahresbericht*, and *Zeitschrift für Pflanzenkrankheiten*, which helped keep the botanists of the day up to date in their reading. Early botanists relied on the German abstracting and indexing tools. *Botanical Abstracts* only began in 1918 and then merged with *Abstracts of Bacteriology* to form *Biological Abstracts* in 1926. For a very interesting and informative discussion on the historical background of scientific communication in the life sciences, see Kronick (1985). In his book, Kronick traces the development of scientific literature from its oral roots to transmission by writing, printing, scholarly letters between scientific peers, newsletter columns, scientific journals, and societies.

Since the early 1900s, science and the literature that must accompany it have grown at an astonishing rate. During the past three centuries, there has been exponential growth in scientific literature (de Solla Price, 1963). Federally funded research, large research laboratories, worldwide scientific research programs, and numerous specialist journals all produced a doubling of the periodical literature every 10 to 15 years during the twentieth century. Since World War II, scientific literature has grown logarithmically, with technological advances in electronic communication and storage having significant consequences on the future of scientific communication.

## Characteristics of Plant Biology Literature

Whether electronic or in print, biological literature can be described in various ways. Kronick (1985) bases his discussion on the distinguishing parameters of size and growth; distribution by country, subject, and language; scatter and use; obsolescence and redundancy; and writing and publishing cycles. The matter is further complicated by the discrepancies that occur between various studies conducted over time. Although the characteristics of the botanical literature do conform overall to the qualities of scientific literature in general, it may be more meaningful to describe the botanical literature in a more specific manner.

During the 1980s, information scientist and publisher Eugene Garfield wrote several essays on the distinctive qualities of the botanical literature. He stated that it has an annual growth rate of 3%, has a doubling time of 25.5 years, and relies more on the older literature than does a faster moving field such as biochemistry (Garfield, 1979). The average number of references per article in plant biology was about 12, compared to 20 in biomedicine (Garfield, 1980). Botanists also cited more book chapters than the average in *Science Citation Index* (Garfield, 1981b). In general, botanists cite life and physical scientists heavily because botanists use methodology developed in the biochemical and molecular biology fields to solve botanical problems (Garfield, 1989). However, the reverse is not true, although many fundamental discoveries in basic biological science were made by botanists (Garfield, 1981a). For example, a number of Nobel prizes have been awarded for plant-related research, from Richard M. Willstätter's 1915 Chemistry Prize for research on plant pigments to Barbara McClintock's 1983 Physiology or Medicine Prize for the discovery of mobile genetic elements in maize. A botanist even won the Peace Prize in 1970 (Norman Borlaug for his Green Revolution).

One way to discuss botanical literature is to divide it into two parts: the descriptive and the functional (Lawrence, 1970). Descriptive botanical literature is primarily used by taxonomists, plant anatomists, and ecologists. It is cumulative and of importance whenever and wherever it occurs, from the fifteenth century's incunabula to last year's monographs, bulletins, or journals. It is a vast literature that is worldwide in scope, multilingual in nature, and chronologically inclusive. The functional botanical literature, on the other hand, is used in such subdisciplines as plant physiology and molecular biology. It depends almost entirely on current serial literature for the most recent information on original research. Functional literature may be found in a wide spectrum of journals and draws from a broad range of other disciplines such as biochemistry. It can be very expensive to obtain due to its wide disciplinary scope and prolific rate of growth.

The descriptive literature described by Lawrence is used primarily by taxonomists. Delendick (1990) examined the citation patterns found in three systematic botany journals (*Brittonia*, *Systematic Botany*, and *Taxon*). Not surprisingly, the author found that many of the references were to quite old materials. About two-thirds of the cited articles were more than 10 years old, and about a quarter were from before 1900. The literature of systematic botany was also quite diffuse, reflecting a core of anywhere from one and a half to three times the size of the core of the hard sciences.

Plant biology tends to be considered a fringe or terminal subdiscipline, not as central or important as research into animals or microbes. For instance, no botanists were included in the list of the 250 most-cited authors for 1977 (Garfield, 1980). When this was pointed out, Garfield's speculation on the cause included the following: 1) many leading botanists were forced by the lack of funding to leave the field of more traditional work for molecular or cell biology; 2) botany is highly diversified, and such very specific areas may not be citing each other; 3) the primary author bias may be significant in botany if senior botanists list students as first author of significant papers; and 4) botany is not a basic science but, instead, is a specialized field that builds on the basic sciences of chemistry and physics.

Citation rates between subdisciplines partly confirm this impression of a lack of centrality. Marton (1983) compared citation patterns in biochemistry and plant physiology journals and found that whereas plant physiologists frequently cited biochemistry journals, the reverse was not true, and yet the two fields had similar patterns of citing material that was more than 10 years old. Biochemical articles contained about 27 citations compared to about 21 for plant physiology articles. Using data from 1955 to 1986, Garfield (1989) created a list of 25 highly cited papers in plant sciences and also developed a list of 80 articles most often cited in plant science core journals. He found that 60% of the cited articles dealt with plant science subjects, while the other 40% were methodology papers. Garfield also found that cited plant science articles had a cited half-life of 6.8 years, the same as the overall average cited half-life in the entire *Science Citation Index*, but of greater age than articles in fast-moving fields such as immunology (4.3 years) or biochemistry and molecular biology (5.4 years).

More recently, it was reported that it took about twice as many articles to account for half the field's citations in the areas of plant and animal sciences than in fields such as computer science or molecular biology (Anonymous, 1999). According to these data, 9.21% of articles in plant and animal sciences accounts for half the citations in the fields, compared to 6.68% for molecular biology. In addition, the percent of never cited articles in plant and animal sciences was 25.79% compared to molecular biology's 14.66%, but in line with noncitation rates in ecology (25.44%). In general, there seemed to be an inverse correlation between the degree of concentration of citations in a field and the noncitation rate.

The *Journal Citations Reports,* or *JCR,* (2003) provides other insights into the literature of plant biology. Review serials such as the *Annual Review of Plant Biology* have among the highest impact rankings (importance of a journal based on the number of times that articles in that journal have been cited) for botanical serials. Five out of the top ten journals in the list of Plant Sciences in 2003 were review periodicals, which is very similar to the rankings of reviews in other biological fields.

In 2003, the highest-ranking serial reporting original research was *Plant Cell*, ranked third. Of the other top 10 journals in 2003 (in descending order: *Annual Review of Plant Biology; Trends in Plant Science; Plant Cell; Current Opinion in Plant Biology; Annual Review of Phytopathology; Plant Journal; Plant Physiology; Plant Molecular Biology; Critical Reviews in Plant Sciences; Plant Cell and Environment*), the five journals reporting original research covered plant physiology, molecular, and cellular biology. The top systematics journal, *Systematic Botany*, ranked 25, closely followed by *Botanical Review* at 29 and *Annals of the Missouri Botanical Garden* at 30. The highest-ranking plant ecology journal, *Journal of Vegetation Science*, came in at 35 out of 136 titles. Of course, as mentioned earlier, many plant biologists publish in the non–plant biology journals such as *Cell* and *Ecology*.

It is interesting to compare these titles with the top 21 botany titles reported by Garfield (1976). Based on 1974 data, the top 10 titles were *Annual Review of Plant Physiology; Botanical Review; Planta; Plant Physiology; Annual Review of Phytopathology; Physiologia Plantarum; Journal of Experimental Botany; Journal of Phycology; American Journal of Botany;* and *Zeitschrift für Pflanzenphysiologie*. Although both *Annual Review* titles are included, all other journals either are general botanical titles, cover specific taxa, or cover either plant diseases or physiology. Plant molecular biology titles are not to be found in this early list, and six out of the top 10 titles from 2003 were not yet in existence in 1974.

# The Future of Plant Biology Literature

The future of botanical literature will surely parallel the future of other forms of the biological literature. Most plant biology journals are available electronically, though small regional publications and specialized systematics journals lag behind. However, journals such as the *American Fern Journal* and *Economic Botany* are participating in the BioOne program (http://www.bioone.org). There are a number of interesting new models being explored by the scientific community, and plant biologists are participating in many of them. These models include Open Access journals in which authors pay a publication fee up front that allows their articles to be read for free by anyone in the world; SPARC alternative journals set up by the Scholarly Publishing and Academic Resources Coalition (http://www.arl.org/sparc/) as inexpensive competitors for more expensive commercially published journals; and many other variations on the traditional publishing model.

Older material has not been ignored. Electronic back files of some important journals are now available from a number of different organizations or programs such as the Ecology and Botany collection from JSTOR (http://www.jstor.org/), Highwire Press (http://highwire.stanford.edu/), and the free back files program at PubMed Central (http://www.pubmedcentral.nih.gov/about/scanning.html). Commercial publishers are also making back files of their journals available.

In addition to these advances and innovations in the journal literature, plant geneticists participate in actively exploring the range of options that the Web and digital media allow. The amazing boom in molecular biology, genomics, and bioinformatics has resulted in an equal boom in data publication and analysis. With the complete genomes of species such as rice, maize, and *Arabidopsis* already available, databases such as *GenBank* (http://www.ncbi.nih.gov/Genbank/index .html) are as important for plant biologists as for animal biologists. Taxonomists are also taking advantage of the Web to compile vast databases such as *The International Plant Names Index* (http://www.ipni.org/index.html), which is much easier to use and more flexible than the old print indexes.

Despite much early hype, e-books in the sciences are growing at a much slower rate than e-journals. However, an increasing number of books are now being published both electronically and in print, although publishers are still experimenting with pricing models. Some e-books can be purchased by individuals or libraries as single items directly from the publisher whereas others are available only to libraries as part of large packages from aggregators such as netLibrary (http://www.netlibrary.com/) that include books from many publishers. A few e-books are Open Access, such as *The Arabidopsis Book* published by the American Society of Plant Biologists and made freely available through BioOne. Unlike journals, in which users are usually interested in only a single article that is often printed out rather than read on screen, e-books face many usability issues. As a result, textbooks, reference books, and methods and protocols are presently the most common e-books. However, most e-books do not take full advantage of the possibilities inherent in the electronic format such as continual updating, internal and external linking, searching across multiple books from different publishers, or the inclusion of other media types such as video or modeling software. The possibilities are intriguing and the future will certainly include many new publishing formats.

# About this Book

This annotated guide to the literature of plant biology attempts to include the most important resources for plant biologists, whether print or electronic; books, journals, and major Web sites are all included. All URLs were last checked in September 2005. Because Web sites have an unfortunate tendency to change URLs or disappear, the authors have created an associated Web site, *Web Resources in Plant Biology*, at http://www.library.uiuc.edu/bix/plantbiology/. This site contains the Web-accessible material annotated in the guide and the URLs will be kept up-to-date.

Only book-length works are covered in this guide, not individual book chapters, articles in journals, or single Web pages. The emphasis is on books that are in print but we do include classic out-of-print works that are widely available in libraries in the United States. The Web sites are included with print works in the sections that are most appropriate rather than treated separately. These sites have been chosen using the same criteria as the print material, namely that they are important, are authoritative, have authors or sponsors with good credentials, and seem likely to remain available in the future.

The material types annotated in this guide include the following:

- Bibliographies and Guides to the Literature—Includes bibliographies, guides to the literature, and guides to Web resources
- Databases, Abstracts, and Indexes—Includes bibliographic databases, indexes, and others
- Serials—Journals and review publications. This section is divided into two parts: general biology journals that are important to botanists and plant-specific journals. The general journals are not annotated
- Dictionaries and Encyclopedias

- Handbooks and Methods—Includes general works, protocols and methods, and data compendia
- Textbooks and Treatises—Both textbooks and treatises (works that summarize a field)
- Associations—Professional societies and organizations, especially those that publish one or more major journals; some research centers and major botanical gardens are also listed

# References

Anonymous. 1999. Citations reveal concentrated influence: Some fields have it, but what does it mean? *ScienceWatch* 10(1). URL: http://www.sciencewatch.com/jan-feb99/ sw_jan-feb99_page1.htm.

Bazzaz, F. A. 2001. Plant biology in the future. *Proceedings of the National Academy of Sciences* 98(10):5441–5445.

Browne, Janet. 2001. History of plant sciences. In *Encyclopedia of Life Sciences.* Vol. 9, 125–130. New York: Nature Publishing Group. URL: http://www.els.net/ [doi:10.1038/npg.els.0003081]

Delendick, Thomas J. 1990. Citation analysis of the literature of systematic botany: A preliminary survey. *Journal of the American Society for Information Science* 41(7):535–543.

de Solla Price, Derek J. 1963. *Little Science, Big Science.* New York: Columbia University Press.

Garfield, Eugene. 1976. Significant journals of science. *Nature* 264(5587):609–615.

Garfield, Eugene. 1979. Trends in biochemical literature. *Trends in Biochemical Sciences* 4 (December):290–295.

Garfield, Eugene. 1980. The 250 most-cited primary authors, 1961–1974. Part I. How the names were selected. In *Essays of an Information Scientist.* Vol. 3, 1977–1978, 326–347. Philadelphia: Institute for Scientific Information.

Garfield, Eugene. 1981a. Journal citation studies. 33. Botany Journals, Part 1: What they cite and what cites them. In *Essays of an Information Scientist.* Vol. 4, 1979–80, 555–562. Philadelphia: Institute for Scientific Information.

Garfield, Eugene. 1981b. Journal citation studies. 33. Botany Journals, Part 2: Growth of botanical literature and highly-cited items. In *Essays of an Information Scientist.* Vol. 4, 1979–80, 563–573. Philadelphia: Institute for Scientific Information.

Garfield, Eugene. 1989. Citation classics in plant science: Their impact on current research. In *Essays of an Information Scientist.* Vol. 10, 1988–89. Philadelphia: Institute for Scientific Information.

Institute for Scientific Information. 2003. *Journal Citation Reports.* Philadelphia: Institute for Scientific Information.

Kronick, David A. 1985. *The Literature of the Life Sciences: Reading, Writing, Research.* Philadelphia: Institute for Scientific Information.

Lawrence, George H. M. 1970. Botanical libraries and collections. In *Encyclopedia of Library and Information Sciences.* Vol. 3, 104–121. New York: Marcel Dekker.

Marton, János. 1983. Causes of low and high citation potentials in science: Citation analysis of biochemistry and plant physiology journals. *Journal of the American Society for Information Science* 34(4):244–246.

Morton, A. G. 1981. *History of Botanical Science: An Account of the Development of Botany from Ancient Times to the Present Day.* New York: Academic Press.

Prather, L. Alan, Orlando Alvarez-Fuentes, Mark H. Mayfield, and Carolyn J. Ferguson. 2004a. The decline of plant collecting in the United States: A threat to the infrastructure of biodiversity studies. *Systematic Botany* 29(1):15–28.

Prather, L. Alan, Orlando Alvarez-Fuentes, Mark H. Mayfield, and Carolyn J. Ferguson. 2004b. Implications of the decline in plant collecting for systematic and floristic research. *Systematic Botany* 29(1):216–220.

Raikhel, Natasha V. 2001. Plant physiology: Past, present, and future. *Plant Physiology* 125(1):1–3.

Raven, Peter H., Ray F. Evert, and Susan E. Eichhorn. 1999. *Biology of Plants*, 6th ed. New York: W. H. Freeman.

Somerville, Chris. 2000. The twentieth century trajectory of plant biology. *Cell* 100: 13–25.

Sundberg, Marshall D. 2004. Where is botany going? *Plant Science Bulletin* 50(1):2–7.

# 2
# General Sources

This chapter contains resources that either are very general or do not fit in another chapter. Many of the more general resources are described here and not in the individual subject chapters; for instance, *Biological Abstracts*, the main database for the life sciences, is listed only in this general chapter because it is appropriate to use for almost any subject in plant biology. Chapter 3, History and Biography, lists indexes and other resources that have long since ceased publication but may be useful for retrospective research. This chapter contains general works covering the biology and taxonomy of individual plant groups such as bryophytes or carnivorous plants; but chapter 10, Systematics and Identification, should also be checked for resources on plant names or information on specific plant species.

## Bibliographies and Guides to the Literature

01    Clewis, Beth. *Index to Illustrations of Animals and Plants.* New York: Neal-Schuman, 1991. 217 p. ISBN 1555700721.

This is useful as a supplement to Munz's and Thompson's *Index to Illustrations* (below) and it follows a similar format. Clewis covers books published in the 1980s and lists 62,000 entries for access to 142 books with illustrations for plants and animals from around the world. The book is arranged by common name with indexes for scientific name and book title.

02    Hutchinson, Barbara S., and Antoinette Paris Greider. *Using the Agricultural, Environmental, and Food Literature.* New York: Marcel Dekker, 2002. 533 p. (Books in Library and Information Science, 61). ISBN 0824708008.

This bibliographic guide covers a range of topics that may be of interest to plant biologists. In particular, the chapters on environmental sciences, field crops, horticulture, and the gray literature may prove useful.

03   Isaacson, R. T., comp. *Flowering Plant Index of Illustration and Information.* Boston, MA: G. K. Hall, 1979. 3 vol. ISBN 0816103011. *1979–1981 Supplement,* 2 vol. ISBN 0816104034.

This set and its supplement are a useful source for locating colored illustrations of flowering plants and can be used to update *Index Londinensis* and *Index Kewensis* (both below). It is appropriate for all botanical and large public libraries. There are cross-references for common and botanical names. See also Clewis's *Index to Illustrations,* above.

04   Kuchler, August Wilhelm, ed. *International Bibliography of Vegetation Maps.* Lawrence, KS: University of Kansas Libraries, 1965–1970. 4 vol. (University of Kansas Publications. Library Series, 21, 26, 29, 36).

Only published vegetation maps are listed in this bibliography, and data include title of the map, date of preparation, color, scale, legend in the original language if Western European, author of the map, when and where published. Arrangement is geographical and contents are Volume 1, Vegetation maps of North America; Volume 2, Vegetation maps of Europe; Volume 3, U.S.S.R., Asia, and Australia; and Volume 4, Africa, South American, and world maps. *Section 1,* 2nd edition, containing South American materials, was published in 1980 by the University of Kansas Libraries (Library Series, 45).

05   Lampinen, R., S. Liu, A. R. Brach, and K. McCree. *The Internet Directory for Botany.* 1996– . URL: http://www.botany.net/IDB/.

A very extensive alphabetical listing of plant biology-related Web sites. It can be searched by keyword, but unfortunately there is no subject categorization. Most of the major associations, botanical gardens, and arboreta with Web sites are included in the list.

06   *Merlot: Biology.* Long Beach, CA: California State University, Center for Distributed Learning, 1997– . URL: http://www.merlot.org/Home.po? discipline=Biology.

Designed for higher education, this site provides links to educational resources such as streaming videos, tutorials, online courses, societies, and so on. At the time of viewing, there were over 100 links to botanical materials.

07   Munz, Lucile Thompson, and Nedra G. Slauson, comps. *Index to Illustrations of Living Things Outside of North America: Where to Find Pictures of Flora and Fauna.* Hamden, CT: Shoe String, 1981. 441 p. ISBN 0208018573.

This and Thompson's *Index to Illustrations*, below, are companion volumes and indexes to illustrations of plants and animals throughout the world. Their formats are identical (see below); this volume includes sources found in guides, handbooks, and encyclopedias dating mainly from 1963 through the 1970s. Both of these indexes are recommended for libraries of all sizes; research libraries will need to augment this information with the more comprehensive sources mentioned below. Updated by Clewis's *Index to Illustrations*, above.

08   *Plant Science Homepage.* Agriculture Network Information Center (AgNIC), 1999. URL: http://citnews.unl.edu/CYT_agnic/SiteForUser/.

Although emphasizing agricultural-related sites, this guide is a good starting place for reliable Web sites dealing with plant biology. It is arranged by type of resource and subject and can also be searched by keyword.

09   Schmidt, Diane, Elisabeth B. Davis, and Pamela F. Jacobs. *Using the Biological Literature: A Practical Guide*, 3rd ed., rev. and expanded. New York: Marcel Dekker, 2002. 474 p. (Books in Library and Information Science, 60). $85.00. ISBN 0824706676.

The third edition of this successful guide covers the reference resources, databases, and Web sites relevant to the basic biological sciences. One chapter covers plant biology.

10   Stapf, O., G. A. Pritzel, W. C. Worsedell, and A. W. Hill. *Index Londinensis to Illustrations of Flowering Plants, Ferns and Fern Allies.* Königstein, Germany: Lubrecht and Cramer, 1979. 6 vol. $1,775.00 (set). ISBN 3874291510 (set).

This index updates Pritzel's *Iconum Botanicarum Index Locupletissimus* and contains and updates the material from that set. The main set covers illustrations published up to 1920 with a supplement covering material from 1921 to 1935. It is continued by *Index Kewensis* supplements (see chapter 10) and can be updated by Isaacson's *Flowering Plant Index* and Clewis's *Index to Illustrations*, both above.

11   Swift, Lloyd H. *Botanical Bibliographies: A Guide to Bibliographic Materials Applicable to Botany.* Königstein, Germany: Koeltz, 1974. 804 p. ISBN 387429076X.

This is an excellent guide to the bibliographic literature of botany and allied areas. Reproduction of the 1970 edition.

12   Thompson, John W., and Nedra G. Slauson, eds. *Index to Illustrations of the Natural World: Where to Find Pictures of the Living Things of North America.* Syracuse: Gaylord, 1977. 256 p. ISBN 0915794128.

This index provides an alphabetical listing of 6,200 North American plants, birds, and animals with citations to where illustrations may be found. There is a scientific name index and a bibliography of sources. This very useful compilation is recommended for all libraries, particularly small public ones; the sources were chosen to be widely available with illustrations that clearly identify the organisms. Useful for the more popular plants, this index can't compete, of course, with the more comprehensive, and retrospective sources such as *Index Kewensis* (see chapter 10), Nissen's *Die botanishche Buchillustration* (see chapter 3), Stapf's *Index Londinensis* (above), Isaacson's *Flowering Plant Index* (above), and Clewis's *Index to Illustrations*, also above.

# Databases, Abstracts, and Indexes

13 *AGRICOLA (AGRICultural OnLine Access)*. Washington, DC: National Agricultural Library, 1970– . Updated daily. URL: http://agricola.nal.usda.gov/.

The online equivalent of the now-ceased *Bibliography of Agriculture,* produced by the National Agriculture Library (NAL). This database covers journal articles, book chapters, government documents, technical reports, and proceedings. *AGRICOLA*'s focus is primarily agricultural; however, it is important to botanists working in the applied area who need to pick up international information from government reports, agricultural experiment stations, and the like. The database uses the same controlled vocabulary used in *CAB Abstracts* (see below). *AGRICOLA* is available from many vendors in several formats including online, on CD-ROM, and through the Web. The database can also be searched for free at the URL listed above, although this search engine is rather clumsy. NAL also publishes an annual *List of Journals Indexed in AGRICOLA*. It can also be accessed at no charge on the Web at http://www.nal.usda.gov/indexing/jia.html. This version includes data on journals dating back to 1992.

14 *AGRIS*. Rome, Italy: U.N. Food and Agriculture Organization, 1975– . URL: http://www.fao.org/agris/.

This database covers agriculture "in the widest sense" according to its Web site. It indexes articles, unpublished scientific and technical reports, theses, conference papers, government publications, and unpublished scientific and technical reports from around the world, making it a good source for the gray literature that is hard to find elsewhere. Like the other agricultural databases (*AGRICOLA* and *CAB Abstracts*), *AGRIS* is a good source of information on plants of economic importance and is especially strong in non-English material. *AGRIS* uses the AGROVOC standardized vocabulary. Users can obtain vocabulary terms in Arabic, Chinese,

Czech, English, French, Portuguese, and Spanish from the FAO's site at http://www.fao.org/agrovoc/. *AGRIS* is available from various vendors and can also be searched for free at the URL listed above. Published in print from 1975 to 1995 as *Agrindex*.

15   *Biological Abstracts*. Vol. 1– . Philadelphia, PA: Thomson, 1926– . Biweekly. $9,850.00, including semiannual cumulative indexes. ISSN 0006-3169.

This is the most comprehensive biological abstracting publication in the English language. It covers world literature including over 9,000 serial and nonserial publications; the emphasis is on basic research papers from primary biological and biomedical journals. The botanical sciences are covered in detail from every facet: general and systematic, ecological, physiological, biochemical, biophysical, and methodological. *Biological Abstracts (BA)* is available as *BA on CD* from 1969 to the present. *BA* and *Biological Abstracts/RRM* (below) are available as a combined database called *BIOSIS Previews*, also covering the literature from 1969 to date. A more limited version of the database, *Basic-BIOSIS*, is also available. It consists of a four-year rolling file covering 300 core journals plus news sources and is aimed at students rather than researchers. The *BIOSIS Previews Search Guide* is a reference manual designed to support users of the *BIOSIS Previews* database; it is very helpful for conducting complex searches. The search guide includes an index to vocabulary, a list of broad subject codes, and helpful hints to use in developing effective strategies for searching the database. The *Serial Sources for the BIOSIS Previews Database* provides an alphabetical list of the serials scanned for inclusion with their abbreviations and publishers' addresses. *BA* and its companion publication *Biological Abstract/RRM* are the instruments of choice for comprehensive access to the literature; their scope and coverage provide the best source available for current botanical research. *BA* was formed by the merger of *Abstracts of Bacteriology* and *Botanical Abstracts*. For articles published before *BA* began, see the classic indexes and bibliographies listed in chapter 3.

16   *Biological Abstracts/RRM (Reports, Reviews, Meetings)*. Vol. 18– . Philadelphia, PA: Thomson, 1980– . Biweekly. $4,800.00, including semiannual cumulative indexes. ISSN 0192-6985.

This publication continues *Bioresearch Index* by the same publisher and is a sister publication of *Biological Abstracts*. *BA/RRM* reports on notes, symposia papers, meeting abstracts, trade journal items, translated journals, review publications, bibliographies, technical data reports, research communications, books, book chapters, and a variety of special taxonomic publications. The literature monitored is the same as BA, and taken together, the two publications cover all aspects of worldwide botanical literature. There are no abstracts. *BA/RRM* is available electronically both separately and as part of *BIOSIS Previews* covering the literature from 1969 to date.

17    *Biological and Agricultural Index*. Vol. 1– . New York: H. W. Wilson, 1964– . Monthly, annual cumulations. Price varies. ISSN 0006-3177.

Formerly *Agricultural Index*, this index covers all aspects of biology and agriculture, including botany. The index scans 225 English language periodicals. There is a subject index with extensive cross-references and complete bibliographic information, as well as an author index. The level of this index is appropriate for undergraduate students or the general public. Also available online, on CD-ROM, and on the Web. In the electronic versions, some citations include abstracts.

18    *Biological Sciences Collection*. Bethesda, MD: Cambridge Scientific Abstracts, 1994– . Price varies.

Provides citations and abstracts to articles, conference proceedings, technical reports, monographs, and selected patents in biomedicine, biotechnology, zoology and ecology, as well as some aspects of agriculture and veterinary science. Comprised of a number of subsets, including *Agricultural and Environmental Biotechnology Abstracts* (see chapter 8); *Algology, Mycology and Protozoology: Microbiology Abstracts Section C*; *Ecology Abstracts*; and a number of other databases of possible interest to plant biologists. The database is made available online and on the Web through CSA's Internet Database Service. Also known as *CSA Biological Sciences*.

19    *Biology Digest*. Vol. 1– . Medford, NJ: Plexus, 1974– . Monthly, September through May. $149.00, including cumulative index. ISSN 0095-2958.

This abstracting publication covers about 200 periodicals in biology, including botany. It was created to meet the needs of high school and undergraduate students, but it is also useful for professional and amateur botanists because it covers some of the more popular literature not included in *Biological Abstracts*. It is a competitor to *Biological and Agricultural Index* and, unlike *BAI*, it provides lengthy abstracts. Each issue contains a keyword subject and author index, plus a feature article on some aspect of the biological sciences. Also available as a subset of the *Biological Sciences Collection* from CSA's Internet Database Service (see above).

20    *CAB Abstracts*. Wallingford, England: CAB International, 1972– . Price varies.

Indexes scholarly, professional, and commercial journals as well as some book chapters, theses, proceedings, and technical reports in the applied life sciences including forestry, grasslands, crop science, horticulture, invasive species, mycology, and plant pathology. Because CAB International (formerly Commonwealth Agricultural Bureaux) is an international nonprofit organization, the database has good coverage for regions outside of North America. The *CAB Thesaurus* provides the classified vocabulary used in *CAB Abstracts* and *AGRICOLA* and is available in print and online. The database is available through several vendors and directly from the publisher.

21 *Chemical Abstracts*. Vol. 1– . Columbus, OH: Chemical Abstracts Service, 1907– . Weekly. $26,000, including indexes. ISSN 0009-2258.

This is the most comprehensive abstracting service for chemistry, covering over 15,000 source materials including journals, book chapters, patents, conference proceedings, and dissertations. *CA* is international in scope, covering all aspects of chemistry in all languages. Although it does not cover plant biology specifically, it does cover botanical subjects from a chemical viewpoint and is essential for information on chemistry and biochemistry. A list of sources abstracted in *CA* is available as *Chemical Abstracts Service Source Index (CASSI)*. *CASSI* is a gold mine of information about research materials pertinent to the chemical sciences. *CA* is available in a number of formats and pricing models aimed at business and academic markets, including *SciFinder* (for business use) and *SciFinder Scholar* (for academic use), on CD-ROM, and online through a number of vendors.

22 *Current Advances in Plant Science (CAPS)*. Vol. 1– . Amsterdam, the Netherlands: Elsevier, 1972– . Monthly. $2,461.00. ISSN 0306-4484.

This current awareness service for over 3,000 biological journals covers all aspects of the plant sciences. Arranged by subject, complete bibliographic information is available for articles scanned; there are no abstracts. This competitor of *Biological Abstracts* is not as comprehensive as *BA*, does not provide as much information, and is less expensive; the technical level of the two publications is equivalent and is aimed at the professional botanist, researcher, and upper-level college student. *CAPS* is part of the *Current Awareness in Biological Sciences (CABS)* database and is available online.

23 *Current Contents/Agriculture, Biology, and Environmental Sciences*. Vol. 1– . Philadelphia, PA: Thomson ISI, 1970– . Weekly. $730.00. ISSN 0011-3379.

This section of the *Current Contents* publications, along with *Current Contents/Life Sciences (CC/LS)* (below), provides a unique service that alerts professional botanists to journal articles and books at their time of publication. The print versions of these serials consist of Tables of Contents (TOCs) from major periodicals and book series. This TOC orientation carries over to the *Current Contents* database, which allows users to browse the TOCs of journals as well as performing the usual subject searches. The database is available from several vendors and in several formats, including online, CD-ROM, and diskette. *CC/ABE* covers about

1,040 journals plus book chapters, commentaries, and meeting abstracts. The Plant Sciences category covers general botany, regional botany, mycology, bryology, forestry, weed science, plant pathology, economic botany, plant nutrition, photosynthesis research, experimental botany, and plant cell research.

24   *Current Contents/Life Sciences.* Vol. 1– . Philadelphia, PA: Thomson ISI, 1958– . Weekly. $1,015.00. ISSN 0011-3409.

Companion to *CC/ABE*, above, and covers about 1,400 journals in the life sciences. Plant biology topics such as plant molecular biology, molecular genetics, plant-microbe interactions, physiology, and cell biology are included in this section. Although there is overlap between the two *CC* sections, the *CC/ABE* section generally covers the applied and integrative fields whereas *CC/LS* covers the cellular and molecular subjects.

25   *Excerpta Botanica.* Vol. 1–65. New York: Gustav Fischer Verlag, 1959–1998. *Sectio A: Taxonomica et Chorologia.* ISSN 0014-4037. *Sectio B: Sociologica.* ISSN 0014-4045.

Produced in conjunction with the International Association for Plant Taxonomy. *Sectio A* provided abstracts in English, French, German, and Spanish for international coverage of articles on systematic botany, herbaria, gardens, and so on; whereas *Sectio B* presented a world bibliography of books and articles dealing with plant geography and ecology. These are important publications because of the auspices under which they are produced; a comprehensive search of the botanical literature should include them.

26   *Index to American Botanical Literature.* Bronx, NY: New York Botanical Garden, 1999– . URL: http://www.nybg.org/bsci/iabl.html.

The index covers both living and fossil American plants and fungi, indexing articles covering general and economic botany, systematics and floristics, morphology, and ecology. The area includes the entire Western Hemisphere, from Greenland to Antarctica. From 1886 through 1995 the index was published in the *Bulletin of the Torrey Botanical Club* and from 1996 to 1998 in *Brittonia.* After that point, it became electronic only and is searchable at the URL listed above. The database includes material added to the index from 1996 to date.

27   *Journal Citation Reports (JCR).* Vol. 1– . Philadelphia, PA: Thomson ISI, 1978– . Annual. Price varies.

Each year, ISI produces *Journal Citation Report (JCR)*, which provides data on which journals were cited the most, were cited most quickly, cited half-lives (i.e., how long articles were cited), and more. This data can be used to determine which journals are more important in a particular field. *JCR*'s Impact Factor, the measure of the frequency with which the average article in a journal has been cited in a particular year, is one of the most frequently used criteria; it is often required in tenure documents and is carefully monitored by journal editors. *JCR*'s publication history is complex; it was first published as part of *SCI* as *SCI Journal Citation Reports* from 1978 to 1988, on microfiche as *SCI JCR* from 1989 to 1994, on CD-ROM from 1995 to date, and is now available on the Web.

28   *PubMed*. Bethesda, MD: National Library of Medicine, 1951– . Updated daily. URL: http://www.ncbi.nlm.nih.gov/entrez/query.fcgi.

*PubMed* is the free version of the National Library of Medicine's *MEDLINE* database and is the access method favored by most biological researchers. As well as indexing the 4,500 journals covered in *MEDLINE*, *PubMed* includes a number of journals in the life sciences that are not included in *MEDLINE* and has links to the National Center for Biotechnology Information (NCBI) molecular biology databases. *PubMed* has a number of valuable features, including direct links to full-text articles, a citation matching feature, and the ability to save searches. Although the emphasis in the database is on medicine, it is useful for botanists because it covers medicinal plants, plant molecular and cellular biology, and a range of other topics. *MEDLINE* is available online and on CD-ROM from a variety of vendors by subscription. The print version of *MEDLINE*, *Index Medicus*, began in 1903 and is still being published. The very useful *List of Serials Indexed for Online Users* is available in print and also on the Web at http://www.nlm.nih.gov/tsd/serials/lsiou.html.

29   *Science Citation Index (SCI)*. Vol. 1– . Philadelphia, PA: Thomson ISI, 1961– . Bimonthly. $15,020.00. ISSN 0036-827X.

In addition to serving as a multidisciplinary index, *SCI* provides information on citations to the older scientific literature, so that users can trace who is using the older papers. Because it is multidisciplinary in nature and covers nearly 6,000 of the most influential international journals, it is also a good database to use for interdisciplinary studies. *Web of Science*, the Web database version of *SCI*, covers the scientific literature from 1945 to date. *SCI* is also available online and on CD-ROM. The same underlying database is used to create *Current Contents* (above) and *Science Citation Index*.

30   *Scirus: For Scientific Information Only*. Amsterdam, the Netherlands: Elsevier Science, 2001– . URL: http://www.scirus.com/.

This free search engine includes only scientific resources, including links to societies, electronic journals, researchers' personal Web pages, course syllabi, and more. Because users can search *Scirus* for subscription-only journal articles as well as Web pages, they may pull up resources that are not available to them; but because the search engine indexes many high-quality free sites, it is worth checking.

# Serials

## General Serials

31   *Biological Reviews of the Cambridge Philosophical Society.* Vol. 1– . New York: Cambridge University Press, 1923– . Quarterly. $208.00. ISSN 0006-3231. Available electronically.

32   *BioScience.* Vol. 1– . Washington, DC: American Institute of Biological Sciences, 1951– . Monthly. $280.00. ISSN 0006-3568. Available electronically.

33   *Nature.* Vol. 1– . New York: Macmillan, 1869– . Weekly. $1,280.00. ISSN 0028-0836. Available electronically.

34   *Philosophical Transactions of the Royal Society of London: Series B, Biological Sciences.* Vol. 224– . London: Royal Society of London, 1934– . Monthly. $1,975.00. ISSN 0962-8436. Available electronically.
    Formerly *Philosophical Transactions of the Royal Society of London. Series B, Containing Papers of a Biological Character.*

35   *Proceedings: Biological Sciences.* Vol. 241– . London: Royal Society of London, 1990– . Bimonthly. $1,175.00. ISSN 0962-8452. Available electronically.
    Formerly *Proceedings of the Royal Society of London. Series B, Containing Papers of a Biological Character.*

36   *Proceedings of the National Academy of Sciences of the United States of America (PNAS).* Vol. 1– . Washington, DC: National Academy of Sciences, 1915– . Weekly. $1,320.00. ISSN 0027-8424. Available electronically.

37   *The Quarterly Review of Biology.* Vol. 1– . Chicago, IL: University of Chicago Press, 1926– . Quarterly. $233.00. ISSN 0033-5770. Available electronically.

38   *Science.* Vol. 1– . Washington, DC: American Association for the Advancement of Science, 1880– . Weekly. $425.00. ISSN 0036-8075. Available electronically.

## Botanical Serials

39   *Advances in Botanical Research.* Vol. 1– . New York: Academic, 1963– . Irregular. Price varies. ISSN 0065-2296.
    This series traditionally reviews progress across the whole spectrum of botanical studies and serves botanists with a wide range of interests. Includes

both thematic and mixed-subject volumes. Merged with *Advances in Plant Pathology.*

40   *American Fern Journal.* Vol. 1– . Washington, DC: American Fern Society, 1910– . Quarterly. $35.00. ISSN 0002-8444. Available electronically.

Publishes "articles and notes based on original scientific research on ferns and allied groups of vascular plants." Most of the articles deal with fern taxonomy.

41   *American Journal of Botany.* Vol. 1– . Ames, IA: Botanical Society of America, 1914– . Monthly. $445.00. ISSN 0002-9122. Available electronically.

Covers all branches of plant sciences. In addition to research articles, the journal also publishes Rapid Communications and Special Papers, which include reviews, critiques, and analyses of controversial subjects. An official publication of the Botanical Society of America.

42   *Annals of Botany (London).* Vol. 1– . Oxford, England: Oxford University Press, 1887– . 13 times per year. $787.00. ISSN 0305-7364. Available electronically.

An international journal publishing in all aspects of plant biology. It includes research papers, short communications, invited and submitted review articles, and book reviews as well as Botanical Briefings, which are short commissioned reviews. The Botanical Briefings are available for free at http://aob.oupjournals .org/botanicalbriefing.shtml; Invited Reviews are also freely available at http:// aob.oupjournals.org/invitedreviews.shtml.

43   *Botanical Review.* Vol. 1– . New York: New York Botanical Garden, 1935– . Quarterly. $115.00. ISSN 0006-8101.

Authors are chosen primarily by invitation, but unsolicited manuscripts are also considered. This journal bills itself as "present[ing] syntheses of the state of knowledge and understanding of individual segments of botany" and serves the function of synthesizing the state of knowledge of the botanical sciences for a broad spectrum of botanists.

44   *The Bryologist.* Vol. 1– . Las Vegas, NV: American Bryological and Lichenological Society, 1898– . Quarterly. $70.00. ISSN 0007-2745. Available electronically.

"Manuscripts on all aspects of bryology and lichenology will be considered." Recent issues include articles on taxonomy, biology, and ecology of mosses and lichens. The journal also publishes book reviews and *Recent Literature on Lichens* and *Recent Literature on Bryophytes* (see Bibliographies and Guides to the Literature, chapter 10).

45    *Canadian Journal of Botany. Journal Canadien de Botanique.* Vol. 29– . Ottawa, Canada: National Research Council of Canada, 1951– . Monthly. $1,165.00. ISSN 0008-4026. Available electronically.

This primary research journal publishes the results of scientific research including articles, notes, reviews, and commentaries in all aspects of botany, in English or French. Continues *Canadian Journal of Research. Section C, Botanical Sciences.*

46    *Critical Reviews in Plant Sciences.* Vol. 1– . Philadelphia, PA: Taylor and Francis, 1983– . Bimonthly. $840.00. ISSN 0735-2689. Available electronically.

Publishes "reviews of timely subjects in the broad discipline of plant science ranging from the molecular biology-biochemistry aspects through the areas of cell biology, plant physiology, genetics, classical botany, ecology, etc. to the practical agricultural applications."

47    *Current Opinion in Plant Biology.* Vol. 1– . London: Elsevier, 1998– . Bimonthly. $1,206.00. ISSN 1369-5266. Available electronically.

Each year the following seven general areas are reviewed: growth and development; plant biotechnology; genome studies and molecular genetics; physiology and metabolism; biotic interactions; cell signaling and gene regulation; and cell biology. Also publishes alerts for useful Web sites and hot papers.

48    *Environmental and Experimental Botany.* Vol. 1– . Amsterdam, the Netherlands: Elsevier, 1961– . Bimonthly. $890.00. ISSN 0098-8472. Available electronically.

Covers research dealing with the physical, chemical, and biological mechanisms and processes that relate the performance of plants to their abiotic and biotic environment. Includes research areas such as radiation botany, plant soil/water/atmosphere/temperature relations, the physiological and/or ecological responses of genotypes or ecotypes, pollution effects on plants, and gravitational botany. Formerly *Radiation Biology.*

49    *European Journal of Phycology,* Vol. 28– . Abingdon, England: Taylor and Francis, 1993– . Quarterly. $404.00. ISSN 0967-0262. Available electronically.

An international journal that publishes papers on all aspects of the ecology, physiology, biochemistry, cell biology, molecular biology, and systematics of algae. Continues *British Phycological Journal.*

50    *Fungal Genetics and Biology: An Experimental Journal.* Vol. 20– . New York: Elsevier, 1996– . Irregular. $521.00. ISSN 1087-1845.

Publishes "experimental investigations of fungi and their traditional allies that relate structure and function to growth, reproduction, morphogenesis, and differentiation." Formerly *Experimental Mycology*.

51   *Grana*. Vol. 10– . Stockholm: Taylor and Francis, 1970– . Quarterly. $293.00. ISSN 0017-3134. Available electronically.

"*Grana* publishes original papers, mainly on ontogony (morphology, and ultrastructure of pollen grains and spores of Eucaryota and their importance for plant taxonomy, ecology, phytogeography, paleobotany, etc.) and aerobiology. Aerobiology involves studies of airborne biological particles, such as pollen, spores, etc., and their launching, dispersal and final deposition. The significance of these particles in medicine (allergology) and plant pathology is of particular interest." Original title *Grana Palynologica*.

52   *International Journal of Plant Sciences*. Vol. 153– . Chicago, IL: University of Chicago Press, 1993– . Quarterly. $588.00. ISSN 1058-5893. Available electronically.

"Topics covered include plant-microbe interactions, development, structure and systematics, molecular biology, genetics and evolution, ecology, paleobotany, and physiology and ecophysiology." Formerly *Botanical Gazette*.

53   *Journal of Bryology*. Vol. 7– . London: Maney, 1972– . Quarterly. $392.00. ISSN 0373-6687. Available electronically.

Publishes "original research papers in cell biology, anatomy, development, genetics, physiology, chemistry, ecology, palaeobotany, evolution, taxonomy, applied biology, conservation, biomonitoring aspects and biogeography of bryophytes, and also significant new check-lists and descriptive floras of poorly known regions." Also publishes short Bryological Notes. Continues the *Transactions of the British Bryological Society*.

54   *Journal of Phycology*. Vol. 1– . Oxford, England: Blackwell, 1965– . Bimonthly. $520.00. ISSN 0022-3646. Available electronically.

The journal publishes articles on "all aspects of basic and applied research on algae" and also contains mini-reviews, notes on articles of interest from other publications, and book reviews.

55   *Mycologia*. Vol. 1– . Lawrence, KS: Allen Press for the Mycological Society of America, 1909– . Bimonthly. $203.00. ISSN 0027-5514. Available electronically.

"Publishes papers on all aspects of the fungi, including lichens." Publishes regular articles, brief notes, invited papers, and reviews.

56   *New Phytologist*. Vol. 1– . Oxford, England: Blackwell, 1902– . Monthly. $1,581.00. ISSN 0028-646X. Available electronically.

Publishes articles covering "all aspects of plant science." The journal is divided into four sections: Function, Environment, Interaction, and Evolution. The journal publishes letters, commentaries, and reviews in its Forum section and also publishes occasional thematic special issues.

57   *Phycologia*. Vol. 1– . Lawrence, KS: International Phycological Society, 1961– . Bimonthly. $450.00. ISSN 0031-8884.

Covers articles on "all aspects of algal biology" including original research articles, reviews, notes and commentaries, book reviews, meetings announcements, and obituaries of prominent phycologists. The official journal of the International Phycological Society.

58   *Plant Biology*. Vol. 1– . New York: Thieme, 1999– . Bimonthly. $579.00. ISSN 1435-8603. Available electronically.

Publishes research papers, rapid communications, and review articles in all areas of plant biology. Also publishes occasional opinion pieces and reviews of hot topics. The official journal of the German Botanical Society and the Royal Botanical Society of the Netherlands, *Plant Biology* was created by the merger of *Acta Botanica Neerlandica* and *Botanica Acta*.

59   *Planta*. Vol. 1– . New York: Springer-Verlag, 1925– . Monthly. $4,182.00. ISSN 0032-0935. Available electronically.

Publishes articles and reviews in "all aspects of plant biology, particularly in molecular and cell biology, structural biology, biochemistry, metabolism, growth, development and morphogenesis, ecological and environmental physiology, biotechnology, and plant-microorganism interactions."

60   *Progress in Botany*. Vol. 36– . New York: Springer-Verlag, 1974– . Irregular. Price varies. ISSN 0340-4773.

The articles in this review series are divided into several categories, including genetics, physiology, ecology, and systematics. Continues *Fortschritte der Botanik*.

61   *Progress in Phycological Research*. Vol. 1– . Amsterdam: Elsevier Biomedical, 1982– . Irregular. Price varies. ISSN 0167-8574.

A review series covering a range of topics dealing with algae. The most recent volume, 13, was published in 1999.

62   *Trends in Plant Science*. Vol. 1– . London: Elsevier, 1996– . Monthly. $1,206.00. ISSN 1360-1385.

A review periodical publishing short reviews and opinion pieces "with broad coverage of basic plant science, from molecular biology through to ecology. There are also research update articles discussing implications of advances in selected hot areas. Other titles in the *Trends in* . . . series are also of interest to botanists: *Trends in Biochemical Sciences, Trends in Biotechnology, Trends in Cell Biology, Trends in Ecology and Evolution, Trends in Genetics,* and *Trends in Microbiology.*

# Dictionaries and Encyclopedias

63   Allaby, Michael, ed. *A Dictionary of Plant Sciences.* 2nd ed. Oxford, England: Oxford University Press, 1998. 508 p. (Oxford Paperback Reference Series). $15.95. ISBN 0192800779.

This compact dictionary contains 5,500 entries from a range of fields associated with plant biology. About a third of the entries define taxonomic groups down to the genus, and there are also brief biographies of prominent botanists. The first edition was titled *Concise Oxford Dictionary of Botany.*

64   Bailey, Jill. *The Facts On File Dictionary of Botany.* New York: Facts On File, 2003. 250 p. (Facts On File Science Library Series). ISBN 0816049106.

Aimed at high school students taking Advanced Placement biology as well as college students, this dictionary contains 2,000 entries covering all aspects of pure and applied plant biology. It includes entries for most taxa at or above the family level. There are two appendixes, one listing scientific units and the other providing a short list of useful Web sites.

65   Bailey, Jill, ed. *The Penguin Dictionary of Plant Sciences.* London: Penguin, 1999. 504 p. (Penguin Reference Books Series). ISBN 0140514031.

Contains 4,000 entries from pure and applied fields of plant biology. There are several appendixes listing the meanings of common scientific names, the names of organic compounds, and scientific units. Unlike Allaby's *A Dictionary of Plant Sciences,* above, this dictionary does not cover plant taxa.

66   Bailey, Liberty H., and Ethel Z. Bailey, comps. *Hortus III: A Concise Dictionary of Plants Cultivated in the United States and Canada.* New York: Macmillan, 1976. 1290 p. $150.00. ISBN 0025054708.

This is an indispensable source for description, botanical names and synonyms, common names, uses, propagation, hardiness, and illustrations of cultivated plants. A glossary and an index to common names are included.

67    Bedevian, Armenag K. *Illustrated Polyglottic Dictionary of Plant Names in Latin, Arabic, Armenian, English, French, German, Italian and Turkish Languages, Including Economic, Medicinal, Poisonous and Ornamental Plants and Common Weeds.* Cairo: Argus and Papazian, 1936. 2 pt. in 1 vol.

Part 1 includes 3,657 entries in English arranged by scientific name, followed by the abbreviated name of the author, synonyms, family name, and common name in seven languages. Part II contains indexes of the common names of plants, referring to entry number in the first part of the dictionary. This is a useful source with an unusual selection of languages. Unfortunately, it is long out of print with no complete substitute at hand.

68    Benvie, Sam. *The Encyclopedia of North American Trees.* Buffalo, NY: Firefly, 2000. 304 p. $35.00; $24.95 (paper). ISBN 1552094081; 1552976416 (paper).

Covering 278 species of trees, this encyclopedia is appropriate for both gardeners and students of botany. It is arranged alphabetically by genus, and each genus with more than three American species has a brief introduction describing the characteristics of the genus. The species accounts include distribution; habitat; size; description of bark, needles or leaves, fruits or seeds; and overall growth habit. The author also provides information on the horticultural and ethnobotanical uses of the trees. A table listing plant hardiness zones for each species is also included, along with a glossary, list of botanical gardens and organizations, bibliography, and index.

69    Brako, Lois, Amy Y. Rossman, and David F. Farr. *Scientific and Common Names of 7,000 Vascular Plants in the United States.* St. Paul, MN: APS, 1995. 295 p. $34.00. ISBN 089054171X (paper).

Published by the American Phytopathological Society, this resource is designed to provide common names for the majority of vascular plants of interest to plant pathologists. This includes plants of economic importance as well as native trees and wildflowers, so it is of use to a wide variety of people. It is in four parts, the first section listing scientific names in alphabetical order by genus and including common names for species within the genus. The second section lists common names, indexed by each word in the common name. The third section lists important synonyms of scientific names, and the fourth section lists genera of plants listed in the book arranged by family.

70    Clason, W. E., comp. *Elsevier's Dictionary of Wild and Cultivated Plants in Latin, English, French, Spanish, Dutch and German.* Amsterdam: Elsevier, 1989. 1016 p. $275.00. ISBN 0444429778.

This dictionary, which gives the Latin and vernacular names of wild and cultivated plants of Europe, was designed to aid in translation of botanical names.

Names are given in Latin, followed by the various other languages. There are also separate indexes for each of the other languages leading back to the main entry.

71  Committee on Standardization of Common Names for Plant Diseases. *Common Names of Plant Diseases*. American Phytopathological Society, 1978–2004. URL: http://www.apsnet.org/online/common/top.asp.

Lists the common names of plant pathogens and diseases for use in American Phytopathological Society publications. Can be searched by keyword or browsed by alphabetical listing.

72  Coombes, Allen J. *Timber Press Dictionary of Plant Names*. Portland, OR: Timber, 1986. 207 p. $12.95. ISBN 0881920231.

The purpose of this book is to "provide a guide to the derivation, meaning, and pronunciation of the scientific names of the more commonly grown plants." Generic and common names are given with their pronunciation, family, derivation, and use in gardens. Selected species are also listed. First published in the U. K. under the title of *Collingridge Dictionary of Plant Names*.

73  Cullmann, Willy, Erich Gotz, and Gerhard Groner. *The Encyclopedia of Cacti*. Portland, OR: Timber, 1987. 340 p. ISBN 0881921009.

Combines a botanist's discussion of cactus systematics with a cactus enthusiast's guide to culture and propagation. Includes a key to cactus genera and an encyclopedic listing of cactus genera, along with excellent color photographs of many species. The authors also include a glossary, a list of the authors of cactus names, and useful addresses. A good choice for either a general or specialized collection.

74  D'Arcy, C. J., D. M. Eastburn, and G. L. Schumann. *Illustrated Glossary of Plant Pathology*. American Phytopathological Society, 2001. URL: http://www.apsnet.org/Education/IllustratedGlossary/.

This lengthy glossary is part of the society's Plant Health Instructor site and provides definitions of a large number of terms used in plant pathology. Almost all of the terms are illustrated with a color photograph or drawing.

75  Dickinson, Colin, and John Lucas, eds. *Encyclopedia of Mushrooms*. New York: Crescent, 1983. 280 p. ISBN 0517374846.

There are introductory chapters on the history, biology, lifestyle, habitat, identification, edible properties, and utilization of mushrooms. The 148-page reference section includes colored illustrations, discussions of the characteristics of the fruiting body, habitat and distribution, occurrence, culinary properties, scientific and common names, and indexes. It is written with an emphasis on natural history and is appropriate for the nonspecialist.

76   *Elsevier's Dictionary of Horticultural and Agricultural Plant Production: In Ten Languages, English, Dutch, French, German, Danish, Swedish, Italian, Spanish, Portuguese, and Latin.* New York: Elsevier, 1990. 817 p. $230.00. ISBN 0444880623.

This is a revised edition of *Elsevier's Dictionary of Horticulture in Nine Languages* (1970) and includes about 500 botanical, agricultural, and landscaping terms as well as selected plant names. It is arranged by the English term, with the other languages listed under the English. There are separate indexes in the other languages leading to the main entry.

77   Gledhill, D. *The Names of Plants.* 3rd ed. New York: Cambridge University Press, 2002. 326 p. $29.99 (paper). ISBN 052181863X; 0521523400 (paper).

This little book consists of two parts: a brief description of botanical nomenclature suitable for students and amateurs, and a glossary that translates the more descriptive scientific names into English. The third edition has been updated to include explanations of the *International Codes* of both *Botanical Nomenclature* (2000) and *Nomenclature for Cultivated Plants* (1995) (see chapter 10 for both codes).

78   Goodman, Robert M. *Encyclopedia of Plant and Crop Science.* New York: Marcel Dekker, 2004. 1300 p. $395.00 (print); $553.00 (online); $593.00 (print plus online). ISBN 0824709446 (print); 0824709438 (online); 0824742680 (print plus online).

Although the emphasis in this encyclopedia is on agricultural topics, it contains many articles discussing basic plant biology including topics such as oxidative stress, secondary metabolites, and the life cycles of plant pests.

79   Graf, Alfred Byrd. *Exotica, Series 4 International: Pictorial Cyclopedia of Exotic Plants from Tropical and Near-tropic Regions.* 11th ed. East Rutherford, NJ: Roehrs, 1982. 2 vol. ISBN 0911266178 (set).

This pictorial record of ornamental or fruited plants and trees is an exhaustive encyclopedia presenting 16,300 photographs, most black and white, and 300 drawings. There are discussions for each plant on its origins, botanical synonyms, cross-references, common name, and directions for care. For authors responsible for naming the plant, consult Bailey's *Hortus III*, above. *Exotica* and its companions *Hortica* and *Tropica* are good starting places for information on a large number of plants.

80   Graf, Alfred Byrd. *Hortica: Color Cyclopedia of Garden Flora in All Climates—Worldwide—and Exotic Plants Indoors.* East Rutherford, NJ: Roehrs, 1992. 1216 p. $195.00. ISBN 0911266259.

A companion to *Exotica*, above, and *Tropica*, below.

81   Graf, Alfred Byrd. *Tropica: Color Cyclopedia of Exotic Plants and Trees: For Warm-Region Horticulture—In Cool Climate the Summer Garden or Sheltered Indoors.* 4th ed. East Rutherford, NJ: Roehrs, 1992. 1152 p. ISBN 0911266240.

Contains over 7,000 photographs of cultivated tropical plants. The brief descriptions include country of origin and native climate.

82   Grebenshchikov, Oleg S. *Geobotanic Dictionary; Russian–English–German–French.* Königstein, Germany: Koeltz, 1979. 226 p. $54.00. ISBN 3874291642.

Geobotanical terminology, principal plant formations and world plant communities, and related terms from plant ecology, soil science, climatology, geomorphology, and phytogeography are included in the 2,660 entries. The contents include a Russian/English/German/French dictionary with English, German, and French indexes.

83   Griffiths, Mark. *Index of Garden Plants.* Portland, OR: Timber, 1994. 1234 p. ISBN 0881922463.

Provides currently accepted botanical names, synonyms, and common names for about 60,000 cultivated plants along with brief descriptions and natural distribution. Arranged by scientific names; common names are cross-referenced to the scientific name. The dictionary also has an introduction outlining plant nomenclature and an extensive illustrated glossary. Names in the index were taken from the *New Royal Horticultural Society Dictionary of Gardening* edited by Anthony Huxley, below, so this volume can be used as a common name index for the dictionary.

84   Heywood, Vernon H., consultant ed. *Flowering Plants of the World.* New York: Oxford University Press, 1993. 335 p. $65.00. ISBN 0195210379.

This encyclopedic treatment presents an introduction to forms, structure, ecology, uses, and classification of the flowering plants of the world; there is also a glossary. More than 300 angiosperm families are described and illustrated, many in full color. The descriptions include information on distribution, significant features, classification, economic uses, number of species, and genera.

85   Hickey, Michael, and Clive King. *The Cambridge Illustrated Glossary of Botanical Terms.* Cambridge, England: Cambridge University Press, 2000. 208 p. $28.00 (paper). ISBN 0521790808; 0521794013 (paper).

Contains over 2,400 terms used to describe vascular plants, most illustrated. The illustrations are in a separate section in the back of the book rather than being integrated with the text. A good source for illustrations of plant parts from roots to fruits.

86    Hogan, Sean, ed. *Flora: A Gardener's Encyclopedia: Over 20,000 Plants.* Portland, OR: Timber, 2003. 2 vol. plus CD-ROM. $99.95. ISBN 0881925381.

The subtitles sum this encyclopedia up nicely; it contains brief descriptions of over 20,000 plant species and varieties arranged alphabetically by genus. Each entry includes information on cultivation, hardiness zones, region of origin, and description. Some entries also include use, taxonomic notes, photographs, and more. Most plants are illustrated by color photographs. Introductory chapters discuss the history of botany and gardening, hardiness zones, nomenclature, and more. Although this is a horticultural encyclopedia, the large number of taxa covered makes it useful for obtaining general information on a wide range of plant genera. See also Graf's trio of guides annotated above and Huxley's *New Royal Horticultural Society Dictionary of Gardening*, below, for similar works.

87    Hora, Bayard, ed. *Oxford Encyclopedia of Trees of the World.* New York: Oxford University Press, 1981. 288 p. ISBN 0192177125.

This attractive and authoritative book covers a broad field in depth, providing a summary of the major genera of trees of the world. Beautiful color photographs and illustrations cover trees of every kind; there is information on the identification of trees. This book is an excellent general source for native and exotic trees of North America. A bibliography, a glossary, and common and Latin name indexes are included.

88    Huxley, Anthony, ed. in chief. *New Royal Horticultural Society Dictionary of Gardening.* New York: Grove's Dictionaries, 1999. 4 vol. $795.00. ISBN 1561590010 (set).

This encyclopedia is one of the most useful and comprehensive items annotated here. Although the emphasis is on cultivated plants, the coverage includes much more, including biographies of famous botanists, over 180 articles on aspects of plant biology and horticulture, a botanical glossary, and a glossary of plant taxonomy. The main portion of the dictionary is an alphabetical list of over 50,000 genera of plants with brief description, distribution, cultivation, and important species. There are over 4,000 line drawings. Not just for gardeners.

89    Jackson, Benjamin D. *A Glossary of Botanic Terms with Their Derivation and Accent.* 4th ed. London: G. Duckworth, 1991. 481 p. $35.00. ISBN 8121100054.

Originally published in 1928, this well-known and frequently reprinted glossary has 25,000 entries providing derivation of terms, accent, and definition. It puts terms into context with the use of their period, and gives authors' names (in parentheses) for authority of the definition. This dictionary may well be used in conjunction with one that is more modern; however, the information that

Jackson provides is unique in many ways and is especially useful for historical work.

90   Jones, David L. *Encyclopaedia of Ferns*. Portland, OR: Timber, 1987. 433 p. ISBN 0881920541.

This encyclopedia includes a great deal of basic information on fern botany as well as fern cultivation and propagation. Approximately half of the volume is dedicated to an encyclopedic listing of fern species, with illustrations for many of the species. Most entries include distribution, size, and information on cultivation.

91   Lincoln, Roger J., Geoffrey Allan Boxshall, and P. F. Clark. *A Dictionary of Ecology, Evolution, and Systematics*. 2nd ed. New York: Cambridge University, 1998. 361 p. $32.00 (paper). ISBN 0521591392; 052143842X (paper).

Over 11,000 entries are covered in this dictionary, which covers the subjects formerly known as natural history. The 21 appendixes are a nice addition, covering a wide range of lists, charts, and tables including the geological time scale, terrestrial biomes, the taxonomic hierarchy, common acronyms, and proof correction marks.

Mabberley, D. J. *The Plant-Book: A Portable Dictionary of the Vascular Plants*. 2nd ed.

See chapter 10 for full annotation. The dictionary includes many English common names as well as accepted scientific names; the list of author abbreviations used in plant nomenclature is a useful bonus.

92   Macura, Paul, comp. *Elsevier's Dictionary of Botany: In English, French, German, Latin, and Russian*. New York: Elsevier/North-Holland, 1979–1982. 2 vol. $209.00 (vol. 1); $209.00 (vol. 2). ISBN 0444417877 (vol. 1); 0444419772 (vol. 2).

The first volume of this dictionary covers over 6,000 plant names, listing common names where known in English, French, German, and Russian as well as the scientific names. Most of the plants are from Europe or are garden plants. The second volume provides translations of nearly 10,000 terms from botany, phytochemistry, horticulture, taxonomy, and other similar fields. Both volumes are arranged with the main section presenting the terms in English with a list of their translations. Separate indexes to the other languages provide access to the terms.

93   Macura, Paul, comp. *Elsevier's Dictionary of Botany: Russian-English*. Boston, MA: Elsevier, 2002. 541 p. $150.00. ISBN 0444512292.

Lists English and Russian scientific names for lichens, fungi, and vascular plants as well as definitions for a number of terms found in the Russian botanical literature. Contains about 60,000 terms.

94    Magill, R. E., ed. *Glossarium Polyglottum Bryologiae: A Multilingual Glossary for Bryology*. St. Louis, MO: Missouri Botanical Garden, 1990. 297 p. $19.95 (paper). (Monographs in Systematic Botany from the Missouri Botanical Garden, vol. 33).

The dictionary defines nearly 1,200 terms from bryology. Definitions are in English and include translations in Latin, French, German, Spanish, Japanese, and Russian. The English terms and their definitions as well as the Latin, French, German, and Spanish translations are also available on the Web at http://www .mobot.org/MOBOT/tropicos/most/Glossary/glosefr.html.

95    Malcolm, Bill, and Nancy Malcolm. *Mosses and Other Bryophytes: An Illustrated Glossary*. Nelson, New Zealand: Micro-Optics Press, 2000. 220 p. ISBN 0473067307.

A heavily illustrated dictionary covering the highly specialized, technical terminology used to describe mosses, liverworts, and hornworts. There are several detailed photographs per page illustrating many of the terms.

96    *Marshall Cavendish Illustrated Encyclopedia of Plants and Earth Sciences*. Bellmore, NY: Marshall Cavendish, 1990. 10 vol. $329.95. ISBN 0863079016.

Although plants and earth sciences may seem an odd combination, these 10 slim volumes contain a great deal of useful information and many beautiful pictures. This encyclopedia consists of articles on a variety of plant biology topics as well as plant descriptions. Volumes 1 through part of Volume 3 consist of a dictionary of plants and plant science, with most plant descriptions only about a paragraph long. The rest of Volumes 3 through 5 are descriptions of flowering plant families, whereas Volumes 6 through 7 are an encyclopedia of plant ecology. Volumes 8 and 9 cover earth sciences, and Volume 10 is an index. An alternative to Huxley's *New Royal Horticultural Society Dictionary of Gardening*, above, less detailed and/or technical, but also less expensive.

97    Massey, J. R., and J. C. Murphy. *Vascular Plant Systematics Glossary*. 1996. URL: http://www.ibiblio.org/botnet/glossary/.

This glossary was taken from chapter 6 of Radford's classic textbook *Vascular Plant Systematics* (see chapter 10). The illustrated glossary covers plant anatomy, general characters used in taxonomy, and terms specific to gymnosperms and angiosperms.

98    Miller, Paul R., and Hazel L. Pollard. *Multilingual Compendium of Plant Diseases*. St. Paul, MN: American Phytopathological Society for the United States Agency for International Development in cooperation with the U.S. Department of Agriculture, 1976–77. (Compendia Series, 2). 2 vol. $48.00 (vol. 2). ISBN 0890540187 (vol. 1); 0890540209 (vol. 2).

Although plant pathology is generally out of the scope of this guide, this particular compendium is included as a communication aid for botanists working with translations. The entries are arranged by Latin name of the host in association with the Latin name of the pathogen, resulting in the name of the disease in English and 20 other languages. Each disease is described in English, Interlingua, French, and Spanish; 22 language indexes refer to the disease descriptions.

99    Mitchell, Alan F. *The Trees of North America*. New York: Facts On File, 1987. 208 p. ISBN 0816018065.

A lavishly illustrated work covering the most common North American trees, along with selected rare species. About 500 species are discussed. The encyclopedia is arranged by group of trees, such as willows, larches, or poplars. Each group has leaves, bark, and general shape illustrated along with a brief text describing the trees. The author also provides a limited amount of information on selecting and cultivating trees. There are also range maps in a separate section.

100    Ness, Bryan D., ed. *Magill's Encyclopedia of Science: Plant Life*. Pasadena, CA: Salem, 2003. 4 vol. $457.00 (set). ISBN 1587650843 (set).

Aimed at high school and college students, this encyclopedia includes 379 essays covering both applied and research-oriented topics. Each essay includes a brief definition, cross-references and list of broader categories, and reading list. Several appendixes include a biographical list of botanists, an outline of plant taxonomy, common-to-scientific and scientific-to-common plant name lists, and a bibliography and Webliography. Topics include agriculture, molecular biology, plant physiology, taxonomy (including information on many families of plants), and more.

101    Pridgeon, Alec M., ed. *The Illustrated Encyclopedia of Orchids*. Portland, OR: Timber, 1992. 304 p. $39.95. ISBN 0881922676.

An attractive encyclopedia describing over 1,100 species of orchids. Although this is only a tiny fraction of the estimated 19,000 species of orchids, most of the most commonly grown species are included. Descriptions are extremely brief, but include distribution and cultivation information. The entries are alphabetical by genus, and the tribe, subtribe, etymology, and pronunciation are included for each genus.

102    Quattrocchi, Umberto. *CRC World Dictionary of Plant Names: Common Names, Scientific Names, Eponyms, Synonyms, and Etymology*. Boca Raton, FL: CRC, 2000. 4 vol. $829.95. ISBN 0849326737 (set).

This astonishing compendium includes just what the subtitle says: the source of scientific names to the level of the genus, plus common names in many languages. The dictionary is arranged alphabetically by scientific name, and each entry provides often detailed information on the etymology of the name; when the genus was named after an individual there is often detailed information on the honoree's career, publications, and biographical sources. Selected species are listed for some genera along with synonyms and common names used in countries around the world. Often many common names are given for a species. The dictionary lacks an index to common names, although it includes an extensive bibliography.

103    Robinson, Richard, ed. *Plant Sciences.* New York: Macmillan Reference USA, 2001. 4 vol. $395.00. ISBN 002865434X (set).

Designed for the use of high school students and undergrads. The nearly 300 essays cover specific plants as well as topics from molecular biology to ecology of plants. There are also biographical essays and information on careers in plant biology. Each essay has cross-references and a bibliography, and most contain illustrations as well.

104    Schroeter, A. I., V. A. Panasiuk, and V. A. Bykov, eds. *Dictionary of Plant Names: Over 100,000 Names of About 10,000 Species and Varieties of Flowering Plants and Fern-Like Plants in Latin, Russian, English and Chinese (Hieroglyphic and Latin Transliteration).* Königstein, Germany: Koeltz Scientific, 1999. 1033 p. $142.00. ISBN 387429398X.

Designed to help identify approved common names of plants from around the world, this dictionary includes synonyms for the scientific name, author of scientific name, and family as well as English, Russian, and Chinese common names. The dictionary includes title pages and introductions in English, Russian, and Chinese.

105    Schubert, Rudolf, and Gunther Wagner. *Pflanzennamen und botanische Fachworter: Botanische Lexikon: Mit einer "Einführung in die Terminologie und Nomenklatur," einem Verzeichnis der "Autornamen" und einem Überblick über das "System der Pflanzen."* 8 ed., neubearbeitete und erw. Aufl. Melsungen, Gemany: Verlag J. Neumann-Neudamm, 1984. 662 p. ISBN 3788804211.

German was formerly *the* language of systematic botany; hence the usefulness of a German botanical dictionary such as this. This *Pflanzennamen* is very similar to other English language botanical dictionaries, with discussions of nomenclature and systematics, a main section containing definitions of technical botanical terms and plant names (to the family or genus level), and a list of botanical authors.

106    Shosteck, Robert. *Flowers and Plants: An International Lexicon with Biographical Notes.* New York: Quadrangle/New York Times Book, 1974. 329 p. ISBN 0812904532.

This dictionary is arranged by common name of flora in North America and Canada. There are several thousand entries that include botanical name, origin of the name, use, and history for each plant. Each page includes at least one line drawing and the accounts are interesting, enjoyable reading. A glossary, bibliography, and index are provided. Biographical sketches of the "notable" figures in botanical history are included, making this dictionary, along with Jaeger's *Source-Book* (see chapter 10), of importance to the historian.

107    Stearn, William T. *Stearn's Dictionary of Plant Names for Gardeners: A Handbook on the Origin and Meaning of the Botanical Names of Some Cultivated Plants*. Portland, OR: Timber, 2002. 363 p. $19.95. ISBN 088192556X (paper).

The purpose of this book is to provide a source of reliable information for gardeners on the significance of botanical names attached to cultivated plants. It is a revised edition of A.W. Smith's *A Gardener's Dictionary of Plant Names* (1972). Stearn provides an introduction to botanical names followed by a dictionary of botanical names, both generic and specific, as well as an introduction to vernacular names and a dictionary of vernacular names. The combination of botanical and vernacular names, plus the accuracy of Stearn's derivations, makes this a valuable tool for both gardeners and botanists working with cultivated plants.

108    Thomas, Brian, Denis J. Murphy, and Brian G. Murray, eds. *Encyclopedia of Applied Plant Sciences*. San Diego, CA: Elsevier Academic, 2003. 3 vol. $995.00. ISBN 0122270509 (set).

Most entries in this encyclopedia outline recent advances in basic plant biology research and indicate their use in applied fields. Each article contains a glossary, cross-references, and further readings.

109    Ulloa, Miguel, Richard T. Hanlin, Samuel Aguilar, and Elvira Aguirre Acosta. *Illustrated Dictionary of Mycology*. St. Paul, MN: APS, 2000. 448 p. $99.00. ISBN 0890542570.

Originally written in Spanish, this dictionary defines about 3,800 terms, including their etymology, and includes about 750 illustrations. It does not include taxonomic terms or the names of fungi although there is an appendix outlining fungal taxonomy.

110    Vaucher, Hugues, comp. *Elsevier's Dictionary of Trees and Shrubs: In Latin, English, French, German, Italian*. New York: Elsevier, 1986. 413 p. $203.00. ISBN 0444425691.

The dictionary provides common names for over 2,300 scientific names from 140 families, 510 genera, and 1,650 species of trees and shrubs found in the temperate Northern and Southern Hemispheres. The main part of the dictionary is arranged by scientific name and lists common names in the appropriate languages along with codes that indicate height, characteristics (evergreen, soil needs, etc.), and an indication of the approximate number of species in the genus. There are separate indexes for each vernacular language.

111   *The Visual Dictionary of Plants.* New York: Dorling Kindersley, 1992. 64 p. (Eyewitness Visual Dictionaries). ISBN 1564580164; 1564580172.

Although out of print and aimed at a juvenile audience, this colorful dictionary is useful for anyone wanting photographic illustrations of different types of plants and/or plant parts. See also Perry's *Photo Atlas for Botany* and Van De Graaff's *A Photographic Atlas for the Botany Laboratory,* both in chapter 7.

112   Watts, Donald, comp. *Elsevier's Dictionary of Plant Names and Their Origin.* New York: Elsevier Science, 2000. 1001 p. $191.00. ISBN 0444503560.

Contains about 30,000 common names for wild and cultivated plants, including English and a few American uses. The terms also include literary and archaic plant names. The author includes brief descriptions of the meaning of the names, if known.

113   White, Richard C., comp. *Elsevier's Dictionary of Plant Names of North America, Including Mexico: In Latin, Spanish (Mexican and European), and English (American).* Boston, MA: Elsevier, 2003. 600 p. $175.00. ISBN 0444512721.

This multilingual dictionary will be most useful for people working in the southwestern United States and northern Mexico, because it provides common names in English and Spanish for 7,000 plants of the region. The main portion of the dictionary is arranged alphabetically by scientific name, and there are also separate indexes to common names in English and Mexican Spanish.

114   Wrobel, Murray, and Geoffrey Creber, comp. *Elsevier's Dictionary of Fungi and Fungal Plant Disease: In Latin, English, German, French, and Italian.* New York: Elsevier, 1998. 400 p. $144.00. ISBN 0444827749.

This multilingual dictionary lists common names for fungi and fungal pathogens. The main section is arranged alphabetically by scientific name. Each entry includes common names in one or more of European languages. There are indexes for each language.

# Handbooks and Methods

115   Association of Applied Biologists. *Descriptions of Plant Viruses.* Wellesbourne, England: Association of Applied Biologists, 1970– . URL: http://www.dpvweb.net/.

Originally published in paper from 1970 to 1989 by CAB International and on CD-ROM in 1998, it is now freely available on the Web. The site provides an introduction to plant viruses, over 400 descriptions of plant viruses, taxonomic information, information on gene sequences, and links to other sites. Formerly titled *AAB Descriptions of Plant Viruses* and *CMI/AABI Descriptions of Plant Viruses*.

116   *Bibliotheca Mycologica*. Vol. 1– . Berlin: J. Cramer, 1967– . Irregular. Price varies. ISSN 0067-8066.

This monographic series "publishes monographs on studies of fungi in the widest sense. This includes papers on the physiology, taxonomy, morphology, ecological aspects, and biochemical aspects of fungi." Most volumes are cataloged separately in libraries.

117   Coyle, Heather Miller, ed. *Forensic Botany: Principles and Applications to Criminal Casework*. Boca Raton, FL: CRC, 2004. 320 p. $119.95. ISBN 0849315298.

Covers topics from the collection and preservation of plant-based evidence at crime scenes to testing methods to an overview of plant biology. Includes case studies and guidelines for using botanical evidence.

118   Day, Robert A. *How to Write and Publish a Scientific Paper*. 5th ed. Phoenix, AZ: Oryx, 1998. 275 p. $40.95; $27.95. ISBN 1573561649; 1573561657 (paper).

Filled with often amusing examples of how not to write a scientific paper, this guide discusses ethical issues and provides detailed information on preparing each part of a paper, from writing the introduction to preparing good tables and illustrations and from submitting the manuscript to dealing with the review process. The author also discusses other forms of scientific writing such as poster sessions, review papers, and book reviews. Day is also author of *Scientific English*, below.

119   Day, Robert A. *Scientific English: A Guide for Scientists and Other Professionals*. 2nd ed. Phoenix, AZ: Oryx, 1995. 148 p. $27.95 (paper). ISBN 0897749898 (paper).

Useful for both native and nonnative English speakers, this guide covers everything from grammar and style to the use of jargon and the rise of English as the *lingua franca* of the scientific world. Appendixes list correct uses of punctuation, problem words, and words to avoid. Day is also author of *How to Write and Publish a Scientific Paper*, above.

120   Francki, R. I. B., Robert G. Milne, and T. Hatta. *Atlas of Plant Viruses*. Boca Raton, FL: CRC, 1985. 2 vol. ISBN 0849365015 (vol. 1); 0849365023 (vol. 2).

This is a comprehensive collection of plant virus electron micrographs; there are 192 examples of all taxonomic groups designated by the International Committee on Taxonomy of Viruses. Data includes information on physical, chemical, structural, cytopathological, and antigenic properties of viruses. This should be of great value for botanical viral research.

121    Galun, Margalith, ed. *CRC Handbook of Lichenology*. Boca Raton, FL: CRC, 1988. 3 vol. $479.85. ISBN 0849335809 (set).

This handbook covers a wide variety of topics about lichens. Volume 1 covers general topics including the history of lichenology, the fungal and algal components and their relationship, reproduction, and physiology. Volume 2 covers ecology and ecophysiology, and Volume 3 concludes with chemical constituents, classification, lichens and pollutants, use of lichens, and cultivation information.

122    Gibson, Arthur C., and Park S. Nobel. *The Cactus Primer*. Cambridge, MA: Harvard University Press, 1986. 286 p. $27.95 (paper). ISBN 0674089901; 067408991X (paper).

Provides detailed information on the biology of the cacti, from anatomy to phylogeny. There is a detailed glossary, and each chapter has an extensive bibliography.

123    Glimn-Lacy, Janice, and Peter B. Kaufman. *Botany Illustrated: Introduction to Plants, Major Groups, Flowering Plant Families*. New York: Van Nostrand, 1984. 146 p. ISBN 0442229690.

This book is written for students of botany and botanical illustration interested in learning more about plants with reference to methods of illustration. The book is divided into three parts: an introduction to botanical facts; a section including bacteria to flowering plants; a section on major flowering plant families. Each page is a separate subject with a separate full page of illustrative examples of scientifically accurate line drawings including a coloring code guide. There are brief explanations about methods and suggestions for sources of plants. This unusual book is included here because of its discussion about drawing materials and its excellent examples of illustration technique.

124    Hill, Stephen A. *Methods in Plant Virology*. Oxford: Blackwell, 1985. 167 p. (Methods in Plant Pathology, 1). ISBN 0632009950 (paper).

Published on behalf of the British Society for Plant Pathology, this methodology handbook presents basic techniques, rationale, materials required, step-by-step procedures, interpretation of results, additional references, and detailed recipes where appropriate. Basic biophysical and chemical knowledge is assumed. Chapters include histological and other basic methods, virus characterization and storage, transmission tests, serological techniques, and electron microscopy. Useful for the student at the bench, this volume also helps provide elementary understanding of plant virology.

125    Holmgren, Noel H., and Bobbi Angell. *Botanical Illustration: Preparation for Publication.* Bronx, NY: New York Botanical Garden, 1986. 74 p. ISBN 0893272728 (paper).

Provides detailed, practical information on creating botanical illustrations. This guide covers equipment needed, techniques for drawing plants, and instructions for creating maps, graphs, and photographs.

126    Juniper, B. E., R. J. Robins, and D. M. Joel. *The Carnivorous Plants.* San Diego, CA: Academic, 1989. 353 p. ISBN 0123921708.

Carnivorous plants have a fascinating range of adaptations for living in their difficult environments, and this book describes their biology in detail. There are sections on habitat, prey attraction mechanisms, digestion, phytochemicals, and evolution. See Slack's handbook by the same name in chapter 10 for information on individual genera.

127    Lee, Welton L., Bruce M. Bell, and John F. Sutton, eds. *Guidelines for Acquisition and Management of Biological Specimens.* Lawrence, KS: Association of Systematics Collections, 1982. 42 p. ISBN 0942924029.

"A Report of the Participants of a Conference on Voucher Specimen Management" that discusses methods of collection, identification, preparation, repository selection, legislation, publication policies, costs, fees, and funding.

128    Lide, David R., ed. in chief. *CRC Handbook of Chemistry and Physics.* 85th ed. Boca Raton: CRC, 2004. 2,712 p. $139.95. ISBN 0849304857.

Revised annually, this is a classic must-have for scientists in all areas, providing reliable and authoritative chemical and physical data. Also available electronically.

129    McMillan, Vicky. *Writing Papers in the Biological Sciences.* 3rd ed. Boston, MA: Bedford/St. Martin's, 2001. 207 p. $24.95 (spiral bound). ISBN 0312258577 (spiral bound).

A straightforward, basic outline of everything from doing literature searches and handling data through writing and revising papers. The author also discusses writing review papers, creating oral and poster presentations, and developing resumes and curriculum vitae.

130    Mead, R., R. N. Curnow, and A. M. Hasted. *Statistical Methods in Agriculture and Experimental Biology.* 3rd ed. Boca Raton, FL: Chapman and Hall/ CRC, 2003. 472 p. $55.75. ISBN 1584881879.

An introductory text explaining basic statistical methods appropriate for students and research workers in agriculture and experimental biology.

131    Peterson, Curt M., and Roland R. Dute. *Plant Biology: Laboratory Manual*. 3rd ed. Dubuque, IA: Kendall/Hunt, 1987. 205 p. ISBN 0840342373 (paper).

Appropriate for a freshman course in biology, this successful lab manual provides nine laboratory exercises beginning with an evolutionary survey of organisms from four different kingdoms, followed by a study of the structure and physiology of seed plants. Appendices provide information on scheduling preparation, materials, supplies, reagents, prepared slides and suppliers, and special techniques. There is liberal use of figures, photographs, and questions that aid understanding.

132    *Plants Database*. Baton Rouge, LA: U.S. Department of Agriculture, Natural Resources Conservation Service, 1990– . URL: http://plants.usda.gov/.

The database provides standardized information about the vascular and nonvascular plants (excluding fungi) of the United States and its territories including names, checklists, distributional data, species abstracts, characteristics, images, references, and much more. Users can get reports on several topics such as invasive or endangered species, culturally significant plants, and alternative crops. This is an excellent place to start for information on a specific plant of the United States.

133    Roth, Charles Edmund. *The Plant Observer's Guidebook: A Field Botany Manual for the Amateur Naturalist*. Englewood, NJ: Prentice-Hall, 1984. 222 p. ISBN 0136807453.

The author describes this book as "a source of tools and strategies for personal investigations into the lives of plants." It is a how-to, hands-on botanical guide for amateurs, students, teachers, camp counselors, and hikers to gathering information about plants, maintaining a journal, using a field guide and keys, conservation, organizing field data, and seeking environmental information. There is a chapter about the plant observer's tool kit, and a bibliography and an index are included.

134    Stevens, Russell B., ed. *Mycology Guidebook*. Seattle, WA: University of Washington Press, 1981. 712 p. ISBN 0295958413.

This manual assembles information to assist teachers in preparing mycological laboratory courses, but its usefulness is much broader. It provides information on field collecting, isolation techniques, culture maintenance, taxonomic groups, ecological groups, fungi as biological tools, and extensive references for culture repositories, stains and media, and available films.

135   Stuessy, Tod F., and S. H. Sohmer, eds. *Sampling the Green World: Innovative Concepts of Collection, Preservation, and Storage of Plant Diversity.* New York: Columbia University Press, 1996. 289 p. $59.50. ISBN 0231101368.

Based on a 1993 symposium by the same name, the chapters in this volume cover the handling of plant specimens, both the actual plants themselves and plant images.

136   Style Manual Committee, Council of Biology Editors. *Scientific Style and Format: The CBE Manual for Authors, Editors, and Publishers.* 6th ed. New York: Cambridge University Press, 1999. 825 p. $60.00. ISBN 0521471540.

The standard style manual for the biological sciences now covers all of the scientific disciplines and is designed for the use of everyone from authors to publishers. It discusses general and special scientific style conventions, describes publication standards for various types of scientific publications, and outlines the publication process from manuscript preparation through proof correction. It also provides a plant sciences section in the section on Special Scientific Conventions that primarily covers nomenclature. This version is a revision of the 5th edition of the *CBE Style Manual.*

137   West, Keith. *How to Draw Plants: The Techniques of Botanical Illustration.* Portland, OR: Timber, 1996. $19.95. ISBN 0881923508.

This book examines in detail the technical aspects of botanical illustrating. It includes a brief outline on the evolution of botanical illustration, with chapters on basic equipment, concepts, plant handling, plants in detail, and the use of various media. There are many lovely black-and-white and color illustrations. Other books of interest by West are *How to Draw and Paint Wild Flowers* (Timber, 1993) and *Painting Plant Portraits: A Step-by-Step Guide* (Timber, 1991).

138   Zweifel, Frances W. *A Handbook of Biological Illustration.* 2nd ed. Chicago, IL: University of Chicago Press, 1988. 137 p. $14.00 (paper). ISBN 0226997006, 0226997014 (paper).

This book discusses the materials and techniques of biological illustration, with emphasis on black-and-white drawing, color illustration, and photography. Also, see Glimn-Lacy's *Botany Illustrated* and West's *How to Draw Plants,* both annotated above.

# Textbooks and Treatises

139   Berg, Linda R. *Introductory Botany: Plants, People, and the Environment.* Ft. Worth, TX: Saunders College, 1997. 466 p. $87.95. ISBN 0030754534.

An introductory text for undergraduates, covering plant biology and diversity. Each chapter includes learning objectives, study outlines, key terms, review and thought questions, and suggested readings. The discussion of plant diversity includes Eubacteria and Archaebacteria, Protista, and fungi as well as the non-vascular and vascular plants.

140   Capon, Brian. *Botany for Gardeners: An Introduction and Guide*. Portland, OR: Timber, 1990. 220 p. $17.95 (paper). ISBN 0881921637; 0881922587 (paper).

For nonscientists, including gardeners and nonmajors. The emphasis is on practical information.

141   Carlile, M. J., Sarah C. Watkinson, and Graham W. Gooday. *The Fungi*. 2nd ed. San Diego, CA: Academic, 2001. 588 p. $78.95; $47.95 (paper). ISBN 0127384456; 0127384464 (paper).

Covering all aspects of fungal biology including taxonomy, anatomy and physiology, genetics, parasitism and mutualism, and biotechnology. The survey of fungal diversity is fairly short. Includes a glossary, and outline of fungal classification. Each chapter contains further readings, a list of Web sites, and review questions.

142   Clewer, Alan G., and D. H. Scarisbrick. *Practical Statistics and Experimental Design for Plant and Crop Science*. New York: Wiley, 2001. 332 p. $150.00; $50.00 (paper). ISBN 0471899089; 0471899097 (paper).

A practical text outlining the statistical methods used in basic and applied plant science research, from simple *t*-tests to nonparametric tests, with emphasis on statistical packages. The text includes tables for all the standard statistical tests, and examples for each test come from plant biology. Despite the title, there is little information on experimental design, the emphasis being on selecting the proper statistical test.

143   Deacon, J. W. *Modern Mycology*. 3rd ed. Malden, MA: Blackwell Science, 1997. 303 p. $86.95. ISBN 0632030771 (paper).

The author emphasizes fungal biology and its importance to humans and the environment rather than taxonomy. The first two editions were published as *Introduction to Modern Mycology*.

144   Graham, Linda E., James M. Graham, and Lee Warren Wilcox. *Plant Biology*. Upper Saddle River, NJ: Prentice Hall, 2003. 497 p. $101.33. ISBN 0130303712.

Designed for freshman or nonmajor plant biology courses, this text covers plant biology and ecology and has chapters on various ecosystems such as deserts or grasslands. Each chapter has an outline of chapter highlights, review questions, and suggestions for applying concepts found in the chapter; however, there are no references or further readings. An associated Web site at http://www.prenhall.com/plantbio/ has study aids and relevant Web sites.

145    Graham, Linda E. and Lee W. Wilcox. *Algae*. Upper Saddle River, NJ: Prentice Hall, 2000. 710 p. $88.00. ISBN 0136603335.

The introductory chapters of this textbook discuss algal biology and roles in a number of areas and two final chapters cover algal ecology. The bulk of the book consists of taxonomic chapters covering each major algal group. It contains a glossary, bibliography, and separate taxonomic and subject indexes. Suitable for use in an introductory course in algae or aquatic ecology.

146    Hoek, C. van den, D. G. Mann, and H. M. Jahns. *Algae: An Introduction to Phycology*. New York: Cambridge University Press, 1994. 623 p. $48.00 (paper). ISBN 0521304199; 0521316871 (paper).

Provides an introduction to the algae as well as a detailed description of each major taxa, from Cyanophyta through the Chlorophyta. The bulk of the text is the systematic descriptions.

147    Kendrick, Bryce. *The Fifth Kingdom*. 3rd ed. Newburyport, MA: Focus, 2000. 386 p. $42.95. ISBN 1585100226 (paper).

Aimed at lower-level undergraduates, this textbook includes more information on the interaction of humans and fungi than other mycological texts, including discussions of such topics as eating fungi, food spoilage caused by fungi, hallucinogenic fungi, and so on.

148    Lack, A. J., and David E. Evans. *Plant Biology*. Oxford, England: BIOS Scientific, 2001. 332 p. (Instant Notes Series). $34.95 (paper). ISBN 1859961975, 038791613X (paper).

A general overview of plant biology for undergraduate courses, covering all major areas from biochemistry to ecology.

149    Lee, Robert Edward. *Phycology*. 3rd ed. New York: Cambridge University Press, 1999. 614 p. $50.00 (paper). ISBN 0521630908; 0521638836 (paper).

A text for an introductory course in algae, this book covers both prokaryotic and eukaryotic algae. It is arranged in systematic order, divided by the evolution of various organelles. The author includes information on the biology of each taxa and use by humans.

150    Mauseth, James D. *Botany: An Introduction to Plant Biology*. 3rd ed. Boston, MA: Jones and Bartlett, 2003. 868 p. plus CD-ROM. $99.95. ISBN 0763721344; 076372517X (CD-ROM).

Suitable for use in an introductory plant biology course. About a third of the book consists of a survey of plants from prokaryotes to vascular plants. Although each chapter contains review questions and links to the associated Web site at http://biology.jbpub.com/botany/, there are no references. The *Plant Biology Tutor* CD-ROM provides images, tutorials, and experimental simulations.

151    Moore-Landecker, Elizabeth. *Fundamentals of the Fungi.* 4th ed. Upper Saddle River, NJ: Prentice Hall, 1996. 574 p. $110.00. ISBN 0133768643.

Another introductory mycology textbook, about half covering fungal systematics. The biology and use of fungi by humans is also covered extensively.

152    Nadakavukaren, Mathew, and Derek McCracken. *Botany: An Introduction to Plant Biology.* St. Paul, MN: West, 1985. 591 p. ISBN 0314852794 (paper).

Introductory text for majors or nonmajors. Includes chapter on plants of economic importance.

153    Northington, David K., Edward L. Schneider, and Daniel C. Scheirer. *The Botanical World.* 2nd ed. Dubuque, IA: Wm. C. Brown, 1996. 480 p. $39.95. ISBN 069724279X; 0697270505 (workbook).

An introductory text for undergraduates and general readers emphasizing plant biology rather than plant diversity. Includes workbook.

154    Raven, Peter H., Ray F. Evert, and Susan E. Eichhorn. *Biology of Plants.* 6th ed. New York: Worth, 1999. 944 p. $92.30. ISBN 1572590416.

First published in 1970, this text is one of the standards. As the title suggests, the emphasis is on plant biology rather than diversity. This edition contains expanded coverage of environmental issues. Each chapter has review questions. There are several appendixes and a glossary, but no references or lists of further readings.

155    Schofield, W. B. *Introduction to Bryology.* New York: Macmillan, 1985. 431 p. $54.95 (paper). ISBN 0029496608; 1930665261 (paper).

Designed for use in a course on bryology, this text covers the systematics and biology of the mosses, liverworts, and relatives. There are also several appendixes designed to further the study of bryophytes, including collecting and culturing bryophytes, techniques for chromosome studies, keys to orders, and a listing of bryophyte floras from around the world.

156    Sengbusch, Peter von, Alice Bergfeld, and Rolf Bergmann. *Botany Online: The Internet Hypertextbook.* International ed. Hamburg, Germany: University of Hamburg, 1990– . URL: http://www.biologie.uni-hamburg.de/b-online/e00/contents.htm.

An introductory undergraduate botany hypertextbook covering all the usual subjects, from the history of plant biology to genetics, cell biology, evolution, and systematics. The text was originally published in German, and at the time of viewing some sections (primarily systematics and ecology) had not been translated into English.

157   Stern, Kingsley Rowland, Shelley Jansky, and James E. Bidlack. *Introductory Plant Biology.* 9th ed. Boston, MA: McGraw-Hill, 2003. 589 p. $113.25. ISBN 0072930381.

An introductory text covering plant anatomy, physiology, genetics, ecology, and breeding. In addition, about half the volume consists of a survey of organisms from bacteria and Protista, to fungi and vascular plants. Each chapter includes a summary, review and discussion questions, additional reading, and links to the associated Web site (http://www.mhhe.com/botany/). Appendixes list scientific names of plants mentioned in the text, biological controls, useful and poisonous plants, houseplants, and metric conversions.

## Associations

158   American Association of Botanical Gardens and Arboreta (AABGA). 100 W 10th St., Ste. 614, Wilmington, DE 19801-6604. Phone: 302-655-7100. Fax: 302-655-8100. E-mail: pallenstein@aabga.org. URL: http://www.aabga.org/.

Directors and staffs of botanical gardens, arboreta, institutions maintaining or conducting horticultural courses, and others. Publishes *American Association of Botanical Gardens and Arboreta-Newsletter,* and *Public Garden.*

159   American Bryological and Lichenological Society (ABLS). Department of Biological Sciences, University of Nevada, 4505 Maryland Parkway, PO Box 454004, Las Vegas, NV 89154-4004. Phone: 702-895-3119. Fax: 702-895-3956. E-mail: lrs@nevada.edu. URL: http://www.unomaha.edu/~abls/.

Professional botanists, botany teachers, and hobbyists interested in the study of mosses, liverworts, and lichens. Maintains moss, lichen, and hepatic exchange clubs. Publishes *Bryologist* and *Evansia.*

160   American Fern Society (AFS). c/o Dr. George Yatskievych, Missouri Botanical Garden, PO Box 299, St. Louis, MO 63166-0299. Phone: 314-577-9522. E-mail: george.yatskievych@mobot.org. URL: http://amerfernsoc.org/.

Promotes the study of ferns and their allies by persons interested in the biology, taxonomy, and horticulture of ferns, club mosses, and horsetails. Publishes *American Fern Journal.*

161   American Orchid Society (AOS). 16700 AOS Lane, Delray Beach, FL 33446-4351. Phone: 561-404-2000. Fax: 561-404-2100. E-mail: theaos@aos .org. URL: http://orchidweb.org/.

Professional growers, botanists, hobbyists, and others interested in promoting all phases of orchidology. Publishes *Orchids* and various handbooks.

162   American Phytopathological Society (APS). 3340 Pilot Knob Road, St. Paul, MN 55121. Phone: 612-454-7250. Fax: 651-454-0766. E-mail: aps@scisoc .org. URL: http://www.apsnet.org/.

Professional educators, researchers, and other interested in the study and control of plant diseases. Publishes *Phytopathology News, Molecular Plant-Microbe Interactions, Phytopathology, Plant Disease: An International Journal of Applied Plant Pathology*, and more.

163   Botanical Society of America (BSA). 4474 Castleman St., St. Louis, MO 63166. Phone: 314-577-9566. Fax: 314-577-9519. URL: http://www.botany.org/.

Professional society of botanists and others interested in plant science. The largest U. S. botanical society, with 15 Special Interest sections covering almost every aspect of plant biology. Publishes *American Journal of Botany* and *Plant Science Bulletin*.

164   Botanical Society of the British Isles (BSBI). 68 Outwoods Road, Loughborough LE11 3LY, United Kingdom. Phone: 44 1283 568136. E-mail: alex@whildassociates.co.uk. URL: http://www.bsbi.org.uk/.

Amateur and professional botanists in England and the Republic of Ireland. Promotes the study of British and Irish flowering plants and ferns. Formerly: Botanical Society of London. Publishes *Watsonia*.

165   British Lichen Society (BLS). Department of Botany, Natural History Museum, Cromwell Road, London SW7 5BD, United Kingdom. Phone: 44 207 9425617. Fax: 44 207 9425529. E-mail: bls@nhm.ac.uk. URL: http://www .thebls.org.uk/.

Professional, academic, and amateur lichenologists involved in research. Publishes *BLS Bulletin, The Lichenologist*.

166   British Phycological Society (BPS). c/o Dr. Jackie Parry, Division of Biological Sciences, Lancaster University, Lancaster LA1 4YQ, United Kingdom. Phone: 44 1524 593489. Fax: 44 1524 843854. E-mail: j.parry@lancaster.ac.uk. URL: http://www.brphycsoc.org/.

Scientists, students, and other interested persons organized to further phycology, the study of algae and seaweed. Publishes *European Journal of Phycology, The Phycologist Newsletter,* and *Seaweeds of the British Isles.*

167   Canadian Botanical Association (CBA)/Association Botanique du Canada (ABC). c/o Christine D. Maxwell, Sec., Biology Department, Trent University, Peterborough, ON, Canada K9J 7B8. Phone: 705-748-1011. Fax: 705-748-1205. E-mail: cmaxwell@trentu.ca. URL: http://www.cba-abc.ca/.

A national organization for Canadian botanists supporting research and education. The association has several sections including ones on conservation, teaching, ecology, systematics, mycology, and structure. Publishes the *CBA/ABC Bulletin.*

168   Council on Botanical and Horticultural Libraries (CBHL). c/o Charlotte Tancin, Secretary, CBHL, Hunt Institute for Botanical Documentation, Carnegie Mellon University, Pittsburgh, PA 15213-3890. Phone: 412-268-7301. Fax: 412-268-5677. E-mail: ct0u@andrew.cmu.edu. URL: http://www.cbhl.net/.

Libraries and collections in botanical or horticultural materials, librarians, bibliographers, booksellers, publishers, researchers, and administrators. Purpose is to initiate and improve communication between persons and institutions concerned with the development, maintenance, and use of botanical and horticultural libraries.

169   International Mycological Associations (IMA). URL: http://www.biologi .uio.no/org/ima/.

National and international societies promoting the study of mycology in all its aspects. Constitutes the section for general mycology within the International Union of Biological Sciences. Publishes *IMA News.*

170   Mycological Society of America (MSA). c/o Kay Rose, Allen Marketing & Management, 810 E 10th St., Lawrence, KS 66044. Phone: 785-843-1235. Fax: 785-843-1274. URL: http://www.msafungi.org/.

Includes both professional and amateur mycologists. Web site includes membership information, links to mycological sites, full text of newsletter, meeting information, and jobs available. Formerly Mycological Section, Botanical Society of America. Publishes *Mycologia* and newsletter *Inoculum.*

171   North American Mycological Association (NAMA). 6615 Tudor Court, Gladstone, OR 97027-1032. Phone: 503-657-7358. E-mail: executivesec@ namyco.org. URL: http://www.namyco.org/.

Amateur and professional mycologists, students, and botanists. Promotes amateur mycology; sponsors field trips and taxonomic and mycological seminars. Publishes *McIlvainea, The Mycophile Newsletter.*

172   Phycological Society of America (PSA). c/o Blackwell Science Inc., Commerce Place, 350 Main St., Malden, MA 02148. Phone: 781-388-8250. Fax: 781-388-8270. E-mail: psa@psaalgae.org. URL: http://www.psaalgae.org/.

Educators, researchers, and others interested in the pure, or applied study and utilization of algae. Publishes *Journal of Phycology, Phycological Newsletter.*

# 3
# History and Biography

This chapter consists primarily of sources introducing the history and biography of the plant sciences. There is no attempt to be comprehensive; the focus is on the general. Most selections are in English and concentrate mainly on American and some British sources, with an emphasis on early American reference materials. Examples include classic histories as well as sources from other areas of plant science. The chapter also includes resources dealing with early botanical illustrations.

Articles of an historical or biographical nature appear in a wide variety of journals but no citations to articles have been included because they are beyond the scope of this guide. Similarly, biographies of individuals have been omitted. Although many of the selections are out of print, they have been included because they are classics and worth consultation if they are available. A few electronic resources are included.

Besides the abstracts and indexes listed in this chapter, the *Kew Record* (see chapter 10) also covers historical and biographical topics. *Biological Abstracts* (chapter 2) also contains a large historical component.

## Bibliographies and Guides to the Literature

173   Bridson, Gavin. *The History of Natural History: An Annotated Bibliography.* New York: Garland, 1994. 740 p. (Garland Reference Library of the Humanities, 991; Bibliographies on the History of Science and Technology, 24). ISBN 0824023196.

This is a guide to the history of natural history. There are sections listing historical sources for personnel, organizations, current awareness, biographies, and natural history libraries; core bibliographies for natural history, botany, and zoology; and historical and bibliographical methods.

174    Bridson, Gavin D. R., and James J. White. *Plant, Animal and Anatomical Illustration in Art and Science: A Bibliographical Guide from the 16th Century to the Present Day.* Detroit, MI: Omnigraphics, 1990. 450 p. ISBN 090675818.

This bibliography is a comprehensive guide to both the primary instructional and iconographical material and the secondary descriptive, historical, bibliographical, and biographical literature. The bibliography is arranged by broad subject with sections for drawing and painting, history, and photography for each subject. Includes lists of references, artist biographies, instructional literature for painting and drawing, and periodicals as well as title, subject, and name indexes.

175    *Catalogue of the Books, Manuscripts, Maps and Drawings in the British Museum (Natural History).* London: The Trustees of the British Museum, 1903–1940. 8 vol. Stechert-Hafner Reprint, 1964.

Author catalog of one of the world's great collections. Volumes 6 through 8 are supplements.

176    *Catalogue of the Manuscripts in the Library of the Linnean Society.* London: Linnean Society, 1934–1948. 4 pt.

This work includes four parts. In particular, Part 1, The Smith papers (The Correspondence and Miscellaneous Papers of Sir James Edward Smith, First President of the Society), 1934, compiled by Warren R. Dawson, covers the history of science and scientific biography as well as the history of botany and of the Linnean Society during the years between 1780 and 1828. The other three parts, by Spencer Savage, were published in 1937, 1940, and 1948, respectively.

177    Darlington, W. *Memorials of John Bartram and Humphrey Marshall. With Names of Their Contemporaries.* New York: Hafner, 1967. 585 p. (Classica Botanica Americana, Supplement, 1).

This book has been called the most frequently cited book today dealing with eighteenth-century botanical history in the American colonies. Contents include discussions of the progress of botany in North America, biographical sketches of John Bartram and Humphrey Marshall, and their correspondence with other well-known botanists and collectors of their day. Facsimile of the 1849 edition.

178    Haller, Albrecht von. *Bibliotheca Botanica.* New York: Johnson, 1967. 2 vol.

This older bibliography provides bibliographical and biographical information for 1,500 primary botanical authors and 3,500 less important writers, illustrators, explorers, and collectors. Reprint of the 1771–1772 edition.

179   Henrey, Blanche. *British Botanical and Horticultural Literature before 1800 Comprising a History and Bibliography of Botanical and Horticultural Books Printed in England, Scotland, and Ireland from the Earliest Times until 1800.* New York: Oxford University Press, 1975. 3 vol. ISBN 0192115480.

This work has stood the test of time very well. Appropriate for large public and research libraries. Volume 1 deals with the history and bibliography of the sixteenth and seventeenth centuries; Volume 2 discusses eighteenth-century botanical history; and Volume 3 is a bibliography of eighteenth-century books. Comprehensive, authoritative, historical, and bibliographical source important for the British Isles.

180   Hunt, Rachel McMasters Miller. *Catalogue of Botanical Books in the Collection of Rachel McMasters Miller Hunt.* New York: Maurizio Martino, 1991. 2 vol. in 3. $150.00. ISBN 1578980283.

This catalog contains a historical introduction to botany, medical aspects of early botanical books, and illustrations of early botanical works, all written by authorities in the field. Valuable information on sources and locations include complete and detailed bibliographic descriptions of botanical books. The compilation consists of Volume 1, Printed books 1477–1700, which lists several manuscripts of the twelfth, fifteenth, sixteenth, and seventeenth centuries; Volume 2, part 1, Introduction to printed books 1701–1800; and Volume 2, part 2, Printed books 1701–1800. Reprint of the 195861 Hunt Botanical Library edition.

181   Jackson, Benjamin D. *Guide to the Literature of Botany: Being a Classified Selection of Botanical Works, Including Nearly 6,000 Titles Not Given in Pritzel's Thesaurus.* Mansfield Center, CT: Martino Fine Books, 1999. 626 p. $65.00. ISBN 1578981484.

This companion to Pritzel's *Thesaurus* (see below) can be used for verification and as a finding aid for the older botanical literature. Nine thousand entries are arranged by subject classification. This is an authoritative bibliography by a botanist/scholar and a "must" for any botanical research collection. Reprint of the 1881 Longmans edition.

182   Johnston, Stanley H. *The Cleveland Herbal, Botanical, and Horticultural Collections: A Descriptive Bibliography of Pre-1830 Works from the Libraries of the Holden Arboretum, the Cleveland Medical Library Association, and the Garden Center of Greater Cleveland.* Kent, OH: Kent State University Press, 1992. 1216 p. $60.00. ISBN 0873384334.

A bibliography of pre-Linnean works, medicinal plants, herbals, horticultural, and botanical works held at the Cleveland Medical Library Association, the Holden Arboretum, and the Garden Center of Greater Cleveland.

183    Junk, Wilhelm. *Bibliographia Botanica*. Berlin: Junk, 1909. 288 p. plus *Bibliographiae Botanicae. Supplementum*. Berlin: Junk, 1916. 764 p.

This is a valuable source for verifying older botanical materials. The bibliography of 6,891 botanical papers and books is arranged by topic in the original volume and supplement, and then by author. There are no indexes. Subjects/ sections include an important list of older botanical periodicals with complete bibliographic information, history, anatomy and physiology, taxonomy, economic plants, illustrations, plants arranged by broad division, and floras. Some entries are annotated in German.

184    *Just's Botanischer Jahresbericht: Systematisch Geordnetes Repertorium der Botanischen Literatur aller Länder*. Berlin–Zehlendorf, Germany: Borntraeger, 1873–1944. 63 vol.

This bibliography of world botanical literature was one of the first library tools developed to aid in keeping up with the swift growth of primary journals during the 1800s. Some records contain abstracts. Includes annual indexes for authors and taxa. *Just's* is useful for retrospective searches and to fill the gap between the Royal Society's *International Catalogue of Scientific Literature* and *Botanical Abstracts* (both below).

185    Kronick, David A., comp. *Scientific and Technical Periodicals of the Seventeenth and Eighteenth Centuries: A Guide*. Metuchen, NJ: Scarecrow, 1991. 332 p. $58.00. ISBN 0810824922.

"The purpose of this guide is to bring together the periodicals and serial titles relevant to the history of science and technology which were published in the seventeenth and eighteenth centuries, and to indicate some of the places they may be located from available national union lists of periodicals and other sources" (from the preface). The main body of the guide is arranged alphabetically by title. Includes title, translations, editor, sources, locations, subjects, microforms, other titles, and indexes. There are subject, personal name, institutional name, and title indexes. Appendixes include microform publishers and formats, abbreviations, and references.

186    Meisel, Max. *A Bibliography of American Natural History: The Pioneer Century, 1769–1865*. Brooklyn, NY: The Premier, 1924–1929. 3 vol.

These volumes aim to trace, bibliographically, the rise and progress of natural history in the United States, which has great relevance to the study of botany. Volume 1 is an annotated bibliography of the publications relating to history, biography, and bibliography of American natural history and its institutions during colonial times and the pioneer century, published up to 1924. There are subject and geographic indexes as well as a selected bibliography of the biographies and bibliographies of the principal American naturalists of the time. Volumes 2 and 3 deal with the institutions that have contributed to American natural history from 1767 to 1865. Volume 3 also contains a bibliography of books, chronological tables, and an index of authors and institutions.

187   Nissen, Claus. *Die botanische Buchillustration, ihre Geschichte und Bibliographie.* 2 Aufl. Stuttgart, Germany: Hiersemann, 1966. 3 vol. in 1. ISBN 3777266140.

The first two volumes are a history of botanical illustration, followed by a bibliography, by author, of 2,400 botanical books containing illustrations. There are indexes by artist, plant, country, and author. Volume 3 is a supplement to the work.

188   *Plant Science Catalog: Botany Subject Index of the U.S. National Agricultural Library.* Boston, MA: G. K. Hall, 1976. 15 vol. ISBN 0816105065.

This photographic reproduction of subject cards from the collection of the National Agricultural Library contains citations to the world botanical literature from antiquity to 1952, including books, serials, proceedings, bulletins, textbooks, voyages, and biographies. Covers major and minor references in any field of plant science except pathology.

189   Pritzel, Georg August. *Thesaurus Literatureae Botanicae.* 2nd ed. Leipzig, Germany: F. A. Brockhaus, 1872. 576 p.

This bibliography includes 11,000 titles by 3,000 authors and covers all botanical fields up to 1870. Pritzel and Jackson (above) are two of the most important sources for information on separately published early botanical literature. Pritzel is supplemented by the Royal Society *Catalogue of Scientific Papers* (below). In Latin. Has been reprinted several times.

190   Rehder, Alfred. *The Bradley Bibliography: A Guide to the Literature of the Woody Plants of the World Published before the Beginning of the 20th Century.* Mansfield Centre, CT: Martino, 2001. 5 vol. $495.00 (set). ISBN 1578982820 (set).

The aim of this set, compiled at the Arnold Arboretum of Harvard University under the direction of Charles Sprague Sargent, is to include titles of all publications relating wholly or in part to woody plants. Books, pamphlets, and articles in serials in all languages are covered up to 1900. Volume 5 is an index to authors, subjects, and titles. Originally published by Riverside Press, 19111918, as no. 3 of the Publications of the Arnold Arboretum.

191   Reuss, Jeremias David. *Repertorium Commentationum a Societatibus Litterariis Editarum.* New York: B. Franklin, 1961. 16 vol. (Burt Franklin Bibliography and Reference Series, 29). $550.00 (set). ISBN 0833729667 (set).

Useful for retrospective work, this index covers publications of learned societies to 1800, making it a precursor to the Royal Society *Catalogue of Scientific Papers* (see below). Volume 2 covers botany and mineralogy. Reprint of the 1801–1821 edition published by Dieterich. In Latin.

192   Royal Botanic Gardens, Kew. Library. *Author Catalogue of the Royal Botanic Gardens Library, Kew, England.* Boston, MA: G. K. Hall, 1974. 5 vol. ISBN 0816110867.

The library of the Royal Botanic Gardens is particularly rich in early botanical books, pamphlets, and reprints, including plant taxonomy and distribution, economic botany, botanical travel and exploration, plant cytology, physiology, and biochemistry. This catalog is organized by author.

193   Royal Botanic Gardens, Kew. Library. *Classified Catalogue of the Royal Botanic Gardens Library, Kew, England.* Boston, MA: G. K. Hall, 1974. 4 vol. ISBN 0816110875.

A companion to the author catalog annotated above, this set provides subject access to the Kew library's holdings. The taxonomic works are classified using Bentham and Hooker's system (see chapter 10 for full annotation) and floras are arranged using a geographical system created at Kew.

194   Sargent, Charles Sprague, and Ethelyn Maria Tucker, comps. *Catalogue of the Library of the Arnold Arboretum of Harvard University.* Cambridge, MA: Printed at the Cosmos Press, 1914–1933. 3 vol. (Publications of the Arnold Arboretum, no. 6).

This work consists of Volume 1, Serial publications and authors and titles; Volume 2, Subject catalogue with supplement to Volume 1; and Volume 3, Serial publications and authors and titles plus Supplement, 1917–1933.

195   Sitwell, Sacheverell, and Wilfred Blunt. *Great Flower Books 1700–1900: A Bibliographical Record of Two Centuries of Finely-Illustrated Flower Books.* New York: Atlantic Monthly, 1990. 189 p. ISBN 0871132842.

This beautiful book includes notes on the flowers chosen for representation and instructive essays. Originally published in 1956 by William Collins (Great Britain).

# Databases, Abstracts, and Indexes

196   *America: History and Life.* Vol. 26– . Santa Barbara, CA: ABC-CLIO, 1989– . 5 times per year. Price varies. ISSN 0002-7065. Available electronically.

Covers the history of the United States and Canada (for the rest of the world see *Historical Abstracts* below) from prehistory to present. Started in 1964, it includes citations and abstracts to journal articles, citations of books and reviews, and citations to abstracts of dissertations completed worldwide. Also available on CD-ROM and online.

197  *Annual Bibliography of the History of Natural History.* Vol. 1–6. London: The Natural History Museum, 1982–1987. ISSN 0268-9936.

This comprehensive bibliography of articles and monographs relating to the history of natural history covers the literature of biology, botany, zoology, entomology, paleontology, mineralogy, forestry, agriculture, geography, and explorations. Publications cited were found in materials in the Natural History Museum libraries and the libraries of the Science Museum, the Victoria and Albert Museum, and the Wellcome Institute for the History of Medicine. The alphabetical list of citations is arranged by author. Includes indexes by subject, biography, and institution.

198  *Botanical Abstracts.* Vol. 1–15. Baltimore: Williams and Wilkins, 1918–1926. ISSN 0096-526X.

This was a monthly abstracting serial, international in scope. It was continued and expanded to all of the biological sciences by *Biological Abstracts.* These abstracts are useful retrospectively.

199  *Botanisches Zentralblatt: Referierendes Organ für das Gesamtgebiet der Botanik.* Vol. 1–179. Cassel, Germany: Theodor Fischer, 1880–1945.

This German abstracting tool for botany stopped being published in 1945 but it is included here because of its coverage of retrospective materials. It picks up from the *Royal Society Catalogue* and continues through the period of the *International Catalogue of Scientific Literature* through the literature covered by *Botanical Abstracts* and the fledgling *Biological Abstracts.* Also known as *Botanisches Centralblatt.*

200  *Historical Abstracts: Bibliography of the World's Historical Literature.* Vol. 52– . Santa Barbara, CA: ABC-Clio, 2001– . Bimonthly. Price varies. ISSN 1531-1120. Available electronically.

Historical coverage of the world from 1450 to the present (excluding the United States and Canada, which are covered in *America: History and Life*; see above). Includes citations and abstracts of articles from over 2,000 journals, citations to historical books reviewed in prestigious journals, and citations to abstracts of dissertations completed worldwide. Also available online and on CD-ROM.

201  *History of Science, Technology, and Medicine Database.* Mountain View, CA: RLG, 1975– . Available electronically.

Available only from RLG, under the auspices of the International Union of the History and Philosophy of Science, this database integrates four separately created bibliographies (*Isis Current Bibliography of the History of Science, Current Bibliography in the History of Technology, Bibliografia Italiana di Storia della Scienza,* and *Wellcome Bibliography of the History of Medicine*) to create the definitive international bibliography for the history of science, technology, and medicine and their influence on culture, from prehistory to the present. Not accessed.

202   Royal Society (Great Britain). *Catalogue of Scientific Papers.* 19 vol. London: C. J. Clay, 1867–1925.

This is the most important listing of retrospective scientific papers for the nineteenth century. The arrangement is by author, with reference to papers in 1,555 worldwide periodicals. Includes transactions of European academies and other learned societies. Each entry provides the author's full name, periodical title, and bibliographic citation for the article; abbreviations and list of journals scanned are included. Subject access is provided by a subject index published by Cambridge University Press, 1908–1914. For materials after 1900, see the *International Catalogue of Scientific Literature,* below. The *Royal Society Catalogue* is a monumental piece of work that must be included in any botanical research library collection. It has been reprinted several times.

203   Royal Society (Great Britain). *International Catalogue of Scientific Literature. M, Botany.* Vol. 1–14. London: Royal Society of London, 1902–1919. $225.00 (set).

This publication serves as a continuation to the *Catalogue of Scientific Papers,* above, and includes original and scientific botanical literature for the period 1901–1914. The M section serves as a botanical subject index to the worldwide scientific literature and is arranged by classification of morphology, anatomy, physiology, pathology, evolution, taxonomy, geographic distribution, and by author. Each annual volume includes a list of journals scanned with their abbreviations. This is a unique source for the period covered that must be included in the collection of any botanical research library. Published for the International Council by the Royal Society.

# Serials

204   *Archives of Natural History.* Vol. 10– . London: Society for the History of Natural History, 1981– . Semiannual. $170.00. ISSN 0260-9541.

A highly respected journal, distributed free to all members of the Society for the History of Natural History. It contains refereed, illustrated papers and reviews of recently published books. Publishes papers on the history and bibliography of natural history in its broadest sense. Includes, among other topics, botany, as well as the lives of naturalists, their publications, correspondence and collections, and the institutions and societies to which they belong. Bibliographical papers concerned with the study of rare books, manuscripts and illustrative material, and analytical and enumerative bibliographies are also published. Continues the *Journal of the Society for the Bibliography of Natural History*.

205   *Biographical Memoirs of the National Academy of Sciences.* Vol. 1– . Washington DC: National Academy Press, 1877– . Irregular. Price varies. ISSN 0077-2933.

This annual publication includes complete biographical information about the deceased members of the National Academy of Sciences. A portrait, bibliography of publications, and complete chronology are provided for each scientist. The full text is available for free at http://www.nap.edu/readingroom/books/biomems/.

206   *Curtis's Botanical Magazine.* Vol. 12– . Cambridge, MA: Blackwell Publishers for the Royal Botanic Gardens, Kew, 1995– . Quarterly. $435.00. ISSN 1355-4905. Available electronically.

In terms of historical significance, *Curtis's Botanical Magazine* is the oldest botanical journal in continuous publication. It was founded in 1787 in London by William Curtis, the owner and editor as well as an eminent English botanist and entomologist. It changed titles at various times: *The Botanical Magazine or Flower Garden Displayed* (1787–1800), *Curtis's Botanical Magazine* (1801–1983), and *The Kew Magazine* (1984–1994). The full text of the first 20 years of the magazine can be viewed at the National Agriculture Library's site at http://www.nal.usda.gov/curtis/.

207   *History and Philosophy of the Life Sciences.* Vol. 1– . Basingstoke, England: Taylor and Francis, 1979– . (Publicazioni della Stazione Zoologica di Napoli, Section 2). Quarterly. $414.00. ISSN 0391-9714. Available electronically.

Devoted to the historical development of the life sciences (biology, medicine) and of their social and epistemological implications with emphasis on the modern Western scientific thought.

208   *Huntia.* Vol. 1– . Pittsburgh, PA: Hunt Botanical Library, Carnegie Institute of Technology, 1964– . Irregular. $60.00 per volume. ISSN 0073-4071.

Publishes articles on all aspects of the history of botany, including exploration, art, literature, biography, iconography, and bibliography.

209   *Isis.* Vol. 1– . Chicago, IL: Published by the University of Chicago Press for the History of Science Society, 1913– . 5 times per year. $300.00. ISSN 0021-1753. Available electronically.

"Since its inception, *Isis* has featured scholarly articles, research notes and commentary on the history of science, medicine, technology, and their cultural influences. Review essays and book reviews on new publications in the field are also included. An official publication of the History of Science Society, this is the oldest (and most widely circulating) English-language journal in the field." Older issues available electronically to subscribers of JSTOR.

210    *Journal of the History of Biology.* Vol. 1– . Dordrecht, the Netherlands: Kluwer Academic, 1968– . 3 times per year. $378.00. ISSN 0022-5010. Available electronically.

This journal "is devoted to the history of the biological sciences, with additional interest and concern in philosophical and social issues confronting biology. While all historical epochs are welcome, particular attention has been paid in recent years to developments during the nineteenth and twentieth centuries. The journal serves both the working biologist who needs a full understanding to the historical and philosophical bases of the field and the historian of biology interested in following developments in the biological sciences."

211    Royal Society (Great Britain). *Biographical Memoirs of Fellows of the Royal Society.* Vol. 1– . London: The Royal Society of London, 1955– . Annual. $230.00. ISSN 0080-4606.

This source includes portraits and biographical information of deceased members of the Royal Society of London. Unlike the United States' National Academy, the Royal Society allows foreign membership. This publication continues the *Obituary Notices of Fellows of the Royal Society.* For obituary notices prior to 1932, consult the *Proceedings of the Royal Society of London.* Back issues are available electronically with a five-year moving wall via a JSTOR subscription.

*Taxon.*
See chapter 10 for full annotation. Includes landmark historical articles.

---

# Dictionaries and Encyclopedias

212    Barnhart, John Hendley. *Biographical Notes upon Botanists.* Boston, MA: G. K. Hall, 1965. 3 vol.

This unique source lists biographical details of botanists from the earliest times to the late 1940s, including information on their lives, academic history, obituary notices, location of portraits, travels, and collections. Maintained in the New York Botanical Garden Library. See also the Hunt Institute's *Biographical Dictionary of Botanists Represented in the Hunt Institute Portrait Collection*, below.

213    Desmond, Ray, and Christine Ellwood. *Dictionary of British and Irish Botanists and Horticulturists: Including Plant Collectors, Flower Painters and Garden Designers*. Rev. and completely updated ed. London: Taylor and Francis, 1994. 825 p. $369.95. ISBN 0850668433.

There are over 13,000 entries for botanists, painters, and garden designers that include biographical information, references in the literature, commemorative plant names, and location of collections, manuscripts, drawings, and portraits. An excellent source of information on the development of botany in Britain and recommended for botanical and historical libraries. Includes subject index.

214    *Dictionary of American Biography*. New York: Charles Scribner's Sons, 1998. 11 vol. plus supplements. ISBN 0684806118 (CD-ROM).

The set, originally published from 1928 to 1936 and reprinted several times since then, records the lives of celebrated women and men who have made significant contributions to American life. Includes over 19,000 biographies covering people who died through 1980. In addition, a comprehensive index to the entire set is available. Botanists are among the outstanding individuals from over 700 fields of endeavor who are chronicled in signed biographies by specialists.

215    Gillispie, Charles Coulston, and Frederic Lawrence Holmes. *Dictionary of Scientific Biography*. New York: Scribner, 1981– . 18 vol. in 10, plus supplements. ISBN 0684169622 (set).

"Published under the sponsorship of the American Council of Learned Societies." Contains more than 5,000 biographies of mathematicians and natural scientists from all countries and all historical periods. Besides biographical information, includes complete bibliographies of the scientists' work and a comprehensive discussion of their scientific contributions.

Holmgren, Patricia K., and Noel H. Holmgren. *Plant Specialists Index*.

See chapter 10 for full annotation. Includes directory type information for institutions and their staff members.

216    Hunt Institute for Botanical Documentation and Hunt Botanical Library. *Biographical Dictionary of Botanists Represented in the Hunt Institute Portrait Collection*. Boston, MA: G. K. Hall, 1972. 451 p. ISBN 0816110239.

The listings in this catalog include 11,000 people represented in 17,000 portraits. Adds biographical information, botanical specialty, and countries of principal activity. Other sources for portraits are Barnhart's *Biographical Notes* (above), *Taxon* (see chapter 10), and Stafleu and Cowan's *Taxonomic Literature* (see chapter 10).

Huxley, Anthony, ed. in chief. *New Royal Horticultural Society Dictionary of Gardening.*

See chapter 2 for full annotation. This encyclopedia includes biographies of several famous botanists.

Jaeger, Edmund C. *A Source-Book of Biological Names and Terms.* 3rd ed.

See chapter 10 for full annotation. Contains biographies of people who have plants and animals named after them.

217   Matthew, H. C. G., and Brian Harrison. *Oxford Dictionary of National Biography: In Association with the British Academy: From the Earliest Times to the Year 2000.* New York: Oxford University Press, 2004. 60 vol. $13,000.00 (set). ISBN 019861411X (set).

A collection of 50,000 specially written biographies of men and women who have shaped all aspects of the British past, from the earliest times to the end of the year 2000. Includes over 10,000 illustrations on a total of 61,792 pages, written by almost 10,000 contributors. The online version, available by subscription at http://www.oxforddnb.com/, includes the full text of both this new edition and the original edition. Online updates will be published three times each year starting in January 2005 and will add new biographies (taking in people who died after 2000) in addition to reference material designed to help readers navigate and interpret the dictionary.

218   Porter, Roy, and Marilyn Bailey Ogilvie. *Biographical Dictionary of Scientists.* 3rd ed. New York: Oxford University Press, 2000. 2 vol. $125.00 (set). ISBN 0195216636 (set).

This new edition features more than 80 new entries. The biographies clearly present each scientist's contributions and provide fascinating insights into the workings of scientific discovery and validation. Includes 150 illustrations, updated historical overviews of the major sciences, chronologies, quotations, bibliographies, tables of scientific discoveries and Nobel Prize winners, and an enlarged glossary.

Quattrocchi, Umberto. *CRC World Dictionary of Plant Names: Common Names, Scientific Names, Eponyms, Synonyms, and Etymology.*

See chapter 2 for full annotation. This dictionary includes biographical information on most individuals who were honored by having plants named after them.

Shosteck, Robert. *Flowers and Plants: An International Lexicon with Biographical Notes.*

See chapter 2 for full annotation. As the subtitle indicates, the dictionary includes biographical sketches.

# Handbooks and Methods

219   Allen, David Elliston Allen. *The Botanists: A History of the Botanical Society of the British Isles Through a Hundred and Fifty Years*. Winchester, England: St. Paul's Bibliographies, 1986. 232 p. $40.00. ISBN 0906795362.

Commissioned by the Botanical Society, this is a very readable, full-scale history written by the Society's official historian. It includes 25 illustrations, membership figures, a list of members and officers, and principal conferences.

220   Anderson, Frank J. *An Illustrated History of the Herbals*. New York: Columbia University Press, 1997. 270 p. $18.95 (paper). ISBN 1583481141 (paper).

This is an herbal sampler portraying the unique character and flavor of selected herbals by illustrations from the herbals themselves. For amateur botanists, and college/public libraries. For a more comprehensive discussion, consult Arber's *Herbals* or Blunt's *The Illustrated Herbal*, both below.

221   Arber, Agnes Robertson. *Herbals: Their Origin and Evolution: A Chapter in the History of Botany, 1470–1670*. 3rd ed. New York: Cambridge University Press, 1986. 358 p. (Cambridge Science Classics). $45.00 (paper). ISBN 0521338794 (paper).

This classic survey "stands as the major survey of the period 1470 to 1670 when botany evolved into a scientific discipline separate from herbalism." First published in 1912, it was extensively revised in the 1938 second edition. This edition also includes two of Arber's later writings and a new introduction and annotations by W. T. Stearn. Appendix I provides a chronological list (not exhaustive) of the principal herbals and related botanical works published between 1470 and 1670. Appendix II is an alphabetical list of the historical and critical works consulted during the preparation of the book.

222   Blunt, Wilfrid, and Sandra Raphael. *The Illustrated Herbal*. Rev. paper ed. New York: Thames and Hudson, 1994. 190 p. ISBN 0500277869 (paper).

Examples from early works about herbs, medicinal plants, printing, and botanical illustration. See also Anderson and Arber, both above.

223   Blunt, Wilfrid, and William T. Stearn. *The Art of Botanical Illustration*. Rev. and enlarged ed. New York: Dover, 1994. 304 p. $19.95 (paper). ISBN 0486272656 (paper).

Lavishly illustrated, this scholarly book deserves its reputation as the definitive and exhaustive historical survey of botanical illustration from prehistoric to modern times. Appendixes include a series of eight articles on botanical drawing, some illustrated books on British plants, and sources of further information.

Brummitt, R. K., and C. E. Powell. *Authors of Plant Names: A List of Authors of Scientific Names of Plants*.
    See chapter 10 for full annotation. Includes birth and death dates of the authors, where known.

224    Campbell-Culver, Maggie. *The Origin of Plants: The People and Plants That Have Shaped Britain's Garden History Since the Year 1000*. London: Eden Project, 2004. 449 p. $14.95 (paper). ISBN 1903919401 (paper).
    History of the introduction of plants in the United Kingdom. Organized in chapters covering the period before the year 1000 and each century after. Chapters include a list of significant dates for the period, the text, and a chronological listing by botanical name of the plants introduced. The text comprises observations on the general botanical situation in Britain and the history of the plant and its introduction, including common name and place of origin.

225    Clarkson, Rosetta E. *The Golden Age of Herbs and Herbalists*. New York: Dover, 1972. 328 p. ISBN 048622869X.
    Originally entitled *Green Enchantment: The Magic Spell of Gardens* (1940), this is a survey and standard reference for garden history and herbal medicine from the Middle Ages to the eighteenth century.

226    Coats, Alice M. *The Book of Flowers: Four Centuries of Flower Illustration*. 2nd ed. New York: Exeter, 1984. 208 p. ISBN 0671070614.
    Limited to flowers as represented on paper or vellum, this book covers the period from 1485 to 1850. Coats introduces her book by discussing flower books from the sixteenth through the nineteenth centuries. There are 126 examples of illustrations, all of them from famous herbals, journals, and the like. Text is oriented toward the history of botanical illustration. Includes a historical bibliography.

227    Coats, Alice M. *The Treasury of Flowers*. New York: McGraw-Hill, 1975. 164 p. ISBN 007011482X.
    Companion volume to the author's *Book of Flowers*, below. Compiled from selections taken from octavo size publications, botanical periodicals, and ordinary gardening books not included in *Book of Flowers*.

228    D'Aniello, Charles A, ed. *Teaching Bibliographic Skills in History: A Sourcebook for Historians and Librarians*. Westport, CT: Greenwood Press, 1993. 385 p. $65.00. ISBN 0313252661.

This book, as the title suggests, is useful for students or beginners who need assistance in using the library for bibliographic research of historical materials. Rationale, definitions, techniques, and sources are reviewed including various examples from card and online catalogs, indexes, databases, and archives.

229 Delaporte, François. *Nature's Second Kingdom: Explorations of Vegetality in the Eighteenth Century.* Cambridge, MA: MIT Press, 1982. 266 p. ISBN 0262040662.

Historical discussion of the progress of phytophilosophy and physiology in the eighteenth century.

230 Desmond, Ray. *A Celebration of Flowers: Two Hundred Years of Curtis's Botanical Magazine.* Kew, England: Royal Botanic Gardens, 1987. 207 p. ISBN 0600550753.

The story of the oldest surviving botanical magazine, a chronicle and pictorial record of over two centuries. For more examples of illustrations from this magazine, see Rix's *The Art of the Botanist*, below. See the annotation for *Curtis's Botanical Magazine* in the Serials section, above, for more information on the journal.

231 Dodge, Bertha Sanford. *Plants That Changed the World.* Boston, MA: Little, Brown, 1959. 183 p.

This book describes some of the plant products, and adventures, that helped to make history. Ornamental plants are not included. The focus is on valuable plants whose introduction may be lost in the mists of history. A bibliography records sources of information.

232 Downie, Mary Alice, and Mary Hamilton, eds. *"And Some Brought Flowers": Plants in a New World.* Markham, Ontario, Canada: Fitzhenry and Whiteside, 2002. 164 p. $18.95. ISBN 1550416162.

This book of unusual travel and exploration writing contains 70 watercolor illustrations of plants, quotations from early explorers and settlers, and 20 pages of short biographies of men and women discussed in the text.

233 Drayton, Richard Harry. *Nature's Government: Science, Imperial Britain, and the "Improvement" of the World.* New Haven, CT: Yale University Press, 2000. 346 p. $50.00. ISBN 0300059760.

The focus of the book is the history of the rise of the Royal Botanic Gardens at Kew during the nineteenth century. In addition to becoming wonderful ornamental gardens, they developed into a pioneering scientific institution. It also delves into the relationships between the history of Britain, Western science, and imperialism. It argues that science, guiding the exploration (and exploitation) of exotic and unknown regions, made conquest seem legitimate and beneficial.

234    Dunthorne, Gordon. *Flower and Fruit Prints of the 18th and Early 19th Centuries: Their History, Makers and Uses, with a Catalogue Raisonne of the Works in Which They Are Found.* New York: Da Capo, 1970. 275 p. (Da Capo Press Series in Graphic Art, 6). ISBN 0306709589.

This book evaluates the quality of the prints from the viewpoint of technique as well as their quality as decorative works of art. The scientific approach is outside its scope. The book is divided into two parts: the first, discussing history and description of prints, includes illustrations; the second includes a catalog of early prints with complete descriptions of each print, artist, engraver, publisher and other identification information. This source may be used for verification, as well as for locating prints of particular plants and artists. The two Blunt and the two Coats books, all above, may be used as companion works.

235    *Ecological Phytogeography in the Nineteenth Century.* New York: Arno, 1977. 468 p. (History of Ecology). ISBN 0405103883.

A collection of reprinted nineteenth-century articles important in the history of phytogeography by giants in the field: Alexander von Humboldt, Auguste De Candolle, William Jackson Hooker, Heinrich Rudolf August Grisebach, and James Starr Lippincott.

236    Elliott, Brent. *Treasures of the Royal Horticultural Society.* Portland, OR: Timber, 1994. 158 p. ISBN 0881922978.

Contains 70 plates of botanical illustrations, arranged chronologically with commentary on the artistic qualities of each plate and a botanical account of the plant shown. The plates, taken from the Royal Horticultural Society's Lindley Library, demonstrate the changing fashions in botanical illustration.

237    Evans, Howard Ensign. *Pioneer Naturalists: The Discovery and Naming of North American Plants and Animals.* New York: Holt, 1993. 294 p. ISBN 0805023372.

This book includes vignettes from the lives of acknowledged naturalists engaged in exploring the United States, including Louis Agassiz, Spencer Fullerton Baird, Nathaniel Lord Britton, Thomas Jefferson, and C. Hart Merriam, to name just a few.

238    Ewan, Joseph, ed. *Short History of Botany in the United States.* New York: Hafner, 1969. 174 p. $25.00. ISBN 0686378709.

Historical review of the centers of botanical activity in the United States from 300 B.C. into the midtwentieth century.

239    Gascoigne, Robert Mortimer. *A Historical Catalogue of Scientists and Scientific Books from the Earliest Times to the Close of the Nineteenth Century.*

New York: Garland, 1984. 1177 p. (Garland Reference Library of the Humanities, 495). ISBN 0824089596.

Over 13,000 scientists, including botanists, from all countries, from antiquity to 1900, are covered in this major reference work. Biographical information, references to sources for additional information, scientific books, plus author and topical indexes are contained in this historical survey of the scientific literature.

240    Green, J. Reynolds, and Julius Sachs. *A History of Botany, 1860 to 1900. Being a Continuation of Sachs History of Botany, 1530–1860.* New York: Russell and Russell, 1967. 543 p.

One of the classic histories of botany; it is a companion to and continuation of Sachs, below. See Weevers, below, for botanical history to 1945. Reprint of the 1909 edition.

241    Greene, Edward Lee. *Landmarks of Botanical History.* Stanford, CA: Stanford University Press, 1983. 2 vol. ISBN 0804710759.

The main body of the two volumes is concerned with Greene's identification and discussion of the landmarks of botany. Part I, first published in 1909, deals with an introduction to the philosophy of botanical history. Part II, taken from Greene's 1915 unpublished manuscript, contains a new introduction, a short biography of Greene, and an appraisal of his somewhat controversial contributions to botany. It discusses the Italian forefathers of the fifteenth century. Appendixes outline pre-Grecian, medieval, and seventeenth-century botany.

242    Hanson, J. B. *History of the American Society of Plant Physiologists.* Rockville, MD: American Society of Plant Physiologists, 1989. 277 p. ISBN 094308816X.

The author describes this record as a "family history, of a sort . . . just one plant physiologist telling another about life in our Society over the past sixty-odd years." Includes information about meetings, officers, award recipients, constitution and bylaws, and references.

243    Harshberger, John William. *The Botanists of Philadelphia and Their Work.* Philadelphia, PA: Press of T. C. Davis and Son, 1899. 457 p.

This contribution to the history of botany in America encompasses the area within a radius of 60 miles of Philadelphia and includes biographical sketches for most of the botanists who lived near Philadelphia. There are 40 illustrations including portraits of scientists and their living quarters, appendixes listing members of botanical clubs and societies, and historical accounts of scientific journals and landmarks.

244    Harshberger, John William. *Phytogeographic Survey of North America: A Consideration of the Phytogeography of the North American Continent, Including Mexico, Central America and the West Indies, Together with the Evolution of North American Plant Distribution.* Monticello, NY: Lubrecht and Cramer, 1976. 790 p. ISBN 3768200035.

In four parts: Part 1, History and Literature of the Botanic Works and Explorations of the North American Continent; Part 2, Geographic, Climatic and Floristic survey; Part 3, Geologic Evolution, Theoretic Considerations and Statistics of North American Plants; and Part 4, North American Phytogeographic Regions, Formations, Associations. A historical survey of the phytogeography of North America makes this a useful book for the botanist and the historian of science. Reprint of the 1911 edition.

245    Haughton, Claire S. *Green Immigrants: The Plants That Transformed America.* New York: Harcourt, Brace, Jovanovich, 1978. 450 p. ISBN 0151370346; 0156364921 (paper).

Haughton very effectively meets her aim of relating the "history and romance, the legend and folklore, of nearly one hundred growing plants, telling where they came from, how they arrived here, and what has happened to them since."

246    Hawks, Ellison, and George Simonds Boulger. *Pioneers of Plant Study.* Freeport, NY: Books for Libraries, 1969. 288 p. (Essay Index Reprint series). $23.95. ISBN 0836911393.

This episodic history traces the work of selected botanists from antiquity to the nineteenth century, their investigations, and important botanical institutions. Includes 18 portraits of botanical pioneers from the earliest times to the nineteenth century. Reprint of the 1928 edition.

247    Humphrey, Harry Baker. *Makers of North American Botany.* New York: Ronald, 1961. 265 p. $29.00 (paper). ISBN 0758147597 (paper).

Includes short biographies (one to three pages) of 122 famous North American botanists; there are no portraits, although references to their obituaries are provided; coverage to 1958.

248    Isely, Duane. *One Hundred and One Botanists.* Ames, IA: Iowa State University Press, 1994. 351 p. $43.95. ISBN 0813824982; 1557532834 (reprint).

Short biographical sketches of important botanists, arranged chronologically, beginning with Aristotle (384 B.C.–322 B.C.), and ending with Winona Hazel Welch (1896–1991). Includes bibliographical references and indexes.

249   Keeney, Elizabeth B. *The Botanizers: Amateur Scientists in Nineteenth-Century America.* Chapel Hill, NC: University of North Carolina Press, 1992. 206 p. $49.95. ISBN 0807820466.
History of amateur botanists active in the 1800s.

250   Linnaeus, Carolus. *Linnaeus' Philosophia Botanica.* 1st English ed. New York: Oxford University Press, 2003. 402 p. $300.00. ISBN 0198501226.
Linnaeus's *"Philosophia Botanica* represents a key stage in the evolution of the scientific classification and naming of plants, and is a classic in the history of science and botany. Amazingly, no complete translation into English had been undertaken since 1775." Translated by Stephen Freer.

251   Miller, Amy Bess Williams. *Shaker Herbs: A History and a Compendium.* New York: Clarkson N. Potter, 1976. 272 p. ISBN 0517524945.
This well-done history of Shaker herbs is a worthy addition to botanical collections. The book is divided into two parts for discussions of herbs from various Shaker communities, and a compendium of herbs detailing their use. A glossary, bibliographies, and index are included.

252   Morton, A. G. *History of Botanical Science: An Account of the Development of Botany from Ancient Times to the Present Day.* New York: Academic, 1981. 474 p. ISBN 0125083823 (paper).
This scholarly book traces in detail the emergence of philosophical concepts within the science of botany.

253   Reeds, Karen Meier. *Botany in Medieval and Renaissance Universities.* New York: Garland, 1991. 392 p. (Harvard Dissertations in the History of Science). ISBN 0824074491.
This book contains the author's 1975 Harvard Ph.D. thesis with the same title and two additional articles that appeared in *Annals of Science* (1976) and *Scholarly Publishing* (1983). The dissertation section documents and discusses the network of scientific communication created by friendships formed at medical schools between teachers and students, as well as the momentous changes in the study and practice of botany during the Middle Ages.

254   Reveal, James L. *America's Botanical Beauty: Illustrations from the Library of Congress.* Golden, CO: Fulcrum, 1996. 162 p. ISBN 1555913369.
Botanical discoveries in North America told through the adventures of early naturalists and explorers. The book is beautifully illustrated with colored pictures drawn from nature by pioneering artists. Originally published in 1992 as *Gentle Conquest.*

255   Rix, Martyn. *The Art of the Botanist*. Guildford, England: Lutterworth, 1981. 224 p. ISBN 0718824822.

Published simultaneously in the United States as *The Art of the Plant World*. The long history of botanical illustration is enhanced with copious examples of art from the plant world. The volume is divided into three parts, discussing early works from antiquity, the golden age of plant illustration, and the changes that the lithographic revolution brought about in the nineteenth and twentieth centuries. There is a list of references and an index for book titles, authors, artists, and engravers.

256   Rodgers, Andrew Denny. *American Botany, 1873–1892: Decades of Transition*. New York: Hafner, 1968. 340 p.

This book covers a crucial period of transition and development in the course of American botany. This very interesting account discusses prominent botanists, their explorations, controversies, and research, relying heavily on primary sources. Reprint of the 1944 edition.

257   Rudolph, Emanuel David, Ronald L. Stuckey and William R. Burk. *Emanuel D. Rudolph's Studies in the History of North American Botany*. Fort Worth, TX: Botanical Research Institute of Texas, 2000. 376 p. (Sida, Botanical Miscellany, no. 19). ISBN 1889878057.

This compilation of papers comprises the interests of a nationally known polar lichenologist and historian of botany in the history of the nineteenth- and early twentieth-century biology and botany. Chapters include botany in textbooks, botany in children's books, botanical teaching, botanical educators, botanical illustration, women in American botany, and writing botanical history.

258   Sachs, Julius, and Isaac Bayley Balfour. *History of Botany, 1530–1860*. New York: Russell and Russell, 1967. 568 p.

This is one of the classic histories of the botanical sciences. It is continued by Green and Sachs's *History of Botany* and then Weevers's *Fifty Years of Plant Physiology*. Reprint of the 1890 edition, which was a translation of *Geschichte der Botanik vom 16. Jahrhundert bis 1860*, published in 1875.

259   Sage, Linda C. *Pigment of the Imagination: A History of Phytochrome Research*. San Diego, CA: Academic, 1992. 562 p. ISBN 0126144451.

An exciting and excellent history of phytochrome research.

260   Saunders, Gill. *Picturing Plants: An Analytical History of Botanical Illustration*. Berkeley, CA: University of California Press in association with the Victoria and Albert Museum, London, 1995. 152 p. $39.95. ISBN 0520203062.

"Explores the purpose and function of the whole range of botanical art, from early woodcut herbals and painted florilegia, botanical treatises and records of new discoveries, to gardening manuals, seed catalogs, and field guides for the amateur enthusiast." Chapters discuss herbals; florilegia and pattern books; the botanical treatise; botanical illustration and plant taxonomy; horticultural illustration; floras and field guides; and herbaria, nature prints, and photographs.

Sengbusch, Peter von, Alice Bergfeld, and Rolf Bergmaan. *Botany Online: The Internet Hypertextbook.*

See chapter 2 for complete annotation. This free online resource includes a chapter on the history of botany.

261    Shteir, Ann B. *Cultivating Women, Cultivating Science: Flora's Daughters and Botany in England, 1760–1860.* Baltimore, MD: Johns Hopkins University Press, 1996. 301 p. $21.95 (paper). ISBN 0801851416 (paper).

Scholarly and heavily annotated "handbook about women who were part of the culture of botany during the formative years of modern science" in England. Includes biographical information on various female writers, illustrators, and teachers related to botany.

262    Stafleu, Frans Antonie. *Linnaeus and the Linnaeans: The Spreading of Their Ideas in Systematic Botany, 1735–1789.* Utrecht, the Netherlands: International Bureau for Plant Taxonomy and Nomenclature, 1971. 386 p. (Regnum Vegetabile, vol. 79).

This book analyzes the work and impact of one of the most dominant figures in plant biology of all times.

263    Stevens, Peter F. *The Development of Biological Systematics: Antoine-Laurent de Jussieu, Nature, and the Natural System.* New York: Columbia University Press, 1994. 616 p. $95.90. ISBN 0231064403.

This book analyzes the history of biological systematics. It discusses the formative years of the so-called natural system of classification in the eighteenth and nineteenth centuries. In particular, it intends to show why systematics has been relegated near to the bottom in the hierarchy of sciences. Appendixes include translations of the works of de Jussieu, and the introduction to Linnaeus's *Genera Plantarum* (see chapter 10 for full annotation).

264    Stuckey, Ronald L., ed. *Development of Botany in Selected Regions of North America before 1900.* New York: Arno, 1978. 210 p. (Biologists and Their World). ISBN 0405107226.

This is a collection of papers written around 1900 and reprinted from recognized journals on the development of botany in the United States, principally in the eastern region. Articles discuss botany from 1635 to 1858 and botany in New York, the District of Columbia, the South, and St. Louis.

265    Tobey, Ronald. *Saving the Prairies: The Life Cycle of the Founding School of American Plant Ecology, 1895–1955.* Berkeley, CA: University of California Press, 1981. 315 p. ISBN 0520043529.

Historical presentation of the "first coherent group of ecologists in the United States, the grassland ecologists of the Midwest."

266    Tyler-Whittle, Michael Sydney. *The Plant Hunters: Being an Examination of Collecting with an Account of the Careers and the Methods of a Number of Those Who Have Searched the World for Wild Plants.* New York: Lyons and Burford, 1997. 281 p. $16.95 (paper). ISBN 1558215921 (paper).

This book discusses "why, how and where some plants have been collected, with an account of a few of the better known collectors." This is an interesting contribution appropriate for scientific and public libraries. Reprint of the original 1970 edition.

267    Weevers, Theodorus. *Fifty Years of Plant Physiology.* Waltham, MA: Chronica Botanica, 1949. 308 p.

This is a continuation of the history of botany begun by Sachs and Green (see both, above). Weevers discusses botanical history from 1895 to 1945 with attention to European, principally Dutch, botanical literature of the period covered.

# Associations

268    History of Science Society. P.O. Box 117360, 3310 Turlington Hall, University of Florida, Gainesville, FL 32611-7360. Phone: 352-392-1677. Fax: 352-392-2795. E-mail: info@hssonline.org. URL: http://www.hssonline.org/main_pg.html.

Funded in 1924 to foster interest in the history of science and its social and cultural relations. Dedicated to understanding science, technology, medicine, and their interactions with society in a historical context. Publishes *Isis* and *Osiris* and several other series, guides, and more.

269    Hunt Institute for Botanical Documentation. 5000 Forbes Avenue, Carnegie Mellon University, Pittsburgh, Pennsylvania 15213-3890. Phone: 412-268-2434. Fax: 412-268-5677. E-mail: huntinst@andrew.cmu.edu. URL: http://huntbot.andrew.cmu.edu/.

"Specializes in the history of botany and all aspects of plant science and serves the international scientific community through research and documentation."

It acquires and maintains authoritative collections of books, plant images, manuscripts, portraits, and data files. Provides publications such as *Huntia* and the *Bulletin of the Hunt Institute for Botanical Documentation* as well as collection catalogs, reference works, and much more.

270   Society for the History of Natural History. c/o The Natural History Museum, Cromwell Road, London, SW7 5BD, U. K. E-mail: info@shnh.org. URL: http://www.shnh.org/.

It "is the only international society devoted to the history of botany, zoology and geology, in the broadest sense, including natural history collections, exploration, art and bibliography." Publishes *Archives of Natural History* and a *Newsletter*.

# 4

# Plant Evolution and Paleobotany

This chapter covers the closely linked subjects of plant evolution and paleobotany. Paleobotany is "the study of fossil plants and plant impressions" (Lawrence, 2000). Fossil plants are not as well known as fossil animals, in part because they are often preserved as random, unconnected bits of leaves, stems, flowers, pollen, and seeds. It is difficult to assemble these fossils into a coherent whole, and thus few complete fossil plants are known. In addition, although the evolution of nonvascular plants and angiosperms has been studied in depth, gymnosperm evolution is not as well known. However, palynology, "the study of pollen and its distribution" (Lawrence, 2000), has been extensively researched and provides insights into ancient ecosystems and climate conditions.

This chapter covers the major reference resources for both paleobotany and plant evolution. Most of the material on fossil plants is found in the geological literature and used by geologists and paleontologists whereas books and resources for plant evolution are part of the biological literature and used by evolutionary biologists.

## Bibliographies and Guides to the Literature

271 *Bibliography of American Paleobotany*. Vol. 1– . Compiled under the auspices of the Paleobotany Section of the Botanical Society of America, 1958/59– . Annual. ISSN 0193-5720.

This bibliography covers paleobotany for all of North America and is arranged by type of literature for books, reviews, and technical reports and by geological period for articles. It also includes a directory of members of the Paleobotany

**75**

Section. Selected years of the bibliography were available at the association's Web site at the time of viewing in late 2005.

272    Boureau, Edouard. *Rapport sur la Paléobotanique dans le Monde. World Report on Palaeobotany.* Königstein, Germany: Published for International Association for Plant Taxonomy by Koeltz Scientific Books, 1956–1973. (Regnum Vegetabile, vol. 7, 11, 19, 24, 35, 42, 57, 78, and 89).

This bibliography indexes the world literature on paleobotany for the time covered. It is arranged with general material first, followed by sections on the geological time periods. Within each section the bibliography is arranged by author.

273    Hardy, Joan E., David Wood, and Anthony P. Harvey, eds. *Information Sources in the Earth Sciences.* 2nd ed. New York: Bowker-Saur, 1989. 518 p. $85.00. ISBN 0408014067.

Although out of date, this bibliographic guide is still a useful resource for locating the classic works in palynology and paleobotany. The guide includes about 50 works on fossil algae, palynology, paleobotany, and paleoecology of plants. Revised edition of *Use of Earth Sciences Literature* by Joan E. Hardy.

274    Kelber, Klaus-Peter, comp. *Links for Palaeobotanists.* URL: http://www.uni-wuerzburg.de/mineralogie/palbot1.html.

This well-organized site provides an annotated list of Web sites of interest to paleobotanists, with an emphasis on the Upper Triassic. The topics covered include taxonomy, anatomy, taphonomy, paleoclimate, evolution, images of plant fossils, and much more.

275    Ward, Dederick C., Marjorie W. Wheeler, and Robert A. Bier, Jr. *Geologic Reference Sources: A Subject and Regional Bibliography of Publications and Maps in the Geological Sciences.* 2nd ed. Metuchen, NJ: Scarecrow, 1981. 560 p. ISBN 0810814285.

Although even more out of date than Hardy et al., above, this guide also lists classic works in paleontology, including palynology and paleobotany. Lists about 25 records for paleobotany and another 20 for palynology.

# Databases, Abstracts, and Indexes

276    *GEOBASE.* New York: Elsevier, 1980– . Price varies. Available electronically.

Indexes 2,060 journals, plus books, conference proceedings, and reports. The database is based on the Elsevier print indexes *Geographical Abstracts: Physical*

*Geography*; *Geographical Abstracts*: *Human Geography*; *Geological Abstracts*: *Ecological Abstracts*; *International Development Abstracts; Oceanographic Literature Review*; and *Geomechanics Abstracts;* which are also available separately. Available online and as a CD-ROM through several vendors.

277  *GeoRef.* Alexandria, VA: American Geological Institute, 1979– . Price varies. Available electronically.

*GeoRef* is the most comprehensive database for the geosciences. It is the electronic equivalent of four major indexes: *Bibliography of North American Geology*; *Bibliography and Index of Geology Exclusive of North America*; *Geophysical Abstracts*; and *Bibliography and Index of Geology.* The database indexes over 3,500 journals plus dissertations, theses, USGS publications, and other document types. It contains over 2.2 million records from North America since 1785 and from other areas of the world since 1933. The database covers paleobotany extensively and can be searched by systematic names for fossils and by geological time periods. The database is available online and as a CD-ROM through several vendors.

*Index to American Botanical Literature.*
See chapter 2 for full annotation. Includes fossils as well as living plants from the Western Hemisphere.

The Royal Botanic Gardens, Kew. *Plant Micromorphology Bibliographic Database.*
See chapter 7 for full annotation. Includes records of interest to paleopalynologists.

278  Söderman, Margareta, Hans Tralau, Britta Lundblad, and Rita Baechler. *Bibliography and Index to Palaeobotany and Palynology, 1971–1975.* Stockholm: Swedish Museum of Natural History and Swedish Natural Science Research Council, 1983. 2 vol. ISBN 9186344145 (vol. 1); 9186344153 (vol. 2).

Continues Tralau's *Bibliography and Index to Palaeobotany and Palynology 1950–1970*, below. It is in the same format and has the same subject coverage.

279  Tralau, Hans. *Bibliography and Index to Palaeobotany and Palynology, 1950–1970.* Stockholm: Almqvist and Wiksell, 1974. 2 vol.

This set, which started out as the author's personal card file, contains extensive coverage of the European and especially Russian literature. Volume 1 contains a bibliography in alphabetical order by a code containing letters from the author's name, a year code, and letters from the title. Each entry also includes information on the presence of figures and tables. Volume 2 contains a keyword-in-context index, very similar to the old print *Biological Abstracts*.

# Serials

## General Serials

280    *Annual Review of Ecology, Evolution, and Systematics.* Vol. 34– . Palo Alto, CA: Annual Reviews, 2003– . Annual. $179.00. ISSN 1543-592X. Available electronically.
Formerly *Annual Review of Ecology and Systematics.*

281    *Evolution: International Journal of Organic Evolution.* Vol. 1– . Lawrence, KS: The Society for the Study of Evolution, 1947– . Bimonthly. $250.00. ISSN 0014-3820. Available electronically.

282    *Trends in Ecology and Evolution.* Vol. 1– . Amsterdam, the Netherlands: Elsevier Science, 1986– . Monthly. $1,309.00. ISSN 0169-5347. Available electronically.

## Botanical Serials

283    *Global and Planetary Change.* Vol. 1– . Amsterdam, the Netherlands: Elsevier, 1988– . 20 issues per year. $1,465.00. ISSN 0921-8181. Available electronically.
"The journal focuses on the record of change in earth history and the analysis and prediction of recent and future changes. Topics include, but are not limited to, changes in the chemical composition of the oceans and atmosphere, climate change, sea level variations, human geography, global geophysics and tectonics, global ecology and biogeography." Continues in part *Palaeogeography, Palaeoclimatology, Palaeoecology.*

*Grana.*
See chapter 2 for full annotation. Publishes articles on spores and pollen, including their use in paleobotany and paleoecology.

284    *Palaeontographica. Beiträge zur Naturgeschichte der Vorzeit. Abt. B: Palaeophytologie.* Vol. 78– . Stuttgart, Germany: E. Schweizerbart'sche Verlagsbuchhandlung, 1933– . Irregular. $338.70 per volume. ISSN 0375-0299.
Part B covers paleophytology, publishing "qualified contributions of paleobotanical and stratigraphic interest" in German, French, and English. Continues in part *Palaeontographica.*

285   *Palynology.* Vol. 1– . Austin, TX: American Association of Stratigraphic Palynologists, 1977– . Annual. $70.00. ISSN 0191-6122.

Published by the AASP. Papers cover all aspects of Quaternary and stratigraphic palynology. "In addition to peer-reviewed papers, *Palynology* includes biographical sketches of the authors, abstracts of the annual meetings, group photos of the meeting participants and instructions to authors."

286   *Review of Palaeobotany and Palynology.* Vol. 1– . Amsterdam, the Netherlands: Elsevier, 1967– . 20 issues per year. $2,102.00. ISSN 0034-6667. Available electronically.

Covers "all fields of palaeobotany and palynology dealing with all groups, ranging from marine palynomorphs to higher land plants. The journal especially encourages the publication of articles in which palaeobotany and palynology are applied for solving fundamental geological and biological problems as well as innovative and interdisciplinary approaches." Includes the occasional obituary.

# Dictionaries and Encyclopedias

287   Allaby, Ailsa, and Michael Allaby. *A Dictionary of Earth Sciences.* 2nd ed. New York: Oxford University Press, 2003. 619 p. (Oxford Paperback Reference). $16.95. ISBN 0198607601.

In addition to the usual geological subjects such as climatology and economic geology, this dictionary has a good coverage of paleobotany terms, including definitions of major plant groups, fossil terminology, and stratigraphy. It is a revised edition of *The Concise Oxford Dictionary of Earth Sciences* and contains over 6,000 entries.

Hoen, Peter. *Glossary of Pollen and Spore Terminology.* 2nd rev. ed.
See chapter 10 for full annotation.

Lincoln, Roger J., Geoffrey Allan Boxshall, and P. F. Clark. *A Dictionary of Ecology, Evolution, and Systematics.* 2nd ed.
See chapter 2 for full annotation. Appendixes include the geological time scale and a chronology of the Quaternary Ice Age.

288   Pagel, Mark D., ed. in chief. *Encyclopedia of Evolution.* New York: Oxford University Press, 2002. 2 vol. $325.00. ISBN 0195122003 (set).

Although most of the essays in this encyclopedia cover animal evolution, there are good discussions of the evolution of the major plant groups as well as evolutionary genetics and general topics applicable to plant evolution. Each article has cross-references and a bibliography.

289    Singer, Ronald, ed. *Encyclopedia of Paleontology*. Chicago, IL: Fitzroy Dearborn, 1999. 2 vol. $355.00. ISBN 1884964966 (set).

There are several good essays covering plants, including the evolution of various plant taxa, general articles on the mechanics of plant design, vegetative features of plants, and adaptive strategies taken by plants. Each essay includes cross-references, works cited, and further reading. The encyclopedia includes a list of paleontology journals.

# Handbooks and Methods

290    Beck, Charles B., ed. *Origin and Early Evolution of Angiosperms*. New York: Columbia University Press, 1976. 341 p. $111.00. ISBN 0231038577.

Most of the papers that make up this book were originally presented in a symposium in 1973. They include general reviews of the state of knowledge of angiosperm evolution relating to topics such as plate tectonics, neoteny, and seeds and seedlings as well as more specific topics. A classic.

291    Beck, Charles B., ed. *Origin and Evolution of Gymnosperms*. New York: Columbia University Press, 1988. 504 p. $108.50. ISBN 023106358X.

The question of the origin of the gymnosperms is neglected compared to the origin of angiosperms. This volume surveys the biology of ancestral gymnosperms and discusses pollen fossils as well as covering the origin of various gymnosperm groups such as conifers.

292    Behrensmeyer, Anna K., et al., eds. *Terrestrial Ecosystems Through Time: Evolutionary Paleoecology of Terrestrial Plants and Animals*. Chicago, IL: University of Chicago Press, 1992. 568 p. $95.00; $35.00 (paper). ISBN 0226041549; 0226041557 (paper).

This book surveys paleoecological topics, including discussing various types of paleoecosystems, including their taphonomy and changes through time. The text also includes an extensive discussion of the ecological characterization of fossil plants.

293    Benton, M. J., ed. *The Fossil Record 2*. New York: Chapman and Hall, 1993. 845 p. $412.95. ISBN 0412393808.

This catalog lists the first and last records of fossils through time. Each record includes the first author of the taxa, *Plant Fossil Record* number, first and last record in the geological periods, records in intervening periods, and comments. The chapter on angiosperms includes records of pollen grains as well. A standard source, the catalog is also available on the International Organisation of Palaeo-botany's *Plant Fossil Record* site, below.

294   Blackmore, Stephen, and S. H. Barnes. *Pollen and Spores: Patterns of Diversification.* New York: Oxford University Press, 1991. 391 p. (The Systematics Association Special Volume, no. 44). $135.00. ISBN 019857746X.

The results of a symposium by the same title held in 1990, this volume covers a variety of topics dealing with paleopalynology, including evolution of spore types and reviews of spores known from various geological periods.

295   Boersma, M., and L. M. Broekmeyer. *Index of Figured Plant Megafossils.* Amsterdam, the Netherlands: Editions Rodopi, 1981. 4 vol. in 6. (Special Publication of the Laboratory of Palaeobotany and Palynology, University of Utrecht).

As the title suggests, this set provides an index to illustrations of plant fossils from scientific publications. Each entry includes citation, geographical information, and chronostratigraphical information. Indexes in each volume sort the fossils by systematics, geological, and chronological order. The set covers the Carboniferous, Triassic, Permian, and Jurassic eras.

296   Boureau, Edouard, ed. *Traité de Paléobotanique.* Paris: Masson et Cie, 1964–1989. 9 vol. in 11.

Volumes 1–7 of this massive handbook cover all the major plant groups, whereas the final volumes provide information on palynology and paleophytogeography.

297   Cleal, Christopher J., ed. *Plant Fossils in Geological Investigation: The Palaeozoic.* New York: Ellis Horwood, 1991. 233 p. (Ellis Horwood Series in Applied Geology). ISBN 0136808778.

Most texts on paleobotany are written by botanists, but Cleal takes a geologist's view of plant fossils, discussing how they are used by geologists working on the Paleozoic period. Topics covered include the biostratigraphy of plants worldwide, plus techniques for studying plant fossils and problems with the taxonomy of extinct plants.

Cronquist, Arthur. *The Evolution and Classification of Flowering Plants.* 2nd ed.

See chapter 10 for full annotation. Cronquist's classic work presents his system of flowering plant classification and discusses what was then known about the origin of angiosperms.

Dahlgren, R. M. T., H. T. Clifford, and P. F. Yeo. *The Families of the Monocotyledons: Structure, Evolution, and Taxonomy.*

See chapter 10 for full annotation. Includes information on the evolution of monocots, as the title suggests.

298    *Fossilium Catalogus. II: Plantae.* 's-Gravenhage, the Netherlands: W. Junk, 1913– . Irregular.

The most important classic catalog of fossil plants, arranged by taxon. Each record includes the original source and remarks. Currently up to Volume 106 (2003).

299    Friis, Else Marie, William G. Chaloner, and Peter R. Crane, eds. *The Origins of Angiosperms and Their Biological Consequences.* New York: Cambridge University Press, 1987. 358 p. ISBN 0521323576; 052131173X (paper).

The articles in this volume were based on a symposium held in 1985. They cover the effects of the evolution of angiosperms on other plants and animals, including insects, herbivorous tetrapods, dinosaurs, and mammals.

300    Gensel, Patricia G., and Henry N. Andrews. *Plant Life in the Devonian.* New York: Praeger, 1984. 380 p. ISBN 0030620023.

Although out of date in some aspects, this is still an excellent source for information on early land plants. The authors discuss pre-Devonian plant fossils and then cover each major plant group present in the Devonian as well as discussing heterospory, palynology, and Devonian plant ecosystems.

301    Gensel, Patricia G., and Dianne Edwards, eds. *Plants Invade the Land: Evolutionary and Environmental Perspectives.* New York: Columbia University Press, 2001. 304 p. (Critical Moments and Perspectives in Earth History and Paleobiology series). $71.00; $35.00 (paper). ISBN 0231111606; 0231111614 (paper).

Based on talks given at the Fifth International Organization of Paleobotany conference in 1996, this volume provides a synthesis of the state of knowledge of the origin of land plants, covering the Ordovician through the Upper Devonian periods. Topics covered include early land dwellers (plant and animal) as well as discussions of the adaptations needed to live on the land.

302    Gifford, Ernest M., and Adriance S. Foster. *Morphology and Evolution of Vascular Plants.* 3rd ed. New York: W. H. Freeman, 1989. 626 p. (Series of Books in Biology). $75.00. ISBN 0716719460.

A revision of the authors' *Comparative Morphology of Vascular Plants* originally published in 1974, this text not only emphasizes the morphology of vascular plants but also covers origin of land plants, early vascular plants, and other paleobotanical topics. The bulk of the book consists of a systematic discussion of the morphology of each major plant group from Rhyniophyta to Magnoliophyta.

303   Graham, Linda E. *Origin of Land Plants*. New York: Wiley, 1993. 287 p. $225.00. ISBN 0471615277.

This book gathers the scattered information on the origin of land plants taken from paleontology, phylogeny, and molecular systematics that has become available since F. O. Bower's classic *Primitive Land Plants* was published in 1935.

Hemsley, Alan R., and Imogen Poole, eds. *The Evolution of Plant Physiology: From Whole Plants to Ecosystems.*

See chapter 9 for full annotation. Examines the evolution of how plants function on both physical as well as biochemical or molecular levels.

304   Hirmer, Max. *Handbuch der Paläobotanik*. Berlin: R. Oldenbourg, 1927– . Multivolume.

This classic handbook provides a catalog of known plant fossils and includes notes, literature, and illustrations. Volume 1 covers Thallophyta, Bryophyta, and Pteridophyta. It appears that this volume was the only one ever published.

305   Hughes, Norman F. *The Enigma of Angiosperm Origins*. New York: Cambridge University Press, 1994. 303 p. (Cambridge Paleobiology series, no. 1). $95.00. ISBN 0521411459.

A continuation of the author's arguments first presented in his 1976 book, *Palaeobiology of Angiosperm Origins*, suggesting that the difficulty in determining angiosperm origins is based more on paleobotanists' methodology than on a lack of evidence. He supports a Cretaceous origin for angiosperms.

306   International Organisation of Palaeobotany. *Plant Fossil Record*. Version 2.2. URL: http://www.biodiversity.org.uk/ibs/palaeo/pfr2/pfr.htm.

This database includes descriptions and occurrences of more than 10,000 extinct plant genera. This version of the database includes most valid plant fossil genera published before 1985. The database also includes maps of the locations of plant fossils. The descriptions include author, citation to original description, type of plant part represented, and age of fossil. The occurrence database lists author, location, and age for each reported discovery of the fossil.

307   Iwatsuki, K., and Peter H. Raven, eds. *Evolution and Diversification of Land Plants*. New York: Springer, 1997. 330 p. ISBN 4431702032.

Combines molecular biology, new methods of analysis, and the fossil record to elucidate the evolution of land plants.

308   Jolivet, Pierre. *Insects and Plants: Parallel Evolution and Adaptations*. 2nd ed. Gainesville, FL: Sandhill Crane, 1992. 190 p. (Flora and Fauna Handbook, no. 2). $69.95. ISBN 1877743100.

Covers a number of interesting topics dealing with the coevolution of insects and plants, including carnivorous plants, pollination, galls, biological control of weeds, and mechanisms of food selection. Translation of *Insectes et Plantes*.

309   Jones, T. P., and N. P. Rowe, eds. *Fossil Plants and Spores: Modern Techniques*. London: Geological Society, 1999. 396 p. $125.00; $48.00 (paper). ISBN 1862390355; 186239041X (paper).

Provides methods and techniques for the study of fossil plants and spores, including information on extraction of fossils, studies of morphology and anatomy, geochemistry, stratigraphy, paleoclimatology, and paleoecology. There are also sections on databases and international laws.

Kapp, Ronald O., Owen K. Davis, and James E. King. *Ronald O. Kapp's Pollen and Spores*. 2nd ed.

See the Identification section of chapter 10 for full annotation. The American Association of Stratigraphic Palynologists published the second edition of this identification guide to North American pollen and spores.

310   Kenrick, Paul, and Peter R. Crane. *The Origin and Early Diversification of Land Plants: A Cladistic Study*. Washington, DC: Smithsonian Institution Press, 1997. 441 p. (Smithsonian Series in Comparative Evolutionary Biology). $55.00; $29.95 (paper). ISBN 1560987308; 1560987294 (paper).

The authors provide a phylogenetic tree of land plants synthesizing the latest data available that is the first attempt to look at morphological data from both fossil and living plants. Introductory material covers both the history of phylogenetic analysis of plants and the place of the plant kingdom in various systems. The remainder of the book consists of detailed discussions of phylogenetic trees for the major plant groups. Appendixes provide descriptions of fossil and extant taxa, and list the data used for analyzing the various taxa.

311   Levin, Donald A. *The Origin, Expansion, and Demise of Plant Species*. New York: Oxford University Press, 2000. 230 p. (Oxford Series in Ecology and Evolution). $95.00; $35.00 (paper). ISBN 0195127285; 0195127293 (paper).

A synthesis of evolutionary biology and ecology, this book provides an overview of the "life cycle" of plant species from origin to extinction. The author discusses the genetic basis of species differentiation, ecological and geographic effects, and macroevolutionary concepts such as speciation rates.

312   Levin, Donald. *The Role of Chromosomal Change in Plant Evolution*. New York: Oxford University Press, 2002. 230 p. (Oxford Series in Ecology and Evolution). $75.00; $38.50 (paper). ISBN 0195138597; 0195138600 (paper).

Synthesizes the scattered body of knowledge about the role of chromosomal evolution in plants at the species and genus level. New technological advances have greatly increased the information available since G. Ledyard Stebbins's *Chromosomal Evolution in Higher Plants* (1971).

313  Niklas, Karl J., ed. *Paleobotany, Paleoecology, and Evolution*. New York: Praeger, 1981. 2 vol. ISBN 0030600383 (set).

A two-volume set of papers originally presented at a symposium in 1979 with papers arranged chronologically by geological time period covered.

314  Silvertown, Jonathan, Miguel Franco, and John L. Harper, eds. *Plant Life Histories: Ecology, Phylogeny, and Evolution*. New York: Cambridge University Press, 1997. 313 p. $42.00. ISBN 0521574951 (paper).

Examines relationships between plant life history traits with a phylogenetic perspective. Chapters in the book cover both theoretical and methodological aspects as well as examining specific traits relating to pollination and mating, seeds, growth, and interactions with insects, microbes, and other plants.

315  Stebbins, G. Ledyard. *Flowering Plants: Evolution above the Species Level*. Cambridge, MA: Belknap Press of Harvard University Press, 1974. 399 p. $58.50. ISBN 0674306856.

Stebbins's classic volume discusses evolutionary trends in flowering plants based on population genetics, developmental biology, and ecology rather than on the more typical emphasis by plant biologists on traditional taxonomy and morphology. The book is in two sections, the first dealing with factors that determine evolutionary trends and the second discussing evolutionary trends in angiosperm phylogeny.

316  Stebbins, G. Ledyard. *Variation and Evolution in Plants*. New York: Columbia University Press, 1950. 643 p. (Columbia Biological series, no. 16).

One of a quartet of books setting out the synthetic theory of evolution, this classic expanded the theory of evolution to cover the unique genetic, physiological, and evolutionary features of plants.

317  Takhtadzhian, A. L. *Evolutionary Trends in Flowering Plants*. New York: Columbia University Press, 1991. 241 p. $65.00. ISBN 0231073283.

Covers the evolutionary morphology of flowering plants with emphasis on the main trends, especially trends in the evolution of vegetative organs, flowers, pollination, fruits, and seeds. The author's name is also transliterated as Armen Takhtajan.

318   Taylor, Thomas N., and Edith L. Smoot, eds. *Paleobotany*. New York: Van Nostrand Reinhold/Scientific and Academic Editions, 1984. 2 vol. (Benchmark Papers in Systematic and Evolutionary Biology, no. 7). ISBN 0442282907 (set).

This set includes classic papers in paleobotany. Volume 1 covers the Pre-cambrian through Permian periods whereas Volume 2 covers the Triassic through Pliocene periods.

319   Tidwell, William D. *Common Fossil Plants of Western North America*. 2nd ed. Washington: Smithsonian Institution Press, 1998. 299 p. $49.95; $24.95 (paper). ISBN 1560987839; 1560987588 (paper).

A well-written and illustrated guide to the fossils of mostly Mesozoic and Cenozoic plants of the West. The author includes methods for studying plant fossils and an illustrated key to leaf shapes. There are many black-and-white illustrations and photographs as well as descriptions of common fossil plants.

320   Tiffney, Bruce H., ed. *Geological Factors and the Evolution of Plants*. New Haven: Yale University Press, 1985. 294 p. $35.00. ISBN 0300033044.

A collection of papers first presented at the third North American Paleonto-logical Association conference in 1982, covering the interaction of organisms and their environment on a geological time scale. The papers discuss topics such as paleophytogeography, paleoclimatology, and the effects of wildfire on plant evolution.

University of California, Berkeley. Museum of Paleontology. *Phylogeny of Life*.

See chapter 10 for full annotation. An excellent source for information on paleobotany of almost every plant taxa at or above the level of the family.

321   Vuorisalo, Timo Olavi, and Pia Kristina Mutikainen, eds. *Life History Evolution in Plants*. Boston: Kluwer Academic, 1999. 348 p. $167.50; $58.00 (paper). ISBN 079235818X; 1402002793 (paper).

Provides an overview of plant life history research, including chapters on the consequences of modularity, modeling and measuring plant life histories, the effects of herbivores and pathogens, senescence, and more.

322   Wyatt, Robert, ed. *Ecology and Evolution of Plant Reproduction*. New York: Chapman and Hall, 1992. 397 p. ISBN 0412030217.

Summarizes knowledge of the ecology and evolution of plant reproduction based on new technical advances and models. The topics include several aspects of pollen viability, competition, and performance; ecological models; sources of variation; and more.

# Textbooks and Treatises

Bell, Peter R., and Alan R. Hemsley. *Green Plants: Their Origin and Diversity.* 2nd ed.

See chapter 10 for full annotation. Includes information on plant evolution and phylogeny.

323   Briggs, D., and S. M. Walters. *Plant Variation and Evolution.* 3rd ed. New York: Cambridge University Press, 1997. 512 p. $80.00; $45.00 (paper). ISBN 0521452953; 0521459184 (paper).

This text takes a more historical view of the study of plant evolution than most texts, providing extensive discussion of historical views as well as more modern theories. Modern topics include DNA analysis, breeding systems, the ecotype concept, genecology, speciation, and conservation.

324   Cleal, Christopher J., and Barry A. Thomas. *Plant Fossils: The History of Land Vegetation.* New York: Boydell, 1999. 188 p. (Fossils Illustrated Series, vol. 3). $110.00. ISBN 0851156843.

A popular introductory survey of plant fossils featuring a systematic survey of plant taxa with reconstructions of representative plants integrated into the text and 128 black-and-whitephotographs of actual fossils. The volume also includes a classification of plants based on Benton's list in *Fossil Record 2* (see Handbooks and Methods section, above).

325   Futuyma, Douglas J. *Evolutionary Biology.* 3rd ed. Sunderland, MA: Sinauer Associates, 1998. 763 p. $94.95. ISBN 0878931899.

A standard text on evolution. This text and Ridley, below, each cover plant evolutionary biology in less depth than animal evolution, and each emphasizes different topics in plant evolution. Futuyma, for instance, covers polyploidy in much more detail than does Ridley.

326   Grant, Verne. *Plant Speciation.* 2nd ed. New York: Columbia University Press, 1981. 563 p. ISBN 0231051123.

A text outlining speciation in higher plants, including evolutionary divergence, natural hybridization, polyploidy, aneuploidy, and specialized genetic systems. The author also provides a good survey of basic topics such as populations and races and the nature of species.

327   Meien, Sergei Viktorovich. *Fundamentals of Palaeobotany.* New York: Chapman and Hall, 1987. 432 p. ISBN 0412271109.

The first half of this textbook consists a systematic survey of the plant king-dom using a slightly different system than most texts. The survey is followed by discussions of paleopalynology, paleoecology, paleofloristics, and the relation-ships between paleobotany and other fields such as stratigraphy, paleoclima-tology, and plate tectonics.

Moore, Peter D., J. A. Webb, and Margaret E. Collinson. *Pollen Analysis*. 2nd ed. See chapter 10 for full annotation.

328   Niklas, Karl J. *The Evolutionary Biology of Plants*. Chicago, IL: University of Chicago Press, 1997. 449 p. $20.00 (paper). ISBN 0226580822; 0226580830 (paper).

This text, written for undergraduate students, is in four parts. The author reviews evolutionary concepts such as adaptation and speciation, the plant fossil record, Sewall Wright's adaptive walks hypothesis, and long-term trends. It provides a synthesis of paleobotany, morphology, biomechanics, population biology, and physiology.

329   Ridley, Mark. *Evolution*. 3rd ed. Oxford, England: Blackwell, 2004. 751 p. $89.95 (paper). ISBN 1405103450 (paper).

One of the standard evolutionary biology textbooks. Each chapter has a summary, study questions, and further readings. The associated Web site at http://www.blackwellpublishing.com/ridley/ contains a number of useful materials, including tutorials, images, and the full text of 20 major papers on evolution.

330   Stewart, Wilson N., and Gar W. Rothwell. *Paleobotany and the Evolution of Plants*. 2nd ed. New York: Cambridge University Press, 1993. 521 p. $65.00. ISBN 0521382947.

One of the most frequently used paleobotany texts, this text was designed for upper-level undergraduates and graduate students and assumes basic knowledge of plant morphology. It includes discussions of controversial topics such as the early evolution of ferns, the origin of seeds, and the origin of angiosperms as well as more accepted topics. The second edition also includes a discussion of paleoecology.

331   Taylor, Thomas N. *Paleobotany: An Introduction to Fossil Plant Biology*. New York: McGraw-Hill, 1981. 589 p. ISBN 0070629544.

A text systematically surveying the fossil plant families.

332   Taylor, Thomas N., and Edith L. Taylor. *The Biology and Evolution of Fossil Plants*. Englewood Cliffs, NJ: Prentice Hall, 1993. 982 p. ISBN 0136515894.

Another highly regarded paleobotany textbook, following a systematic ap-proach. The authors also include chapters on Precambrian life, fungi and lichens, algae, and plant-animal interactions. There are numerous illustrations. Includes some material from the first author's *Paleobotany: An Introduction to Fossil Plant Biology*, though it is not technically a second edition.

333   Thomas, Barry A., and Robert A. Spicer. *The Evolution and Palaeobiology of Land Plants*. Portland, OR: Dioscorides, 1987. 309 p. (Ecology, Phytogeography and Physiology series, vol. 2). ISBN 0709924348; 0709924763 (paper).

This introductory text is arranged by geological time period, covering the first land plants, the initial phase of diversification, and then the second and third phases. It covers the evolutionary history of vascular plants in the context of plant fossils and the biology of extant plant species. A new edition is planned.

334   Traverse, Alfred. *Paleopalynology*. Boston, MA: Unwin Hyman, 1988. 600 p. ISBN 0045610010; 0045610029 (paper).

This text is a laboratory-based introduction to paleopalynology, which the author defines broadly as the study of microfossils found in maceration preparations of sedimentary rocks. These microfossils are mostly pollen and spores but also include some other types of fossils. The text includes information on why students should study palynology, the biology and morphology of spores and pollen, and applications.

335   Willis, K. J., and J. C. McElwain. *The Evolution of Plants*. New York: Oxford University Press, 2002. 378 p. $49.50. ISBN 0198500653.

Rather than following the usual systematic arrangement, this undergraduate textbook surveys plant life through time. The authors also discuss ancient DNA, mass extinctions, and other topics. The text has a companion Web site at http://www.oup.co.uk/best.textbooks/biology/plantevol/ featuring Web links and copies of the biome maps and illustrations used in the text.

# Associations

336   American Association of Stratigraphic Palynologists (AASP). c/o Dr. Thomas D. Demchuk, 600 N. Dairy Ashford, Box 2197, Houston, TX 77252-2197. Phone: 281-293-3189. Fax: 281-293-3833. E-mail: tdemchuk@swbell.net. URL: http://www.palynology.org/.

AASP is a member organization of the Geological Society of America, the American Geological Institute, and the International Federation of Palynological Societies. The Association publishes *Palynology*, *AASP Newsletter*, the AASP Foundation Contribution Series of monographs, and other miscellaneous publications.

337   International Federation of Palynological Societies. URL: http://www.geo
.arizona.edu/palynology/ifps.html.

A federation of 24 regional, national, linguistic, and specialist palynological
organizations of the world. Publishes a biannual newsletter, *Palynos*, which is
available at the Federation's Web site.

338   International Fossil Algae Association. Tonći Grgasović, Institute of Geology, Sachsova 2, P. O. Box 262, HR-10000 Zagreb (Croatia). E-mail: tonci@
igi.hr. URL: http://www.ku.edu/~ifaa/index.html.

A nonprofit organization interested in promoting all aspects of the study of
fossil algae. The Association's Web site includes membership information, an
electronic library of fossil algae resources, and images of fossil algae.

339   International Organisation of Paleobotany. URL: http://iop.biodiversity
.org.uk/.

Most of the organization's work centers around the Plant Fossil Record Database. Its Web site had not been updated for several years at the time of viewing.

340   Palaeontological Association. c/o Dr. T. J. Palmer, Institute of Earth Sciences, University of Wales-Aberstywyth, Aberystwyth SY23 3DB, U. K. Phone:
44 1970 627107. Fax: 44 1970 622659. E-mail: palass@palass.org. URL: http://
www.palass.org.

A British professional association covering all areas of paleontology, including paleobotany. The Association publishes the journal *Palaeontology* as
well as *Palaeontology Newsletter*. The Association's Web site provides information on the society and links to other paleontology Web sites.

Paleobotanical Section. Botanical Society of America. URL: http://www
.dartmouth.edu/~daghlian/paleo/.

The section, a member society of the American Geological Institute, is affiliated with the International Organization of Paleobotany. Publishes the *Bibliography of American Paleobotany*. See chapter 2 for full annotation of the
Botanical Society of America.

# Reference

Lawrence, Eleanor, ed. 2000. *Henderson's Dictionary of Biological Terms*. 12th ed. New
York: Prentice Hall.

# 5
# Ethnobotany

The term *ethnobotany* was first used during a lecture in 1895 by John M. Harchberger, botanist from the University of Pennsylvania (Cotton, 1996). Over the course of the twentieth century, ethnobotany has become a very interdisciplinary scientific field. Anthropology, archaeology, botany, ecology, history, geography, linguistics, medicine, pharmacognosy/pharmacology, phytochemistry, and religion are just some of the areas that have become involved with ethnobotanical research. Interpretations of exactly what ethnobotany encompasses have varied and continue to vary. In the beginning, definitions were limited more to the economic benefits of plant use by "aboriginal" peoples (Cotton, 1996). As time passed, the concept evolved to include other aspects of plant use, such as the use of plants for religious and spiritual needs. The terms put forward as to which peoples were to be studied in relation to their plant use broadened significantly—advancing from primitive to native to indigenous to local peoples, even those locals from the industrialized world (Minnis, 2000). "The study of the use of plants by humans" covers most variations propositioned (Allaby, 1998). As the discipline matured, so did the research methodology with an enlightenment of realizing the rights and contributions of indigenous peoples (Minnis, 2000). This chapter contains resources discussing and identifying edible, poisonous, and medicinal plants but not agricultural crop plants. See also chapters 2 and 10 for other titles that mention ethnobotanical uses.

# Bibliographies and Guides to the Literature

341   Andrews, Theodora, William L. Corya, and Donald A. Stickel. *A Bibliography on Herbs, Herbal Medicine, "Natural" Foods, and Unconventional Medical Treatment*. Littleton, CO: Libraries Unlimited, 1982. 339 p. ISBN 0872872882.

The title describes quite well this valuable compilation of 749 popular and scientific monographs, field guides, reference works, periodicals, and annotated cookbooks.

Arber, Agnes Robertson. *Herbals: Their Origin and Evolution: A Chapter in the History of Botany.*

See chapter 3 for full annotation. This classic survey "stands as the major survey of the period 1470 to 1670 when botany evolved into a scientific discipline separate from herbalism."

Johnston, Stanley H., comp. *The Cleveland Herbal, Botanical, and Horticultural Collections: A Descriptive Bibliography of Pre-1830 Works from the Libraries of the Holden Arboretum, the Cleveland Medical Library Association, and the Garden Center of Greater Cleveland.*

See chapter 3 for full annotation. A bibliography of pre-Linnean works, medicinal plants, herbals, and horticultural and botanical works.

342   Simon, James E., Alena F. Chadwick, and Lyle E. Craker. *Herbs: An Indexed Bibliography, 1971–1980: The Scientific Literature on Selected Herbs, and Aromatic and Medicinal Plants of the Temperate Zone*. Hamden, CT: Archon, 1984. 770 p. ISBN 0208019901.

This comprehensive bibliography on the major commercially significant herbs of the temperate zone was the 1985 winner of the Oberly Award for excellence in bibliographic literature from the Science and Technology Section of the Association of College and Research Libraries. References concern scientific details about the science of herbs. Part 1 is arranged by herb common name, part 2 presents literature arranged by subject, and part 3 lists references that include books, bibliographies, reports, conferences, and symposia.

# Databases, Abstracts, and Indexes

343   *Anthropology Plus*. Mountain View, CA: Research Libraries Group, 2002– . Price varies. Available electronically.

*Anthropology Plus* brings together into one resource the highly respected *Anthropological Literature* from Harvard's Tozzler Library and *Anthropological Index to Current Periodicals* from the Library of the British Museum, Department of Ethnography (Museum of Mankind). *Anthropology Plus* provides extensive worldwide indexing of most of the material in the journals received by these two great libraries in anthropology, archaeology, and interdisciplinary studies for both core periodicals as well as local and lesser-known journals. Coverage is from the late nineteenth century to the present. Updated monthly (British Museum records) and quarterly (Harvard records). A search for the term *ethnobot?* in late 2004 yielded nearly 2,500 citations, so this is a good source for articles on the ethnobotanical use of plants.

344  *NAPRALERT (NAtural PRoducts ALERT)*. Chicago, IL: College of Pharmacy, University of Illinois at Chicago. Program for Collaborative Research in the Pharmaceutical Sciences. Available electronically.

NAPRALERT "is the largest relational database of the world literature describing the ethnomedical or traditional uses, chemistry, and pharmacology of plant, microbial, and animal (including marine) extracts . . . [as well as] considerable data on the chemistry and pharmacology of secondary metabolites." Approximately 50% of the indexed literature in this database is for the period of 1975 to the present. The balance is selected material that dates back to 1650. This database is available online through various subscription options.

*PubMed*. URL: http://www.ncbi.nlm.nih.gov/entrez/query.fcgi.

See chapter 2 for full annotation. *PubMed* includes peer-reviewed articles dealing with research concerning the medical use of plants, so it is useful for ethnobotanists. Relevant Medical Subject Headings (MeSH) include Phytotherapy; Plant Extracts; Plants, Medicinal; Eclecticism, Historical; and Medicine, Traditional. Some keyword search terms that might be useful are *ethnomedicine, folk remedy(ies), home remedy(ies), folk medicine, indigenous medicine,* and *primitive medicine.*

# Serials

345  *Advances in Economic Botany*. Vol. 1. Bronx, NY: New York Botanical Garden, 1984– . Irregular. Price varies. ISSN 0741-8280.

"This series is an international forum for the publication of original monograph-length research papers, collections of papers, and symposia dealing with the uses and management of plants" that integrates pure and applied studies.

346   *Economic Botany.* Vol. 1– . New York: New York Botanical Garden, 1947– . Quarterly. $122.00. ISSN 0013-0001. Available electronically.

Published for the Society for Economic Botany (SEB). "Devoted to past, present, and future uses of plants by man" with emphasis on scientific papers relating to "uses" rather than growing of plant materials. Issues contain original research and review articles, book reviews, annotated bibliotheca, and notes on economic plants. There is a chronological article title index for Volumes 1 through 50 (1947—1996) available from the SEB Web site at http://www.econbot .org/home.html, as well as free full-text access to this journal for Volumes 54 (2000) to the present at http://www.econbot.org/journal/back_issues.html.

347   *Herbalgram.* Vol. 1– . Austin, TX: Herb Research Foundation; American Herbal Products Association, 1984– . Quarterly. $250.00. ISSN 0899-5648. Available electronically.

Published for the American Botanical Council (ABC). This peer-reviewed scientific journal covers medicinal plant research, research and book reviews, conference reports, legal and regulatory updates, plant patents, and ABC news. ABC members have free access to the electronic version of *Herbalgram* from issue 22 (1990) to the present. An issues list, journal departments list, author list, and topic index are also provided on its Web site at http://www.herbalgram.com/.

348   *Journal of Ethnobiology.* Vol. 1– . Chapel Hill, NC: Society of Ethnobiology, 1981– . Semiannual. $80.00. ISSN 0278-0771.

Publication of the Society of Ethnobiology. This peer-reviewed journal deals with research in "the interdisciplinary study of the relationships of plants and animals with human cultures worldwide." Topics include ethnobotany, paleoethnobotany, and ethnoecology, and other biological and anthropological areas. *Index of Journal Articles Presented in the Journal of Ethnobiology from 1981– 1999* is available at http://www.cieer.org/pdf/journal_eb_index.pdf.

349   *Journal of Ethnopharmacology.* Vol. 1– . Limerick, Ireland: Elsevier, 1979– . 18 times a year. $2,122.00. ISSN 0378-8741. Available electronically.

Published for the International Society for Ethnopharmacology (ISE). Original papers on "experimental investigation of the biological activities of plant and animal substances used in the traditional medicine of past and present cultures" are presented in this peer-reviewed journal. The multidisciplinary scope of this publication includes ethnobotanical approaches and field studies concerning indigenous use of plants for medicinal purposes.

350   *Journal of Herbs, Spices and Medicinal Plants.* Vol. 1– . Binghamton, NY: Haworth, 1992– . Quarterly. $285.00. ISSN 1049-6475. Available electronically.

This refereed journal provides a central place for interested educators and researchers around the world to find research, book reviews, and other information on herbs, spices, and medicinal plants.

351 *Planta Medica*. Vol.1– . Stuttgart, Germany: Georg Thieme Verlag. 1953– . Monthly. $838.00. ISSN 0032-0943. Available electronically.

This peer-reviewed international journal of natural products and medicinal plant research publishes original articles and reports and is the official organ of the Society for Medicinal Plant Research. Articles deal with pharmacology, toxicology, medicinal applications, biochemistry, physiology, *in vitro* cultures, biological activities, and phytochemistry. Letters, phytochemical notes, and book reviews are featured.

# Dictionaries and Encyclopedias

352 Bown, Deni. *New Encyclopedia of Herbs and Their Uses*. New York: DK, 2001. 448 p. $40.00. ISBN 078948031X.

This encyclopedia begins with such topics as the history of herbs, herbs that changed the world, major herbs of each continent or regions, and the use and cultivation of herbs. Although historically the passing of information relating to herbal use has been oral, this volume has a unique section listing selected herbal manuscripts and print records (c. 300 B.C.—1835) with a brief overview about herbs in print. The genus and species, growth habit, size, hardiness, properties, and various uses are described for over 1,000 herbs from around the world. High-quality glossy pages are loaded with beautiful color illustrations and photographs. Includes index of common names and subject index.

353 Buckingham, J. *Dictionary of Natural Products*. New York: Chapman and Hall, 1993. 7 vol. $6,349.95 (set). ISBN 0412466201 (set).

A massive undertaking covering over 130,000 natural products and their derivatives. It is arranged alphabetically by name of compound. Each entry has chemical, structural, and bibliographic information, as well as two index volumes with indexes by species, type of compound, name, molecular formula, and CAS registry number. Annual supplements, Volume 8 (1995) to Volume 10 (1998). Chapman and Hall/CRC Press also produce the *Dictionary of Natural Products on CD-ROM* (2000, $6,600.00, ISBN 0412491508) with updates every six months. Web access is also available via Chapman and Hall/CRC *CHEMnet-BASE* at http://www.chemnetbase.com/scripts/dnpweb.exe. Browse, perform searches and view search hitlists for free; subscription required to view or print the full product entries.

354    Chevallier, Andrew. *Encyclopedia of Herbal Medicine*. 2nd American ed. New York: DK, 2000. 336 p. $40.00. ISBN 0789467836.

Chevallier expands his outstanding earlier first edition, *Encyclopedia of Medicinal Plants* (1996), with results of the latest research as well as discussion about quality control and safety regarding the use of herbs. Almost every aspect of herbs as medicinal plants is covered in this extremely comprehensive work. History and herbal traditions from every continent are reviewed. One hundred key medicinal plants are listed alphabetically by Latin plant name (genus and species) followed by common name(s), habitat and cultivation, related species, key constituents and key actions, research information, tradition and current uses, parts used, key preparations and their uses, and self-help uses. Additionally, over 450 other medicinal plants are listed with their characteristics and uses. Instructions for growing, harvesting, and processing of medicinal herbs are provided, as well as directions for how to make various other types of medicinal products from them. There are sections on remedies for common ailments with an index of herbs by ailments, glossary, bibliography, general index, and more. High-quality color photographs and illustrations abound in this beautifully designed volume.

355    Coffey, Timothy. *The History and Folklore of North American Flowers*. New York: Facts On File, 1993. 384 p. ISBN 0816026246.

Compendium of the use of approximately 700 species of North American wildflowers from precolonial times to the twentieth century, including folklore and use as medicines and food. Contains an extensive list of common names for each of the species.

356    Duke, James A., and Rodolfo Vásquez. *Amazonian Ethnobotanical Dictionary*. Boca Raton, FL: CRC, 1994. 215 p. $99.95 (paper). ISBN 0849336643 (paper).

This volume contains over 1,000 descriptions for about 20% of the Amazonian flora. Plants are listed alphabetically by scientific name, followed by author, family name, local name(s), English name when available, comments (uses, poison or toxicity when known), and local sources when known. There are over 200 black-and-white illustrations of selected plants. Plants are additionally listed in the index of common names with cross-references to their scientific names and in the medicinal index for applications.

357    Kowalchik, Claire, and William H. Hylton, eds. *Rodale's Illustrated Encyclopedia of Herbs*. Emmaus, PA: Rodale, 1998. 545 p. $19.95 (paper). ISBN 0878576991; 087596964X (paper).

Herb and topic profiles are interspersed and entered alphabetically in this comprehensive encyclopedia. Herb profiles provide information such as history, evolution, plant description, growing time and conditions, range, habitat, varied uses, pests and diseases, and cultivation/harvesting/storage, with toxicities prominently noted. Topic profiles go into further detail on herbal bathing, cooking, companion planting, crafts, dyes, dangers, gardening, growing, healing, houseplants, herbs, scents, and lotions. There are black-and-white illustrations with some color photographs for selected plants.

358    Phillips, Roger, and Nicky Foy. *The Random House Book of Herbs*. New York: Random House, 1990. 192 p. ISBN 0679732136 (paper).

Nicely illustrated book of herbs, this volume is a guide to about 400 herbs, arranged by type of use (teas, medicinal, etc.). Also includes addresses of suppliers and major herb gardens.

359    Rätsch, Christian. *The Dictionary of Sacred and Magical Plants*. Santa Barbara, CA: ABC-CLIO, 1992. 223 p. ISBN 0874367166.

This unusual dictionary lists plants that have been used in magical or spiritual settings. About 125 of the best-known magical plants from around the world are included, plants such as coffee, aloe, peyote, witch hazel, and mandrake. Their use in traditional rituals is described, along with their scientific name, pharmacology, and further references.

360    Ross, Ivan A. *Medicinal Plants of the World: Chemical Constituents, Traditional and Modern Medicinal Uses*. Totawa, NJ: Humana, 1999–2005. 2 vol.; $99.50 (vol. 1); $110.00 (vol. 2); $125.00 (vol. 3). ISBN 1588292819 (vol. 1, 2nd ed.); 0896038777 (vol. 2, 1st ed.); 1588291294 (vol. 3); 0585224021 (electronic, set, 1st ed.); 1592593658 (electronic, vol. 1, 2nd ed.); 1592598870 (electronic, vol. 3).

Common names, botanical description, origin and distribution, chemical constituents, pharmacological activities, and clinical trials are summarized for 51 major medicinal plant species between the two volumes. Sections on nomenclature, descriptive terminology, and glossary terms are provided. Volume 1 has an index of scientific and common names, and Volume 2 has a cross-references section. An extensive reference list completes each plant species chapter. Small black-and-white photographs of each plant species accompany its description, as well as color plates for most entries. The second edition of Volume 1 is available electronically, as well as the first editions of both Volumes 1 and 2. Volume 3 adds 28 different plant species to the collection (not seen).

361    Skelly, Carole J. *Dictionary of Herbs, Spices, Seasonings, and Natural Flavorings*. New York: Garland, 1994. 484 p. ISBN 0815314655.

Plants are listed in alphabetical order by common name. Each entry includes information on uses, safety, scientific names, and alternate common names.

362   Stuart, Malcolm, ed. *The Encyclopedia of Herbs and Herbalism*. Enderby, England: Black Cat, 1994. 304 p. ISBN 0748100121.

This outstanding book discusses cultivation, preservation, uses, history, folklore, and chemistry of herbs and includes superb color photographs, drawings, and diagrams. The first portion of the encyclopedia consists of chapters discussing various aspects of herbalism, followed by a reference section describing 420 of the most important herbs, their use, cultivation, distribution, and constituents. The herbs are in alphabetical order by scientific name.

# Handbooks and Methods

363   Alexiades, Miguel N., and Jennie Wood Sheldon, eds. *Selected Guidelines for Ethnobotanical Research: A Field Manual*. Bronx, NY: New York Botanical Garden, 1996. 306 p. (Advances in Economic Botany, vol. 10). $22.95 (paper). ISBN 0893274046 (paper).

Protocols, data collection, quantitative methods, and ethics are presented to assist the researcher in "identifying and implementing field techniques suitable to a research question and site." Methods for collecting herbarium specimens, mushrooms, and bryophytes are described. Introduction contains a literature review of the science of ethnobotanical research and its challenges.

364   Ammirati, Joseph F., James A. Traquair, and Paul A. Horgen. *Poisonous Mushrooms of the Northern United States and Canada*. Minneapolis, MN: University of Minnesota Press, 1985. 396 p. ISBN 0816614075.

This carefully researched book contains excellent colored plates and line drawings, plus definitive descriptions and keys. It provides an overview of poisonous mushrooms that inhabit the northern United States with technical information on habitat, habit, occurrence, characteristics, and useful literature. It is aimed at researchers, physicians, and amateurs and will provide an outstanding, standard reference source. Besides discussing fungal structure and taxonomy, the book also deals with toxicity and the major categories of fungal poisoning.

365   Angier, Bradford. *Field Guide to Edible Wild Plants*. Harrisburg, PA: Stackpole, 1974. 255 p. $19.95 (paper). ISBN 0811706168; 0811720187 (paper).

"A quick all in color identifier of more than 100 edible wild foods growing free in the United States and Canada." There are alphabetically arranged descriptions of 116 free growing, edible plants, all with illustrations in color. Information includes habitat, distribution, growth and development, edible parts, how to prepare and store, and general uses. The book is written by a well-known author for camping and outdoor living, and its size is suitable for fieldwork. It would be most useful in public libraries and for students.

366   Angier, Bradford. *Field Guide to Medicinal Wild Plants*. Mechanicsburg, PA: Stackpole, 1978. 320 p. $19.95 (paper). ISBN 0811720764 (paper).

Another book by Angier, this is a popular guide to interesting or valuable plants used for medicinal purposes. Arranged by common name, it gives family, other common names, characteristics, distribution, uses, and full page color illustrations for each plant. It is designed as a field guide, and like the previous book, is appropriate for the lay reader or amateur botanist. Color illustrations throughout.

367   Blumenthal, Mark, ed. *The Complete German Commission E Monographs, Therapeutic Guide to Herbal Medicines*. Austin, TX: American Botanical Council, 1998. 685 p. $165.00. ISBN 096555550X.

Commission E is a panel of experts first created by the German Ministry of Health in 1978 to evaluate the safety and effectiveness of herbal and phytochemical medicines. Commission E used a bibliographic review of 100 to 200 global scientific references for each herb to evaluate safety and effectiveness. They examined traditional use; chemical data; experimental, pharmacological, and toxicological studies; clinical studies; field and epidemiological studies; patient care records submitted from physicians' files and occasionally unpublished data from manufacturer. Their findings, published in the *Bundesanzeiger* (*German Federal Gazette*) as monographs, are recognized as being the most complete and exact available on herbs and phytomedicines. This guide contains the English translation of Germany's *Commission E Monographs* for 380 approved and unapproved herbs. The introduction gives a very detailed examination about the use, sales, marketing, standards, and regulations of herbs in the United States and Europe. There are therapeutic indexes on herbal uses, indications, contraindications, side effects, pharmacological actions, drug interactions, and duration of administration. There are a chemical glossary and index; a taxonomic cross-reference index alphabetized by English name and followed by botanical name, plant family, pharmacopeial, and German name; and excerpts from the German *Pharmacopoeia* on selected herbal drugs for quality standards. Includes appendices for abbreviations and symbols, weights and measures, *German Federal Gazette*, ESCOP [European Scientific Cooperative on Phytotherapy] Monographs, World Health Organization (WHO) Monographs, general glossary, general references to sources used for the translation from German to English, and general index. The references for literature used by the Commission members were not included in the *Commission E Monographs* and are available only to lawyers or scientific organizations for disputes/conflicts through the

*Bundesinstitut für Arzneimittel und Medizinprodukte (BfArM)* [*Federal Institute for Drugs and Medical Devices*]. URL: http://www.bfarm.de/de/index .php.

368    Bresinsky, Andreas, and Helmut Besl. *A Colour Atlas of Poisonous Fungi: A Handbook for Pharmacists, Doctors, and Biologists.* London: Wolfe, 1990. 295 p. $160.00. ISBN 0723415765.

Over 200 illustrations and photographs provide a guide to the world of poisonous fungi. The authors provide an overview of poisoning by fungi, and directions for collection, examination, and identification of samples. There is a glossary, a 20-page bibliography, and an index of terms that also includes illustrations and chemical structures. Refer to Frohne's *Colour Atlas of Poisonous Plants*, below, for a companion volume describing poisonous plants.

369    Brown, Dan. *Cornell University Poisonous Plants Information Database.* Ithaca, NY: Cornell University Animal Science Department, 2003. URL: http://www.ansci.cornell.edu/plants/.

Scientific and common names, primary poisons, and species most affected can be found in the *Poisonous Plants* database. Details include the poisonous parts of the plant as well as a color photo, when available. There are alphabetical listings for both the botanical and common names. There is a list of toxic plant agents with links to associated stereochemistry and information for related classes of agents. Poisonous plants of concern to particular animals are provided as well as details about safety issues concerning the medicinal use of plants for livestock.

370    Castner, James L., S. Lee Timme, and James A. Duke. *A Field Guide to Medicinal and Useful Plants of the Upper Amazon.* Gainesville, FL: Feline, 1998. 154 p. ISBN 0962515078 (paper).

Physical descriptions and local uses for approximately 120 plant species of the Upper Amazon are covered in this field guide, with additional in depth material on five of these species. Over 200 high-quality photographs, some color, are included. Entry is alphabetical by Latin name with heading of common name. Appendixes for plant names by Latin name, English name, and Spanish name.

371    Duke, James A. *Handbook of Phytochemical Constituents of GRAS Herbs and Other Economic Plants, Herbal Reference Library.* Boca Raton, FL: CRC, 2001. 654 p. $179.00. ISBN 0849338654.

Covers all GRAS (generally-recognized-as-safe) herbs, including approximately 250 food and medicinal plants. This unannotated catalog lists over 1,000 plants by species and their more than 15,000 phytochemical components in alphabetical order with coded primary reference sources.

372    Duke, James A., and Stephen Beckstrom-Sternberg, comps. *Dr. Duke's Phytochemical and Ethnobotanical Databases*. URL: http://www.ars-grin.gov/duke/.

James A. Duke is a prolific and renowned USDA ethnobotanist and herbal researcher. Several types of searches can be done from this Web site: Plant Searches for chemicals and activities in a particular plant, Chemical Searches, Activity Searches, and Ethnobotany Searches for ethnobotanical uses concerning a particular plant. Contains links to other databases and information of interest. No longer being updated, but a valuable resource nonetheless.

373    Fischer, David W., and Alan Bessette. *Edible Wild Mushrooms of North America: A Field-to-Kitchen Guide*. Austin, TX: University of Texas Press, 1992. 254 p. $35.00 (paper). ISBN 0292720793; 0292720807 (paper).

This field guide contains identification information for over 100 species of edible mushrooms and 19 poisonous species. How to find and gather mushrooms are covered with special considerations, plus more than 70 recipes are featured. General details are given followed by key identifying characteristics, plant descriptions, fruiting characteristics, similar species, and edibility.

374    Foster, Steven. *101 Medicinal Herbs: An Illustrated Guide*. Loveland, CO: Interweave, 1998. 240 p. ISBN 1883010519 (paper).

Using literature from scientific studies, the author has provided conditions, dosages, and cautions for selected herbs along with their sources, traditional use, and current use. Herbs are entered by their common name and then the botanical name with color photographs. There is a therapeutic cross-references list.

375    Foster, Steven, and James A. Duke. *A Field Guide to Medicinal Plants and Herbs of Eastern and Central North America*. 2nd ed. Boston, MA: Houghton Mifflin, 2000. 424 p. (Peterson Field Guide Series). $30.00; $19.00 (paper). ISBN 0395988152; 0395988144 (paper).

Over 500 plant species from eastern and central North America are arranged by physical description (flower color, number of petals, etc.) for ease of identification when the plant identity is not known. Common name(s), part used, scientific name, family name, and description including growth habit, height, characteristics, and where found, related species, and any warnings are covered. There is a glossary for botanical and medical terms, an index to plants with page numbers for both description and photograph, and an index to medical topics.

376    Foster, Steven, and Christopher Hobbs. *A Field Guide to Western Medicinal Plants and Herbs*. Boston, MA: Houghton Mifflin, 2002. 442 p. (Peterson Field Guide Series). $30.00; $22.00 (paper). ISBN 039583807X; 0395838061 (paper).

Nearly 500 plants from western North America are grouped by physical description (flower color, number of petals, etc.). This format is useful to identify specimens when the name is not known. Entered by common name(s) followed by parts used, scientific name, family name, and brief description including where found, uses, related species, and any warnings. Common terms are used when available. There is a glossary for botanical and medical terms, an index to plants with page numbers for both description and photograph, and an index to medical topics.

377    Frohne, Dietrich, and Hans Jurgen Pfander. *A Colour Atlas of Poisonous Plants: A Handbook for Pharmacists, Doctors, Toxicologists, and Biologists.* London: Wolfe, 1984. 291 p. (Wolfe Atlases Series). ISBN 0723408394.

This comprehensive, authoritative reference provides morphological, pharmacological, toxicological, and therapeutic details for possible cases of poisoning by plants. The introduction discusses problems of poisoning by plants and toxicologically significant plant constituents before launching into details for the most important plants with alleged or actual toxic properties. Each entry includes colored photographs, scientific and common names, botanical description, and information on toxicology, symptoms, treatment, and so on. A bibliography and an index are included. See Bresinsky and Besl, above, for a sister volume on poisonous fungi. New edition forthcoming in 2005 with the title *Poisonous Plants: A Handbook for Doctors, Pharmacists, Toxicologists, Biologists, and Veterinarians*, second edition.

378    Hall, Ian, et al. *Edible and Poisonous Mushrooms of the World.* Portland, OR: Timber, 2003. 371 p. $39.95. ISBN 0881925861.

Approximately 280 types of mushrooms are detailed. The introduction includes information on identifying and naming mushrooms, precautions about edible versus poisonous mushrooms, and the mushroom market. The first section focuses on the cultivation of mushrooms. The second section discusses mushroom collecting, including mushroom myths, toxins, poisoning syndromes and symptoms, and rules for picking. The last section gives identification descriptions for edible and poisonous species. Printed on high-quality paper. Beautiful color photographs of species with annotations indicating whether edible or poisonous.

379    Johnson, Timothy. *CRC Ethnobotany Desk Reference.* Boca Raton, FL: CRC, 1999. 1211 p. $179.95. ISBN 084931187X.

Nearly 30,000 plant species from around the world are listed alphabetically by species name with accession numbers. Aspects such as common name, family, range, action, treatment use, contents, indigenous use, use, body habitat, and comments are keyed by number, and data for these aspects in the species description, when known, are headed by the keyed number. An index with common names, health conditions, and locations are listed with accession numbers of relevant plant species. The author created and maintains an electronic database, *Herbage*, 4th edition, available for purchase on CD-ROM. "Much of the information contained in [the *Herbage* database] can be found in [this] book."

380    Keeler, Richard F., and Anthony T. Tu. *Plant and Fungal Toxins.* New York: M. Dekker, 1983. 934 p. (Handbook of Natural Toxins, vol. 1). $295.00. ISBN 0824718933.

Includes 20 papers from 38 expert contributors that collate and interpret results from field observations and laboratory investigations on plant and fungal poisoning. Toxins are grouped by effects on cardiovascular or pulmonary systems, carcinogenic effects, reproductive effects, psychic or neurotoxic effects, gastrointestinal or hepatic effects, effects on species interactions, and usefulness in medicine. The text provides contemporary information on chemistry, source, gross and histopathologic effects, and the mechanism of action. There are author and subject indexes. This is a useful resource for both research and applied areas.

381    Kingsbury, John Merriam. *Poisonous Plants of the United States and Canada.* Englewood Cliffs, NJ: Prentice-Hall, 1964. 626 p. (Prentice-Hall Biological Science Series). ISBN 0136850162.

Long a standard, this book updates and augments *Poisonous Plants of the United States* by W. C. Muenscher (1939). Kingsbury is authoritative for the time it was written.

382    Kunkel, Günther. *Plants for Human Consumption: An Annotated Checklist of the Edible Phanerogams and Ferns.* Königstein, Germany: Koeltz Scientific, 1984. 393 p. $92.00. ISBN 3874292169.

The author has compiled a checklist of about 12,650 species of edible flowering plants and ferns. The information provided for each species includes the area in which it is found and brief notes on which part of the plant is eaten and whether it is known to be poisonous. A list of the main references is also included.

383    Lampe, Kenneth F., and Mary Ann McCann. *AMA Handbook of Poisonous and Injurious Plants.* Chicago, IL: American Medical Association, 1985. 432 p. ISBN 0899701833 (paper).

This authoritative reference is advertised as a convenient field guide to the identification, diagnosis, and management of human intoxications from plants and mushrooms of the United States, Canada, and the Caribbean. It is designed for health care professionals and is appropriate for all reference libraries. There are color photographs to aid in identification, introductory materials pertaining to epidemiology of plant poisoning, botanical nomenclature, scientific and common name indexes, and sections on systemic plant poisoning, plant dermatitis, and mushroom poisoning. Each plant is discussed according to description, distribution, toxic part, toxin, symptoms, management, and references to the literature.

384    Larone, Davise Honig. *Medically Important Fungi: A Guide to Identification*. 4th ed. Washington, DC: ASM, 2002. 408 p. $79.95. ISBN 1555811728.

This identification guide is written for the laboratory technician who must identify disease-causing fungi in the laboratory. The book includes chapters on identifying fungi both in clinical specimens and in cultures; detailed descriptions of the yeasts, molds, and other fungi; and laboratory techniques for identifying the fungi.

385    Martin, Gary J. *Ethnobotany: A Methods Manual*. Sterling, VA: Earthscan, 2004. 268 p. (People and Plants Conservation Manuals: Volume 1). $39.95 (paper). ISBN 1844070840 (paper).

This methods manual was created as a central part of the People and Plants Initiative of the World Wide Fund for Nature and UNESCO, and its associate, the Royal Botanic Gardens, Kew (U. K.). It was written in response to a growing interest and need for systematic scientific design of projects, collection of data, and documentation for making inventories of useful plants in a collaborative fashion with disciplines such as botany, ethnopharmacology, anthropology, ecology, economics, and linguistics. Guidelines are included that "promote the welfare of local people, equitable distribution of resources, sustainable development, and protection of natural areas even as we carry out scientifically rigorous research."

386    McGinnis, Michael R., Richard F. D'Amato, and Geoffrey A. Land. *Pictorial Handbook of Medically Important Fungi and Aerobic Actinomycetes*. New York: Praeger, 1982. 160 p. $24.95 (paper). ISBN 0030583640 (paper).

This handbook is a simple, complete guide for the identification of commonly encountered clinical laboratory molds, aerobic actinomycetes and yeasts. It is well illustrated with drawings and micrographs; the quality is high, and the descriptions are concise with accurate pictorial references. It is very similar in scope and intent to Larone's *Medically Important Fungi* (above); however, Larone has more information on tests whereas McGinnis includes micrographs as well as drawings. The descriptions in Larone are perhaps less technical.

387    McKenna, Dennis J., Kenneth Jones, and Kerry Hughes. *Botanical Medicines: The Desk Reference for Major Herbal Supplements*. 2nd ed. New York: Haworth Herbal, 2002. 1138 p. $169.95; $79.95 (paper). ISBN 0789012650; 0789012669 (paper).

An extensive review and analysis of the current scientific, peer-reviewed literature for 35 plant species (including *Ephedra*) widely used for herbal medicines forms the foundation for this meticulous and comprehensive compilation. Chapters are divided into nine sections: botanical data (classification and nomenclature: scientific name, family name, and common names; and description including where found and physical details of plant); history and traditional uses; chemistry; therapeutic applications; preclinical studies; clinical studies; and dosage profile (contraindications, drug interactions, pregnancy and lactation, side effects, special precautions, toxicology). Each section is resplendent with references to document evidence and substantiate use or nonuse. Includes appendixes on quality in botanical supplements and key provisions of DSHEA (Dietary Supplement Health and Education Act, 1994). Former title: *Natural Dietary Supplements: A Desktop Reference.*

388   Miller, Amy Bess Williams. *Shaker Medicinal Herbs: A Compendium of History, Lore, and Uses.* Pownal, VT: Storey, 1998. 215 p. $35.00. ISBN 1580170404.

This well-done history of Shaker herbs is a worthy addition to botanical collections. The book is divided into two parts for discussions of herbs from various Shaker communities and a compendium of over 300 herbs, shrubs, and trees detailing their uses. Contains Shaker botanical drawings, seed labels, catalogs, and diary excerpts.

389   Moerman, Daniel E. *Medicinal Plants of Native America.* Ann Arbor, MI: Museum of Anthropology, University of Michigan, 1986. 2 vol. (Research Reports in Ethnobotany, contribution 2; Technical Reports of the University of Michigan Museum of Anthropology, no. 19). ISBN 0915703092 (paper, set).

Volume 1 lists medicinal plants by genus. Information provided for each species includes how it is used and by which tribe. Volume 2 supplies tables for indication, plant family, Native American culture, and plant common names. The preface calls this set a "comprehensive, taxonomically validated, overview of the medicinal plants used by Native Americans."

390   Moerman, Daniel E. *Native American Ethnobotany.* Portland, OR: Timber, 1998. 927 p. $79.95. ISBN 0881924539.

Beginning with an overview of plant use by Native Americans, this compilation, arranged by scientific names (genera and species, families, synonyms) followed by common names and ethnobotanical information (drug, food, fiber, other), provides comprehensive coverage of approximately 4,000 plants with over 44,000 tribal uses. There is an index of tribes, with each tribe listed with use categories (drug, food, fiber, dye, other). There are also indexes of usage, plant name synonyms, and common names of plants. The database *Native American Ethnobotany* was the content source for this book (see entry below).

391    *Native American Ethnobotany: A Database of Foods, Drugs, Dyes and Fibers of Native American Peoples, Derived from Plants.* URL: http://herb.umd .umich.edu/.

Over 44,500 items can be found in this freely accessible database that is hosted by the University of Michigan–Dearborn. Plant species are entered into the system by scientific name, which in most cases hyperlinks to the USDA Plants Database. Common name and plant use(s) with citation of use source are referenced for over 4,000 species and over 240 plant families. Drugs, dyes, fibers, foods, and cleaning agents are just some of the plant uses indexed here. Entries link to the U. S. Department of Agriculture *Plants Database* at http://plants.usda.gov/, which provides color photographs and botanical details. The book *Native American Ethnobotany* is based on this database (see above).

392    *PDR for Herbal Medicines.* 2nd ed. Montvale, NJ: Medical Economics Company, 2000. Various pagings. $59.95. ISBN 1563633612.

As one would expect from the publishers of *the* standard in prescription drug reference, *Physicians' Desk Reference (PDR),* the *PDR for Herbal Medicines* can be considered a comprehensive source of authoritative information on herbal medicines. Currently approval is not required from the Food and Drug Association for manufacture or distribution of dietary supplements (including herbs or other botanicals). This compendium utilizes evaluations on the safety and effectiveness of over 300 herbal drugs done by the German Commission E, a panel of experts created by the German Ministry of Health, which is recognized as being the most exact and correct available. Over 400 additional herbs are included as a result of an extensive literature search. The Scientific and Common Name Index lists herbs alphabetically by scientific name and by common name. The entry by scientific name contains standard sections beginning with scientific name, followed by common name, botanical description, actions and pharmacology, indications and usage, contraindications, precautions and adverse reactions, overdosage, dosage, and literature bibliography. Several indexes are provided including a therapeutic category index, primary indications index, homeopathic indications index, side effects index, and drug/herb interactions index. Additionally guides are provided on safety, herb identification with nearly 400 color photographs, and product identification. See Blumenthal's *The Complete German E Monographs,* above, for background details about the German Commission E.

393   Pearsall, Deborah M. *Paleoethnobotany: A Handbook of Procedures.* 2nd ed. San Diego, CA: Academic, 2000. 700 p. $149.95; $79.95 (paper). ISBN 0125480423; 0125480369 (paper).

Paleoethnobotany history and development; macroremains, phytolith, and pollen analysis (fossil pollen grains as a record of human contact with plants useful to archaeological study), techniques, and procedures; and approaches to predicting diet and health of prehistoric humans are covered in this textbook.

394   *People and Plants Handbook: Sources for Applying Ethnobotany to Conservation and Community Development.* Issue 1– . Paris: WWF, UNESCO, RGB, Kew, 1996– . Irregular. URL: http://www.unesco.org/mab/publications/peptitle.htm.

Publication of the World Wide Fund for Nature and UNESCO, and their associate, the Royal Botanical Gardens, Kew (UK), as part of the People and Plants Initiative (http://peopleandplants.org/). Created to provide "information on ethnobotany, conservation and development, and to enable ethnobotanists and others in developing countries to be in touch with one another and with a wider global network." Sources of information, ethics, methods of assessing biological resources and local knowledge, resource centers and programs, interviews, and advice from the field are some of the many topics covered in this publication. Beginning with Issue 8 (2002), the *Handbook* moved from theme-focused issues to issues with news about the practices and activities of the People and Plants program.

395   Peterson, Lee. *A Field Guide to Edible Wild Plants of Eastern and Central North America.* Boston, MA: Houghton Mifflin, 1999. 374 p. (Peterson Field Guide Series). $19.00 (paper). ISBN 039592622X (paper).

"More than 370 edible wild plants, plus thirty-seven poisonous look-alikes, are described here, with 400 drawings and seventy-eight color photographs showing precisely how to recognize each species. Also included are habitat descriptions, lists of plants by season, and preparation instructions for twenty-two different food uses." Chapter topics are flowering plants (sorted by color), woody plants (sorted by description of leaves), miscellaneous plants, finding edible plants, and food uses.

396   Prance, Ghillean, T. ed. *The Cultural History of Plants.* New York: Routledge, 2005. 432 p. $150.00. ISBN 0415927463.

This reference describes the role of plants in social life, regional customs, and natural landscapes. Covers over 1,000 plants. Not seen.

397 Schultes, Richard Evans, and Siri Von Reis, eds. *Ethnobotany: Evolution of a Discipline*. Portland, OR: Dioscorides, 1995. 414 p. $49.95. ISBN 0931146283.

Published on the one hundredth anniversary of ethnobotany as a distinct science, international experts reflect on the discipline's history and current theory and practice in a compilation of 36 papers.

398 Silverman, Maida. *A City Herbal: Lore, Legend and Uses of Common Weeds*. 3rd ed. Woodstock, NY: Ash Tree, 1997. 181 p. $13.95 (paper). ISBN 1888123001 (paper).

A selected group of city plants, each with its own full-page line drawing, comprise this specialized herbal. Alphabetized by common name followed by scientific name, folk names, location found in urban areas, botanical description, historical lore/legends/uses, and suggested uses. Earlier editions entitled *A City Herbal: A Guide to the Lore, Legend, and Usefulness of 34 Plants That Grow in the City*.

399 Sturtevant, E. Lewis. *Sturtevant's Edible Plants of the World*. New York: Dover, 1972. 686 p. ISBN 0486204596 (paper).

This unabridged reprint of the 1919 version is a valuable, although dated, addition to the plant literature. The scope is worldwide, the bibliography detailed. "Using over 560 ancient and modern sources," details about origin, spread, cultivation, when first plant first eaten, parts of plants eaten, and myths for nearly 3,000 species are described. This work is considered one of the most accurate and complete guides on the topic. Fully referenced.

400 Torkelson, Anthony R. *The Cross Name Index to Medicinal Plants*. Boca Raton, FL: CRC, 1996–1999. 4 vol. $1,689.95 (set). ISBN 0849326354 (set).

Although not intended to be the last word on medical plant taxonomy, this work will be of use to anyone seeking to untangle the myriad of common and scientific plant names. Volumes 1 and 2 provide nearly 30,000 common names of various plants alphabetically followed by the most-cited scientific name (genus and species) below it. Volume 3 provides the scientific name for more than 4,000 medicinal plant species, with the taxonomic classification noted most frequently in a review of literature. Beneath the scientific name are listed common names with the source country, language, and/or alternate scientific name(s). Volume 4 (*Plants in Indian Medicine, A–Z*) "lists more than 12,000 common names in 100 languages, dialects and regions for over 1900 medicinal plants. Both scientific and common names of medicinal plants are cross indexed to each other." The data draw heavily from Ayurvedic medicinal uses.

401    Van Wyk, Ben-Erik, and Michael Wink. *Medicinal Plants of the World: An Illustrated Scientific Guide to Important Medicinal Plants and Their Uses.* Portland, OR: Timber, 2004. 480 p. $39.95. ISBN 0881926027.

Over 320 medicinal plants alphabetically ordered by scientific names are described by physical description, origin, parts used, therapeutic category, uses and properties, preparation and dosage, active ingredients, pharmacological effects, warnings, and regulatory status, if any (based on, for example, medicinal plant monographs from the German Commission E, European Scientific Cooperative on Phytotherapy, and the World Health Organization). Numerous high-quality color photographs document the appearance of entries. The history of traditional medicine from around the world, various plant parts and their uses, active ingredients of plant drugs, quality and safety, efficacy of medicinal plant products (levels of evidence), health disorder and medicinal plants, and quick guide to commercialized medicinal plants round this volume out. See Blumenthal's *The Complete German E Monographs*, above, for background details about the German Commission E.

402    Wagner, Hildebert, and Sabine Bladt. *Plant Drug Analysis: A Thin Layer Chromatography Atlas.* 2nd ed. New York: Springer, 1996. 384 p. $260.00. ISBN 3540586768.

Identification and purity can be checked for nearly 230 medicinal plants utilizing this atlas of thin layer chromatography (TLC) analysis. Chapters are grouped by types of drugs contained in plants and contain data on preparation of extracts, TLC process, drug detection, specific plant source with related major drug constituents, stereochemical structures, and chromatograms for specific samples with analysis details. Includes 184 chromatograms.

403    Wichtl, Max, ed. *Herbal Drugs and Phytopharmaceuticals: A Handbook for Practice on a Scientific Basis.* 3rd ed. Boca Raton, FL: CRC, 2004. 704 p. $279.95. ISBN 0849319617.

Translation of *Teedrogen und Phytopharmaka*, which in Germany is considered a major reference of authoritative information on medicinal herbs and phytomedicine for pharmacists and physicians. References to British and U. S. resources were added to this English version. Entered by scientific name, over 200 herbal medicines are described with common names, illustration and description, plant source, synonyms, origin, constituents, indications, drug interactions, side effects, tea preparations, phytomedicine uses, authentication details (characteristic microscopic features), adulterations, storage, regulatory status (Canada, U. K., and United States), and supporting literature. Color photographs of herbs and herb parts are presented, many times with stereochemical structures, transverse sections, and other black-and-white illustrations. A general section includes information about tea uses, preparation, and therapeutic limitations; residues in herbal drugs; various monographs created by commissions and bodies; and phytopharmaceuticals definition, preparation, quality, purity, safety, and governmental approvals.

# Textbooks and Treatises

404   Balick, Michael J., and Paul Alan Cox. *Plants, People, and Culture: The Science of Ethnobotany*. New York: Scientific American Library, 1996. 228 p. (Scientific American Library Series, no. 60). ISBN 0716750619; 0716760274 (paper).

In this text the authors provide an introduction to the relationship of people with plants and its effect on human culture, both past and present, which is enhanced by their extensive fieldwork experience in Central and South America, the Caribbean, Oceania, and Southeast Asia. Ethnobotanical drugs, fieldwork issues, preparation of specimens, protecting indigenous people and their property rights, plant uses, and indigenous and other perspectives on conservation are just some of the topics presented in this book. Numerous color photos and illustrations.

405   Cotton, C. M. *Ethnobotany: Principles and Applications*. New York: Wiley, 1996. 424 p. $80.00 (paper). ISBN 047195537X (paper).

This ethnobotany textbook covers its history and development, plant biology, research methods, traditional botanical and phytochemical knowledge, evolutionary relationship of humans with plants, and applications, including benefits and problems.

406   Ford, Richard I., ed. *The Nature and Status of Ethnobotany*. 2nd ed. Ann Arbor, MI: Museum of Anthropology, University of Michigan, 1994. 428 p. (Anthropological Papers, no. 67). $18.00 (paper). ISBN 0915703386 (paper).

Originally published in 1978 and considered widely as the standard text on ethnobotany, this reprint adds a new introduction and references to the original text on its history, theoretical issues, epistemology, resource utilization, anthropogenic plants, and prehistoric economics.

407   Levetin, Estelle, and Karen McMahon. *Plants and Society*. 3rd ed. Boston, MA: McGraw-Hill, 2003. 508 p. $84.38 (paper). ISBN 0072909498 (paper).

This introductory text covers botanical principles, plants as a source of food, commercial products derived from plants, plants and human health, the impact of algae and fungi on human affairs, and plants and the environment. Topics are comprehensively covered. Each chapter begins with a content outline with chapter concepts, and ends with chapter summary, review questions, and further readings.

# Associations

408    The American Society of Pharmacognosy (ASP). c/o David J. Slatkin, Treasurer, P. O. Box 28665, Scottsdale, AZ 85255-0161. Phone: 623-572-3500. Fax: 480-513-2782. E-mail: jon_clardy@hms.harvard.edu. URL: http://www .phcog.org/.

This international scientific organization works to "promote the growth, and development not only of pharmacognosy but all aspects of those sciences related to and dealing in natural products." Co-publishes the *Journal of Natural Products* with the American Chemical Society.

409    Herb Society of America (HSA). 9019 Kirtland Chardon Rd., Kirtland, OH 44094. Phone: 440-256-0514. Fax: 440-256-0541. E-mail: herbs@herbsociety .org. URL: http://www.herbsociety.org/.

Society members are scientists, educators, and others interested in botanical and horticultural research on herbs and culinary, economic, decorative, fragrant, and historic use of herbs. The Society maintains plant collections, seed exchanges, symposia, and annual conferences. The National Herb Garden (http:// www.usna.usda.gov/Gardens/collections/herb.html) was designed and donated to the National Arboretum in Washington, DC, by the HSA. The Society operates a library on botany and horticulture, conducts slide shows and lectures, maintains speakers' bureau, and bestows awards. Publishes *The Herbarist*, membership directory, and newsletter.

410    International Council for Medicinal and Aromatic Plants (ICMAP). c/o Professor Dr. Chlodwig Franz, President, Institute for Applied Botany, University of Veterinary Medicine Vienna, Veterinärplatz 1, A-1210 Vienna, Austria. Phone: +43 1 250 77 3101. Fax: +43 1 250 77 3190. E-mail: Chlodwig.Franz@ vu-wien.ac.at. URL: http://www.icmap.org/.

The Council was created by nine international organizations to foster cooperation concerning knowledge, education, and training concerning medicinal and aromatic plants. Publishes the international *Newsletter on Medicinal and Aromatic Plants*.

411    International Society for Ethnopharmacology (ISE). c/o Professor Dr. Elaine Elisabetsky, President, Universidade Federal do Rio Grande do Sul, Caixa

Postal 5072, 90041-970 Porto Alegre RS, Brazil. Fax: +55 51 3316 3121. E-mail: elisasky@ufrgs.br. URL: http://www.ethnopharmacology.org/.

International scientists dedicated to interdisciplinary study of the physiological actions of plant, animal, and other substances used in indigenous medicines of past and present cultures. Official journal of ISE is the *Journal of Ethnopharmacology*. Web site includes information about the Society, its annual meetings and biennial congresses, upcoming conferences of other organizations, and newsletter.

412    International Society of Ethnobiology (ISE). c/o Executive Secretary, International Society of Ethnobiology, 250 Baldwin Hall, Department of Anthropology, University of Georgia, Athens, GA 30602. E-mail: ise@uga.edu. URL: http://guallart.dac.uga.edu/ISE/.

"Non-profit charitable organization dedicated to the research, study, promotion, and enhancement of ethnobiology." The Society was the first international scientific organization that formally acknowledged full respect and compensation for indigenous peoples concerning human rights, compensation for knowledge and resources, and sharing of research findings (Declaration of Belém, 1988). Web site includes information about the Society, its biennial international congress, and links to related sites.

413    Society for Economic Botany (SEB). P. O. Box 7075, Lawrence, KS 66044. Phone: 785-843-1235; 800-627-0629. Fax: 785-843-1274. E-mail: info@econbot.org. URL: http://www.econbot.org/home.html.

Botanists, anthropologists, pharmacologists, and others interested in scientific studies of useful plants. Seeks to develop interdisciplinary channels of communication among groups concerned with past, present, and future uses of plants. Publishes *Economic Botany* journal, Membership Directory, *Plants and People* newsletter, and occasional symposium volumes. Web site includes information about the Society, its annual meeting, related news, and free full-text access to its newsletter and recent issues (2002 to date) of its journal, *Economic Botany*.

414    Society for Medicinal Plant Research (Gesellschaft für Arzneipflanzenforschung-GA). c/o Dr. Renate Seitz, Secretary. Emmeringerstr. 11, D-82275 Emmering, Germany. Phone: 49 8141 613749. Fax: 49 8141 613749. E-mail: ga-secretary@t-online.de. URL: http://www.ga-online.org/.

Scientists in 70 countries who promote medicinal plant research. Organized to serve as an international focal point for such interests as pharmacognosy, pharmacology, phytochemistry, plant biochemistry and physiology, chemistry of natural products, plant cell culture, and application of medicinal plants in medicine. Publishes newsletter and *Planta Medica* journal. Web site includes information about the Society, selected workshop documents, and its annual congress and other meetings.

415   Society of Ethnobiology (SE). c/o Margaret Scarry, Secretary-Treasurer, Department of Anthropology, CB 3115, Alumni Building, University of North Carolina, Chapel Hill, NC 27599-3155. Phone: 919-962-3841. Fax: 919-962-1613. E-mail: scarry@email.unc.edu. URL: http://www.ethnobiology.org/.

"Non-profit professional organization dedicated to the interdisciplinary study of the relationships of plants and animals with human cultures worldwide." Publishes *Journal of Ethnobiology*. Web site includes information about the Society, its annual conferences, and links to related resources.

# References

Allaby, Michael. 1998. *Dictionary of Plant Sciences*. New York: Oxford University Press.

Cotton, C. M. 1996. *Ethnobotany: Principles and Applications*. New York: John Wiley.

Minnis, Paul E., ed. 2000. *Ethnobotany: A Reader*. Norman, OK: Oklahoma University Press.

# 6
# Ecology

Plant ecology is the study of the "collective phenomena of plants" (Nicolson, 2000, 1) within their environment. Connections and relations of plants among themselves and variables relating to their geography were studied in the late eighteenth century (Nicolson, 2000). The early focus of characterizing plants based on morphology and physiology evolved after Darwin published *On the Origin of Species* in 1859 to include considering a plant's adaptive function in nature. By the early twentieth century, researchers for the most part embraced the view "that plants grow together in definite, ordered, and repeating communities" (Nicolson, 2000, 2). In 1935 the concept of ecosystem was conceived—the idea that all types of living things and "associated inanimate material" were interconnected and should be studied as a unit; it incorporated the plant ecology concepts of succession and climax that play a major role in ecosystem theory (Nicolson, 2000). Ever more sophisticated computer modeling assists plant ecologists with increasingly complex and multidimensional research about plants and their environment—and none too soon, because there are new environmental factors that are sure to affect plants and their ecology (e.g., global dimming [Chang, 2004] and recognition of unexpectedly rapid declines in global magnetic field strength [Broad, 2004]).

The body of literature focused on plant ecology is limited. The ecology of plants is directly related to plant-animal interactions; so to do comprehensive research concerning plant ecology, it is necessary to also look at animal ecology and the ecology literature as a whole. Because ecology is dependent on environmental conditions, it is also of benefit to understand associated environmental science research. Related plant ecology fields are micrometeorology, soil science, plant anatomy, plant physiology, plant evolution, plant geography, and ecological biochemistry (Crawley, 1997).

**115**

# Bibliographies and Guides to the Literature

416    Davis, Stephen D. et al. *Plants in Danger: What Do We Know?* Gland, Switzerland: International Union for Conservation of Nature and Natural Resources (IUCN), 1986. (IUCN Conservation Library). 461 p. ISBN 2880327075 (paper).

This compilation on endangered plants provides useful bibliographies on endangered plants of countries around the world, including general information on the floristics and vegetation of the country; lists of checklists, floras, field guides, botanical gardens, voluntary organizations, and other useful addresses; and information on threatened plants and the laws protecting them. Funded by the World Wildlife Fund, United Nations Environment Programme (UNEP), the Trust Fund for the U.N. Environment Stamp Conservation Fund, Exxon Corporation, and the Natural Environment Research Council on behalf of the European Research Council.

# Databases, Abstracts, and Indexes

417    *Ecology Abstracts*. Bethesda, MD: Cambridge Scientific Abstracts (CSA), 1982– . Monthly. $1,550.00. ISSN 0143-3296. Available electronically.

"*Ecology Abstracts* focuses on how organisms of all kinds—microbes, plants, and animals—interact with their environments and with other organisms. Included are relevant papers on evolutionary biology, economics, and systems analysis as they relate to ecosystems or the environment." Over 300 journal titles are selectively indexed. The print version continues *Applied Ecology Abstracts, 1975–1979,* and includes an annual index on CD-ROM. The *Ecology Abstracts* Web version is a subfile of both the *Biological Sciences Collection* (see chapter 2) and *Environmental Sciences and Pollution Management* databases, which are available via the CSA Internet Database Service.

*Excerpta Botanica. Sectio B: Sociologica.*

See chapter 2 for full annotation. *Sectio B* includes books and articles on plant biogeography and ecology.

418    *Index Holmiensis: A World Phytogeographical Index.* Vol. 1– . Stockholm, Sweden: Swedish Museum of Natural History, 1969– . Irregular. Price varies.

This world index of plant distribution maps provides complete bibliographic data and information on area covered. The volumes are arranged alphabetically by genus. Volume 9, published in 1998, was the most recent available at the end of 2005.

# Serials

## General Serials

419  *American Naturalist*. Vol. 1– . Chicago, IL: University of Chicago Press, 1867– . Monthly. $433.00. ISSN 0003-0147. Available electronically.

420  *Annual Review of Ecology, Evolution, and Systematics*. Vol. 34– . Palo Alto, CA: Annual Reviews, 2003– . Annual. $179.00. ISSN 1543-592X. Available electronically.
Formerly *Annual Review of Ecology and Systematics*.

421  *Ecology*. Vol. 1– . Washington, DC: Ecological Society of America, 1920– . Monthly. $630.00. ISSN 0012-9658. Available electronically.

422  *Oecologia*. Vol. 1– . Heidelberg, Germany: Springer-Verlag, 1968– . Monthly. $4,284.00. ISSN 0029-8549. Available electronically.
Formerly *Zeitschrift für Morphologie und Ökologie der Tiere*.

423  *Oikos: A Journal of Ecology*. Vol. 1– . Copenhagen, Denmark: Nordic Society OIKOS, 1949– . Monthly. $778.00. ISSN 0030-1299. Available electronically.

424  *Theoretical Population Biology*. Vol. 1– . Amsterdam, the Netherlands: Elsevier, 1970– . 8 times per year. $938.00. ISSN 0040-5809. Available electronically.

425  *Trends in Ecology and Evolution*. Vol. 1– . Amsterdam, the Netherlands: Elsevier Science, 1986– . Monthly. $1,309.00. ISSN 0169-5347. Available electronically.

426  *Wetlands: The Journal of the Society of Wetland Scientists*. Vol. 1– . Wilmington, NC: Society of Wetland Scientists, 1981– . Quarterly. $125.00. ISSN 0277-5212. Available electronically.

## Botanical Serials

427  *Aquatic Botany*. Vol. 1– . Amsterdam, the Netherlands: Elsevier, 1975– . Monthly. $1,229.00. ISSN 0304-3770. Available electronically.
"An International Scientific Journal dealing with Applied and Fundamental Research on Submerged, Floating and Emergent Plants in Marine and Freshwater Ecosystems."

428    *Environmental and Experimental Botany.* Vol. 16– . New York: Pergamon, 1976– . Bimonthly. $890.00. ISSN 0098-8472. Available electronically.

*Environmental and Experimental Botany* "publishes research papers on the physical, chemical, and biological mechanisms that relate to performance of plants to their abiotic and biotic environments." Formerly *Radiation Botany.*

429    *The Journal of Ecology.* Vol 1– . Oxford, England: Blackwell Scientific, 1913– . Bimonthly. $734.00. ISSN 0022-0477. Available electronically.

*The Journal of Ecology* publishes "original research papers on all aspects of ecology of plants (including algae) in both aquatic and terrestrial ecosystems," including "descriptive, experimental, historical and theoretical studies of plant communities, populations, individuals, and their interactions with other organisms (e.g., animals, microbes)." Official journal of the British Ecological Society.

430    *Journal of Vegetation Science.* Vol. 1– . Knivsta, Sweden: Opulus, 1990– . Bimonthly. $110.00. ISSN 1100-9233. Available electronically.

The *Journal of Vegetation Science* publishes papers on all aspects of vegetation science with a focus on plant communities, including plant geography, landscape ecology, palaeoecology, ecophysiology, and description of ecological communities. The journal is the official organ of the International Association for Vegetation Science.

*Plant, Cell and Environment.*

See chapter 9 for full annotation. Provides "insights into the ways that plants respond to their environment," including physiological ecology and plant function at the community level.

431    *Plant and Soil.* Vol. 1– . Dordrecht, the Netherlands: Kluwer Academic, 1948– . 20 times a year. $3,913.00. ISSN 0032-079X. Available electronically.

Research and review articles "dealing with the interface of plant biology and soil sciences" will be found in this journal, including ones about plant–water relations, symbiotic and pathogenic plant-microbe interactions, and related ecology.

432    *Plant Ecology: An International Journal.* Vol. 128– . Dordrecht, the Netherlands: Kluwer Academic, 1997– . Monthly. $2,727.00. ISSN 1385-0237. Available electronically.

"*Plant Ecology* publishes original scientific papers dealing with the ecology of vascular plants and bryophytes in terrestrial, aquatic and wetland ecosystems" and "descriptive, historical, and experimental studies of any aspect of plant population, physiological, community, ecosystem, and landscape ecology as well as on theoretical ecology." Review articles, symposium proceedings, and book reviews are included. Formerly titled *Vegetatio.*

# Dictionaries and Encyclopedias

433   Allaby, Michael. *A Dictionary of Ecology.* 2nd ed. New York: Oxford University Press, 1998. 448 p. $16.95 (paper). ISBN 0192800787 (paper); 0192800787 (electronic).

With over 5,000 entries, this dictionary has definitions for all aspects of ecology and environmental sciences, including plant physiology, molecular ecology, conservation, and management of habitats. Also contains biographical notes.

434   Collin, P. H. *Dictionary of Environment and Ecology.* 5th ed. London: Bloomsbury, 2004. 254 p. $17.95. ISBN 0747572011.

Over 8,000 environmental and ecological terms are addressed in this edition. Selected entries have sentence examples from publications to help better understand the use of the term. Some entries have additional synonyms, brief notes, and comments. Supplemental information at the back of the volume includes the outline criteria for threatened species, a list of critically endangered species, and recent manmade and natural disasters. Previous edition titled *Dictionary of Ecology and the Environment.*

435   *Encyclopedia of the Biosphere.* Detroit, MI: Gale, 2000. 11 vol. ISBN 0787645060 (set).

This work "features comprehensive coverage of the Earth's greatest ecosystems, their characteristics and their operations." Each volume describes environmental factors, plant and animal ecology, human influences, and biosphere reserves of a particular ecosystem such as deserts or savannahs.

436   Grebenshchikov, Oleg S. *Geobotanic Dictionary: Russian-English-German-French.* Königstein, Germany: Koeltz, 1979. 226 p. $54.00. ISBN 3874291642.

Geobotanical terminology, principal plant formations and world plant communities, and related terms from plant ecology, soil science, climatology, geomorphology, and phytogeography are included in the 2,660 entries. The contents include a Russian/English/German/French dictionary with English, German, and French indexes.

Lincoln, Roger J., Geoffrey Allan Boxshall, and P. F. Clark. *A Dictionary of Ecology, Evolution, and Systematics.* 2nd ed.

See chapter 2 for full annotation. Includes plant ecology terms; an appendix provides a map of phytogeographical regions as well.

437   Moore, D. M., ed. *Plant Life*. New York: Oxford University Press, 1991. 256 p. ISBN 0195208633.

This attractive volume offers a phytogeographical tour of plant life around the world, arranged by geographical area. It includes much useful information on the more conspicuous plants of an area, as well as the ecology of different zones.

438   NatureServe. *NatureServe Explorer: An Online Encyclopedia of Life*. Arlington, VA: NatureServe, 2004. (Version 4.0). URL: http://www.natureserve .org/explorer.

Includes data for nearly 23,000 plants listed under the U. S. Endangered Species Act and over 5,000 ecological communities. Scientific name, common name, status, and distribution are given with summary report, conservation status, distribution map, life history, and comprehensive report. Images are provided when available.

439   Resinger, H., and J. M. Gutierrez, comp. *Elsevier's Dictionary of Terrestrial Plant Ecology: English-Spanish and Spanish-English*. New York: Elsevier, 1992. 664 p. $151.00. ISBN 0444889779.

The half title of this dictionary is *Diccionario de Ecologia Vegetal Terrestre*. The dictionary features plant ecology terms (including *plant physiology, population dynamics, forestry,* and *biostatistics*). The words or phrases are first given in English with a brief English definition, followed by the Spanish equivalent. A separate section reverses the system, with Spanish terms, their Spanish definition, and English equivalent. This dictionary would be useful for general botany as well.

# Handbooks and Methods

440   Alien Plant Working Group. *Weeds Gone Wild: Alien Plant Invaders of Natural Areas*. Washington, DC: Plant Conservation Alliance, 2003. URL: http:// www.nps.gov/plants/alien/index.htm.

Background information on invasive species, related definitions, and identified problems and solutions for invasions are described. A list of invasive species listed by scientific name is provided with common names, where found, associated national parks, and information sources. Fact sheets for aquatics, herbs, vines, shrubs, and trees are illustrated with color photographs and contain plant descriptions, native range, distribution and habitat in the United States, management options, suggested alternative native plants, selected links to relevant people and organizations, and other information.

441    Ayensu, Edward S., and Robert A. DeFilipps. *Endangered and Threatened Plants of the United States.* Washington, DC: Published jointly by the Smithsonian Institution and the World Wildlife Fund, 1978. 403 p. ISBN 0874742226.

This publication introduces the concepts of "endangered and threatened," discusses habitats and conservation, and provides lists of endangered and extinct plant species in the United States. Bibliographies, descriptions of methods, examples of computer programs, and maps are included.

442    Beacham, Walton, Frank V. Castronova, and Suzanne Sessine, eds. *Beacham's Guide to the Endangered Species of North America.* Detroit, MI: Gale, 2001. 6 vol. $675.00 (set). ISBN 0787650285 (set).

Lichens, fern allies, true ferns, conifers, dicots, and monocots are covered in Volumes 3 through 6 of this set. Species are entered by common name followed by scientific name with summary details and color photograph. More elaborate details about the species physical description, behavior, habitat, distribution, threats, and conservation/recovery with contact information for appropriate organizations and references come after the summary section. For the most current list of endangered plant species, see the *Species Information: Threatened and Endangered Animals and Plants* site, below.

443    Causton, David R. *An Introduction to Vegetation Analysis: Principles, Practice, and Interpretation.* Boston, MA: Unwin Hyman, 1988. 342 p. ISBN 0045810249.

The aim of this volume is to aid the student and teacher in understanding the principles, methods, and interpretation of vegetational and environmental data acquired in the field. Causton is predominantly concerned with ordination and classification analysis rather than phytosociology.

444    Cronk, Quentin C. B., and Janice L. Fuller. *Plant Invaders: The Threat to Natural Ecosystems.* Sterling, VA: Earthscan, 2001. 241 p. (People and Plants Conservation Manuals). $45.00 (paper). ISBN 1853837814 (paper).

This handbook was created as a central part of the People and Plants Initiative of the World Wide Fund for Nature (WWF) and the United Nations Educational, Scientific, and Cultural Organisation (UNESCO) and its associate, the Royal Botanic Gardens, Kew (U. K.), with monies from the Darwin Initiative for the Survival of Species (Department of the Environment, U. K.) and the Tropical Forestry Program (U. S. Department of Agriculture). The problem of invasive plants is reviewed, as well as practical information on how to respond. A list of invasive species, regions invaded, and regions of origin are presented along with life form, seed dispersal, seed production, breeding system, invasive category, and other notes when known.

*Ecological Phytogeography in the Nineteenth Century.*

See chapter 3 for full annotation. A collection of reprinted nineteenth-century articles.

445    *Ecosystems of the World.* Vol. 1– . New York: Elsevier, 1977– . Irregular. Price varies.

This monographic series covers "the structure and functioning of all major types of ecosystems." Each volume focuses on an individual ecosystem or biome; coverage includes a global perspective. Volumes are published out of sequence.

446    Falk, Donald A., Constance I. Millar, and Margaret Olwell, eds. *Restoring Diversity: Strategies for Reintroduction of Endangered Plants.* Washington, DC: Island, 1996. 505 p. $45.00; $40.00 (paper). ISBN 1559632968; 1559632976 (paper).

In 1993 a conference on reintroduction of native species was organized by the Center for Plant Conservation, a national organization dedicated wholly to native plant conservation. Issues on the topic from this meeting are further investigated in this book. Biology, environmental, policy, and legal aspects are covered with case study accounts for recovery efforts and restoration projects of individual rare species. Model guidelines are provided for developing a rare plant reintroduction plan.

447    Gibson, David J. *Methods in Comparative Plant Population Ecology.* New York: Oxford University Press, 2002. 344 p. $57.50 (paper). ISBN 0198505620 (paper).

Covers the scope of plant population ecology, how to frame the research question, basic design considerations, statistics, experimental treatments, measurement of individual and population parameters, environmental measurements, spatial patterns, life tables, and modeling. Intended for upper undergraduate and graduate levels, as well as experienced plant population ecology researchers.

448    Greig-Smith, Peter. *Quantitative Plant Ecology.* 3rd ed. Berkeley, CA: University of California Press, 1983. 355 p. (Studies in Ecology, vol. 9). ISBN 0520050800.

The author successfully provides guidance on the most profitable means of obtaining and handling ecological data, put into perspective with a broad survey of the quantitative approach to plant ecology.

449    Grime, J. Phillip. *Plant Strategies, Vegetation Processes, and Ecosystem Properties.* 2nd ed. New York: Wiley, 2001. 417 p. $190.00. ISBN 0471496014.

Having boldly proposing hypotheses in the first edition (1979) for the existence of predictable primary plant strategies that control vegetation structure and composition, the author now examines them considering the abundance of related literature since 1979.

450    Guarino, Luigi, V. Ramanatha Rao, and Robert Reid. *Collecting Plant Genetic Diversity: Technical Guidelines.* Wallingford, England: CAB International, 1995. 748 p. $150.00. ISBN 0851989640.

This work was created to bring together generic and specific, theoretical and practical information on collecting plant germplasm in the research of plant genetic diversity.

451    Hendry, G. A. F., and J. P. Grime, eds. *Methods in Comparative Plant Ecology: A Laboratory Manual.* New York: Chapman and Hall, 1993. 252 p. $157.00. ISBN 0412462303.

Over 90 diagnostic techniques are described and explained by experts for investigating the effects on plants of contrasting ecology. The book is divided into chapters discussing general procedures and methodologies, methods of comparative study, DNA, environmental impacts, growth, leaves, metabolism, mineral nutrients, roots, seeds, shoots, toxicity, and quantitative synthesis. There are indexes for species and subjects. This book is a sister publication to the text *Comparative Plant Ecology: A Functional Approach to Common British Species,* edited by J. P. Grime et al. (Chapman and Hall, 1988) (not reviewed).

452    *Invasivespecies.gov.* Washington, DC: National Invasive Species Council, 2003. URL: http://www.invasivespecies.gov/databases/main.shtml.

This gateway site is brimming with information about federal and state invasive species activities and programs. Links are provided to species profiles; geographic information; vectors and pathway; numerous expertise, general, terrestrial plant, terrestrial animal, aquatic plant, aquatic animal, microbial, and regional databases; and laws and regulations.

453    IUCN/SSC Invasive Species Specialist Group. *Global Invasive Species Database.* URL: http://www.issg.org/database/welcome/.

The Invasive Species Specialist Group is part of the Species Survival Commission (SSC) of The World Conservation Union (IUCN). This database includes details about invasive microbes, plants, and animals species, such as taxonomic, common, and synonym names; description; biology, ecology, native and alien range, management information; references; contacts; links; and images. There are lists of all species and all countries that are in the database, recommended readings, and links to several invasive species sites.

454    Kearns, Carol Ann, and David William Inouye. *Techniques for Pollination Biologists.* Niwot, CO: University Press of Colorado, 1993. 583 p. ISBN 0870812793.

This book provides practical information for experimental field studies of pollination biology. There is a thorough discussion of plants and flower visitors, with chapters for plants, flowers, pollen, nectar, mating systems, animals, environmental measurements, experimental considerations, and appendixes for pollen literature, sources of equipment and supplies, chemicals and stains, and computer programs.

455    Levin, Donald A. *The Origin, Expansion, and Demise of Plant Species.* New York: Oxford University Press, 2000. 230 p. (Oxford Series in Ecology and Evolution). $95.00; $35.00 (paper). ISBN 0195127285; 0195127293 (paper).

Species are examined in the context of life stages—origin or birth, expansion, differentiation and loss of cohesion, and decline and extinction. Looking at plant species as dynamic life forms, the author studies them in relation to their "passage from birth to death" using ecological and genetic theory, merging evolutionary biology and ecology in the process.

456    *List of Rare, Threatened and Endemic Plants in Europe: 1982 Edition.* 2nd ed. Strasbourg, France: Council of Europe, 1983. 357 p. (Nature and Environment Series, no. 27). ISBN 9287102147.

As well as listing the rare plants of Europe by species, this document includes analysis of the rare plants by country.

457    Littler, Mark S., and Diane S. Littler, eds. *Handbook of Phycological Methods: Ecological Field Methods: Macroalgae.* New York: Cambridge University Press, 1985. 617 p. $190.00. ISBN 0521249155.

"This fourth volume of the *Handbook of Phycological Methods*, with its field oriented perspective, is the first comprehensive treatment of methodologies in the field of marine benthic algal ecology." Sponsored by the Phycological Society of America.

458    Lowe, David W., John R. Matthews, and Charles J. Moseley, eds. *The Official World Wildlife Fund Guide to Endangered Species of North America.* Washington, DC: Beacham, 1990–1994. 4 vol. ISBN 0933833172 (vol. 1–2); 0933833296 (vol. 3); 0933833334 (vol. 4).

Endangered plant species are covered in Volume 1 of the original two-volume set, and updated in Volumes 3 and 4. Distribution maps, black-and-white photographs, description, habitat, historical and current range, conservation and recovery data, and bibliography for each species are included. There are also color photographs of some of the more spectacular species.

459    Missouri Botanical Garden. *National Collection of Endangered Plants.* St. Louis, MO: Center for Plant Conservation. URL: http://www.centerforplant conservation.org/NC_Choice.html.

The National Collection of Endangered Plants is an initiative of the Center for Plant Conservation (CPC). It "contains plant material for more than 600 of the country's most imperiled native plants... and is a back up in case a species becomes extinct or no longer reproduces in the wild." Plant profiles, participating CPC institutions, and other details can be accessed from the National Collection Web site.

460   National Biological Information Infrastructure. *NBII Invasive Species Information Node (ISIN)*. Reston, VA: National Biological Information Infrastructure. URL: http://invasivespecies.nbii.gov/.

The *Invasive Species Information Node* is a repository of invasive species information, such as species lists, maps, control and restoration recommendations, and current projects, including the Species Information database. Database details include taxonomic rank and serial number, scientific name, common name(s), USDA NRCS Code, links to more information, and photos when available. A system for reporting invasive species via this Web site is currently being developed. The National Biological Information Infrastructure "is a joint effort, led by the U. S. Geological Survey, to build a distributed electronic 'federation' of biological data and information from many sources... on our nation's plants, animals, and ecosystems."

*Plants Database.*

See chapter 2 for full annotation. Data for the following are included: invasive and noxious plants, invasive and threatened plants, and wetland indicator status.

461   Pugnaire, Francisco, and Fernando Valladares, eds. *Handbook of Functional Plant Ecology*. New York: Marcel Dekker, 1999. 901 p. (Books in Soils, Plants, and the Environment). $250.00. ISBN 0824719506.

An introduction and opinions are given on future directions of several topics in functional plant ecology. The role of structure and growth form in plant performance, physiological ecology, habitats and plant distribution, populations and communities are covered, along with new approaches such as resistance to air pollutants, canopy photosynthesis modeling, ecological applications of remotes sensing, and generalization across species.

462   Secretariat of the Convention on Biological Diversity. *Handbook of the Convention on Biological Diversity*. Sterling, VA: Earthscan, 2001. 690 p. $110.00; $45.00 (paper). ISBN 1853837482; 1853837377 (paper).

The Convention on Biological Diversity from Earth Summit 1992 in Rio de Janeiro was ratified by some 180 parties on "conservation and biological diversity, the sustainable use of its components, and the equitable sharing of benefits arising out of the utilization of genetic resources." The Conference of the Parties has met on many occasions to work out action plans for the Convention decisions. Additionally it has adopted the Cartagena Protocol on Biosafety Treaty that provides international regulations concerning free trade and environmental protection. The Convention, the Biosafety Protocol, and every decision of the Conference of the Parties (previously published separately) have been brought together in this handbook. This book comes with a CD-ROM edition.

463   *Species Information: Threatened and Endangered Animals and Plants.* Washington, DC: U.S. Fish and Wildlife Service, 2003. URL: http://endangered.fws.gov/wildlife.html#Species.

Endangered species information is accessed via the Threatened and Endangered Species Database System (TESS) for federally listed animals and plants. Over 700 endangered plant species have been identified. They are grouped by taxonomic groups (Flowering Plants or Non-Flowering Plants) and listed alphabetically by common name, then scientific name with links to status details regarding information on Recovery Plans, Specials Rules, and Critical Habitat for specific designations, life history, Federal Register documents, Habitat Conservation Plans, petitions received, and refuges the species has been reported on. A wealth of information can be obtained here such as state lists, maps, proposed and candidate species information, delisted species, species by lead region, statistics, laws/policies, Virtual News Room, news releases, and so on. The text of the Endangered Species Act can be accessed through the link *Laws, Policies and Federal Register Notices* at this site.

464   SSC Redlist Programme, IUCN. *2004 IUCN Red List of Threatened Species.* Cambridge, England: IUCN Species Survival Commission, 2004. URL: http://www.redlist.org/.

The Species Survival Commission of The World Conservation Union (IUCN) compiles and manages the *IUCN Red List of Threatened Species* and "is the world's most comprehensive inventory of the global conservation status of plant and animal species [and] is recognized as the most authoritative guide to the status of biological diversity." The list provides information about taxonomy, *ICUN Red List* assessment (including category, classification, and justification); distribution; summary data (biome, major habitat[s], major threat[s], and population trend); and data sources for each selected species. More details on the background of the *IUCN Red List* can be found at http://www.iucn.org/themes/ssc/RedList2003/English/backgroundEn.htm.

465   U.S. Department of Agriculture Forest Service. *USDA Forest Service Forest Inventory and Analysis Program.* Washington, DC: U.S. Department of Agriculture Forest Service, 2004. URL: http://www.fia.fs.fed.us/.

"Forest Service Research and Development (R&D) scientists carry out basic and applied research to study biological, physical, and social sciences related to very diverse forests and rangelands." The USDA Forest Inventory and Analysis Program (FIA) provides information on forest ecosystems. There are links to a number of databases such as the Phase 3 (Forest Health) Data Set Archives (tree crown and damage data, lichen species diversity, ozone damage, soil data, etc.); and the Climate Change Atlas for 80 Forest Tree Species of the Eastern United States (life histories, disturbance attributes, ecological attributes, forest type maps, and listed species for different climate change scenarios).

466   U.S. Department of Agriculture Forest Service. *USDA Fire Effects Information System.* Washington, DC: U.S. Department of Agriculture Forest Service, 2004. URL: http://www.fs.fed.us/database/feis/.

This database is produced by the U.S. Department of Agriculture (USDA) Forest Service to "provide up-to-date information on the effects of fire on plants and animals." The USDA Fire Effects Information System database includes documented information on taxonomy, distribution, basic biology, and ecology of over 900 plant species.

467   U.S. Environmental Protection Agency. *Ecosystems.* Washington, DC: U.S. Environmental Protection Agency, 2004. URL: http://www.epa.gov/ebtpages/ecosystems.html.

The EPA regularly monitors the country's ecological resources for possible effects of environmental pollutants and creating environmental guidelines and standards to manage environmental risks. The fourth goal of the EPA's five goals delineated in the *2003–2008 EPA Strategic Plan: Direction for the Future* is to "Protect, sustain, or restore the health of people, communities, and ecosystems using integrated and comprehensive approaches and partnerships." Search *Ecosystems Subtopics* for information about plants in aquatic ecosystems, ecological monitoring, ecological restoration, endangered/exotic species, and terrestrial ecosystems.

468   Weber, Ewald. *Invasive Plant Species of the World: A Reference Guide to Environmental Weeds.* Cambridge, MA: CABI, 2004. 548 p. $140.00. ISBN 0851996957.

Over 400 nonagricultural invasive plant species are included in this guide. Each plant species is entered alphabetically by its scientific name followed by its "life form" (common name), synonyms, and commercial use, if any. Native and introduced geographic distribution is indicated. Invaded habitat types, plant species description, ecology, and control are presented with references.

# Textbooks and Treatises

469    Agrawal, Shashi Bhushan, and Madhoolika Agrawal, eds. *Environmental Pollution and Plant Responses.* Boca Raton, FL: Lewis, 1999. 393 p. $99.95. ISBN 1566703417.

This text "presents and analyzes the most current research on the causal factors contributing to the deteriorating environmental quality and its effect on plant performance."

470    Ambasht, R. S., and Navin K. Ambasht, eds. *Modern Trends in Applied Terrestrial Ecology.* New York: Kluwer Academic, 2002. 367 p. $166.00. ISBN 0306473321.

The editors brought together renowned scholars on ecology from around the world to write about the history and latest thinking on selected topics, such as applied ecology of biodiversity, restoration and management of degraded tropical forest landscapes, nutrient export from tropical rain forests, ozone stress impacts on plant life, influences of elevated levels of $CO_2$ on plants, and the ecological implications and methodical approaches for plant cover. Includes black-and-white tables, graphs, and photographs.

471    Barbour, Michael G. and William Dwight Billings, eds. *North American Terrestrial Vegetation.* 2nd ed. New York: Cambridge University Press, 2000. 708 p. $69.95, $60.00 (paper). ISBN 0521550270, 0521559863 (paper).

The vegetation structure, response to disturbance, community/environment relations, nutrient cycling and productivity, autecological behavior, paleobotany, modern environment, human-caused vegetation changes, successional changes following disturbance, habitat loss and restoration/preservation programs, and quantitative description of major vegetation types are covered here. Black-and-white photographs, tables, and graphs included.

472    Barbour, Michael G., et al. *Terrestrial Plant Ecology.* 3rd ed. Menlo Park, CA: Addison Wesley Longman, 1999. 649 p. $102.00. ISBN 0805305416.

"Covering the entire breadth of modern plant ecology" the authors present background and basic concepts, characteristics of species and community as ecological units, and related environmental factors in understandable words. Many black-and-white photographs, illustrations, and tables are throughout the text.

473   Barth, Friedrich G. *Insects and Flowers: The Biology of Partnership.* Princeton, NJ: Princeton University Press, 1991. 408 p. (Princeton Science Library series). ISBN 0691025231 (paper).

Although the focus of this book is zoological, there is much botanical material featured here concerning the ecological relationship between insects and flowers. Flower reproduction, forms, pollination, pollen, nectar, and other attributes are described, along with flowers' symbiotic relationship with insects. There are numerous black-and-white illustrations, tables, and graphs; as well as 16 black-and-white and 24 color plates.

474   Bazzaz, F. A. *Plants in Changing Environments: Linking Physiological, Population, and Community Ecology.* New York: Cambridge University Press, 1996. 320 p. $120.00; $38.99 (paper). ISBN 0521391903; 0521398436 (paper).

Ecosystem disturbance and recovery, plant and community responses, and resulting changes in the environment are holistically explained. There are black-and-white tables, graphs, and illustrations throughout. A second edition of this title is due November 2005.

475   Begon, Michael, Martin Mortimer, and David J. Thompson. *Population Ecology: A Unified Study of Animals and Plants.* 3rd ed. Malden, MA: Blackwell Science, 1996. 247 p. $58.95. ISBN 0632034785.

Concentrating on the similarities of plant and animal biological processes, this introductory textbook has three parts: single-species populations, interspecific competition and predation, and synthesis and expansion of the chapters in the first two parts as to regulation and determination of population size, interactions between populations, and metapopulations.

476   Bell, J. N. B., and Michael Treshow, eds. *Air Pollution and Plant Life.* 2nd ed. New York: Wiley, 2002. 465 p. $130.00; $65.00 (paper). ISBN 0471490903; 0471490911 (paper).

Research on air pollution and plants has expanded since the first edition in 1984, along with the expansion of air pollution. Historical highlights of air pollution, air pollutant pathways, atmospheric pollution burdens, and deposition to surfaces with vegetation uptake, physiological/biochemical/stress effects on whole plant/community, major pollutant categories and combinations, and ecosystem impacts from air pollution are examined.

477   Bovey, Rodney W. *Woody Plants and Woody Plant Management: Ecology, Safety, and Environmental Impact.* New York: Marcel Dekker, 2001. 564 p. (Books in Soils, Plants, and the Environment). $195.00. ISBN 082470438X.

This text brings together in one place the most important information about woody plant management and its environmental effects. The significance and botanical nature of woody plants, the history and development of woody plant management (fire, biological, mechanical, and chemical control methods), herbicide residues/spray drift and impact on the environment, ecological impact of woody plant management, and nonchemical methods of woody plant control are among featured topics.

478   Crawley, Michael J., ed. *Plant Ecology*. 2nd ed. Malden, MA: Blackwell Science, 1997. 717 p. $56.95 (paper). ISBN 0632036397 (paper).

Aspects of plant ecology are comprehensively encapsulated in this book. Presents theoretical models and experimental data along with text. There are many black-and-white illustrations and tables, with 14 color plates.

479   Cronk, Julie K., and M. Siobhan Fennessy. *Wetland Plants: Biology and Ecology*. 488 p. $99.95. Boca Raton, FL: Lewis, 2001. ISBN 1566703727.

"Presents a synthesis of wetland plant studies and reviews from biology, physiology, evolution, genetics, community and population ecology, environmental science, and engineering."

480   Fitter, Alastair H., and Robert K. M. Hay. *Environmental Physiology of Plants*. 3rd ed. San Diego, CA: Academic, 2002. 367 p. $52.95 (paper). ISBN 0122577663 (paper).

This third edition of an established and successful university textbook provides an introduction to plant growth and development, and influence of the environment. Radiant energy, mineral nutrients, water, temperature, toxins and toxic environments, and plant interactions among plants and with other organisms are covered. There are numerous black-and-white tables/graphs and 16 color plates.

481   Gurevitch, Jessica, Samuel M. Scheiner, and Gordon A. Fox. *The Ecology of Plants*. Sunderland, MA: Sinauer, 2002. 523 p. $94.95. ISBN 0878932917.

Various relationships between plants and their environments are discussed in this textbook: individual plants, plant populations, communities, and global patterns. Basic to advanced levels will find this title of interest. Black-and-white and bicolored illustration, tables, and graphs with black-and-white photographs throughout.

482   Howe, Henry F., and Lynn C. Westley. *Ecological Relationships of Plants and Animals*. New York: Oxford University Press, 1988. 273 p. $31.95 (paper). ISBN 0195044312, 0195063147 (paper).

Evolutionary ecology, herbivory, mutualisms, and ancient and modern and plant communities are covered in this textbook on the relationships of plants and animals for upper-level undergraduates and graduate students. Contains black-and-white photographs, graphs, and tables.

483    Inderjit, K. M. M. Dakshini, and Chester L. Foy, eds. *Principles and Practices in Plant Ecology: Allelochemical Interactions.* Boca Raton, FL: CRC, 1999. 589 p. $159.95. ISBN 0849321166.

Background and research are presented on the chemicals released from plant and microorganisms, and effects of these chemicals on ecosystems. Includes black-and-white photographs, tables, and illustrations. Also has stereochemical structures for selected compounds and interactions.

484    Lambers, H., F. Stuart Chapin III, and Thijs L. Pons. *Plant Physiological Ecology.* New York: Springer-Verlag, 1998. 540 p. $69.95. ISBN 0387983260.

"Physiological mechanisms that underlie ecological observations" with the interaction of plants with their physical, chemical, and biological environments are encompassed. There are 356 black-and-white illustrations, tables, graphs, photographs, and selected stereochemical structures.

485    Larcher, Walter. *Physiological Plant Ecology: Ecophysiology and Stress Physiology of Functional Groups.* 4th ed. New York: Springer-Verlag, 2003. 513 p. $59.95. ISBN 3540435166.

Topics covered in this text are the environment of plants, carbon utilization and dry matter production, utilization of mineral elements, water relations, environmental influences on growth and development, and stress effects on plants. Includes numerous black-and-white illustrations and photos, maps, graphs, tables, stereochemical structures, and four color plates.

486    Meff, Gary K., and C. Ronald Carroll. *Principles of Conservation Biology.* 2nd ed. Sunderland, MA: Sinauer, 1997. 729 p. $86.95. ISBN 0878935215.

Comprehensive course text for advanced undergraduate and graduate-level courses on conservation biology, and conservation biologists and practitioners.

487    Myers, Judith H., and Dawn Bazely. *Ecology and Control of Introduced Plants.* New York: Cambridge University Press, 2003. 313 p. (Ecology, Biodiversity, and Conservation). $110.00; $40.00 (paper). ISBN 0521355168; 0521357780 (paper).

This book contains information, case studies, and impact techniques concerning invasion of plant species into native plant communities, predicting invasions, plant disease introduction, and control of introduced plants, including biological control.

488    Primack, Richard B. *Essentials of Conservation Biology.* 3rd ed. Sunderland, MA: Sinauer, 2002. 698 p. $75.95. ISBN 0878937196.

This text provides a comprehensive overview of major conservation biology concepts. Serves as a core background or course text for this field, as well as a supplemental text for broader areas of study such as general biology and ecology courses.

489    Ricklefs, Robert E. *Ecology.* 4th ed. New York: Freeman, 2000. 822 p. $99.95. ISBN 071672829X.

This is an excellent textbook about the fundamentals of ecology. The content topics include ecosystems, population ecology, population interactions, community ecology, and evolutionary ecology.

490    Silvertown, Jonathon, and Deborah Charlesworth. *Introduction to Plant Population Biology.* 4th ed. Malden, MA: Blackwell Science, 2001. 347 p. $55.95 (paper). ISBN 063204991X (paper).

"Topics covered include variation and its inheritance, genetic markers including molecular markers, plant breeding systems, ecological genetics, intraspecific interactions, population dynamics, regional dynamics and metapopulations, competition and coexistence, and the evolution of breeding systems and life history." The earlier editions were entitled *Introduction to Plant Population Ecology.*

491    Tivy, Joy. *Biogeography: A Study of Plants in the Ecosphere.* 3rd ed. New York: Wiley, 1993. 452 p. $69.00 (paper). ISBN 0470220783; 0582080355 (paper).

Biosphere, ecosystems, and biotic resources characteristics and interactions are elaborated on, including man's influence as an ecological factor/participant.

492    Walter, Heinrich, and Siegmar-Walter Breckle. *Walter's Vegetation of the Earth: The Ecological Systems of the Geo-Biosphere.* 4th ed. New York: Springer-Verlag, 2002. 527 p. $69.95 (paper). ISBN 3540433155 (paper).

This revised and enlarged update of Heinrich Walter's classic textbook "summarizes our knowledge of the earth's ecology and constitutes the basis for a deeper understanding of the larger interrelations on a global scale." Previous edition: *Vegetation of the Earth and Ecological Systems of the Geobiosphere*, 3rd edition.

# Associations

493    British Ecological Society (BES). 26 Blades Court, Deodar Road, Putney, London, England, SWI5 2NU, UK. Phone: +44 (0)20 8871 9797. Fax: +44 (0)20

8871 9779. E-mail: info@britishecologicalsociety.org. URL: http://www.britishecologicalsociety.org.

The BES provides "academic journals, teaching resources, meetings for scientists and policy makers, career advice and grants for ecologists." Publishes the *Journal of Ecology*.

494   Ecological Society of America (ESA). 1707 H Street NW, Suite 400, Washington, DC 20006-3915. Phone: 202-833-8773. Fax: 202-833-8775. E-mail: esahq@esa.org. URL: http://www.esa.org/.

The Ecological Society of America (ESA) promotes ecological science through its activities and services. Action alerts, science policy, statements, resolutions, position papers, news updates, and other communications are available on its Web site, as well as lots of educational information for students and teachers. There is a Plant Population Biology Section to foster member research and interactions. ESA publishes *Bulletin of the Ecological Society of America*, *Ecology*, *Ecological Monographs*, *Ecological Applications*, and *Frontiers in Ecology and the Environment*.

495   International Association for Vegetation Science (IAVS). Alterra, Green World Research, Postbus 47, NL-6700 AA Wageningen, the Netherlands. Phone: +31317 47 79 14. Fax: +31317 42 49 88. E-mail: Joop.Schaminee@wur.nl. URL: http://www.iavs.org/.

The IAVS promotes research, education, publication of research results, networking opportunities, and disseminates information regarding vegetation science. Publishes the *Journal of Vegetation Science*.

# References

Broad, William J. 2004 July 13. Will the compasses point south? *New York Times*. Section F:1(column1).

Chang, Kenneth. 2004 May 13. Globe grows darker as sunshine diminishes 10% to 37%. *New York Times*. Section A:22(column 2).

Crawley, Michael J., ed. 1997. *Plant Ecology*. 2nd ed. Malden, MA: Blackwell Science.

Nicolson, Malcolm. 2000. History of plant ecology. In *Encyclopedia of Life Sciences*. Vol. 9, 122–124. New York: Nature Publishing Group. URL: http://www.els.net/ [doi:10.1038/npg.els.0003288].

# 7
# Anatomy, Morphology, and Development

Plant anatomy is defined as the internal structure of plants. Classically it refers to the aspects of structure that can be observed when viewing thin sections of plants with a light microscope. Robert Hooke, in 1665, was the first to look at plant material (a thin slice of oak cork) through a compound microscope, where he observed tiny, hollow, room-like structures that he called cells. These were actually just the cell walls of dead cells. Later anatomists have used anatomy to deduce the function and interrelationships of cells, tissues, and organs such as leaves, roots, stems, and reproductive structures. Many genetically engineered manipulations of plant genomes affect the plant's anatomy, so this science remains a part of the core curriculum at most universities, even though in some circles it may be considered passé.

Morphology, on the other hand, refers to the outer structure of plants—their shape and the relationships between the various organs. Current morphological research might be interested in how plants change their conformations in order to adapt to environmental stresses, or how the leaves of a plant might be bred to have a leaf orientation that is more drought resistant.

The third plant specialty covered in this chapter, development, refers to the changes plants undergo through time as they mature or go from the vegetative state to the reproductive state (e.g., flower development). Developmental biologists will study changes in the anatomy as well as the morphology of plants. Tools that are used to study plant development include plant physiology, plant hormones, plant cell and tissue culture, molecular biology, and genetic engineering, so the reader is referred to chapters 8 and 9 for additional resources pertinent to the study of plant development.

**135**

The primary bibliographic databases for anatomy, morphology, and development are *CAB Abstracts, Biological Abstracts,* and *AGRICOLA.* One will also find ISI's *Web of Science* (*Science Citation Index*) covers this topic well. These bibliographic resources have been thoroughly described in chapter 2.

Although there are no specialized dictionaries to cover the topics of this chapter, many of the texts include fine glossaries that will serve as dictionaries. For anatomy, refer to the textbooks listed in this chapter, especially Dickison's *Integrative Plant Anatomy* or Fahn or Mauseth's identically titled *Plant Anatomy.* For morphological terms, refer to Bold's *Morphology of Plants.*

## Bibliographies and Guides to the Literature

496   The Royal Botanic Gardens, Kew. *Plant Micromorphology Bibliographic Database.* URL: http://www.rbgkew.org.uk/bibliographies/PA//PAhome.html.

A "database of references relevant to the anatomy and pollen/spore morphology of flowering plants, gymnosperms and ferns." One may search by family, subject, genus, or author. Although freely accessible, more citations will be shown to those who go through the free registration procedure.

## Serials

### General Serials

497   *Annual Review of Cell and Developmental Biology.* Vol. 11– . Palo Alto, CA: Annual Reviews, 1995– . Annual. $197.00. ISSN 0743-4634. Available electronically.

Formerly *Annual Review of Cell Biology.*

498   *Current Opinion in Genetics and Development.* Vol. 1– . London: Current Biology Ltd., 1991– . Bimonthly. $1,309.00. ISSN 0959-437X. Available electronically.

499   *Development.* Vol. 99– . Cambridge, England: The Company of Biologists, 1987– . Semimonthly. $3,130.00. ISSN 0950-1991. Available electronically.

Continues the *Journal of Embryology and Experimental Morphology.*

500   *Developmental Biology.* Vol. 1– . New York: Elsevier, 1959– . Semimonthly. $5,681.00. ISSN 0012-1606. Available electronically.

501   *Developmental Cell.* Vol. 1– . Cambridge, MA: Cell, 2001– . Monthly. $843.00. ISSN 1534-5807. Available electronically.

502   *Genes and Development.* Vol. 1– . Cold Spring Harbor, NY: Cold Spring Harbor Laboratory in association with the Genetical Society of Great Britain, 1987– . Biweekly. $1,058.00. ISSN 0890-9369. Available electronically.

503   *Protoplasma: An International Journal of Cell Biology.* Vol. 1– . Vienna: Springer-Verlag, 1926– . 16 times per year. $2,027.00. ISSN 0033-183X. Available electronically.

504   *Seminars in Cell and Developmental Biology.* Vol. 7– . Oxford: Elsevier, 1996– . Bimonthly. $528.00. ISSN 1084-9521. Available electronically.
    Merger of *Seminars in Developmental Biology* and *Seminars in Cell Biology.*

## Botanical Serials

*American Journal of Botany.*
    See chapter 2 for full annotation. Most issues include articles on anatomy, morphology, development, and morphogenesis.

*Canadian Journal of Botany. Journal Canadien de Botanique.*
    See chapter 2 for full annotation. This primary research journal includes a section for anatomical or morphological papers.

505   *Flora.* Vol. 1– . Jena, Germany: Urban and Fischer Verlag, 1818– . Bimonthly. $669.00. ISSN 0367-2530. Available electronically.
    With a focus on whole-plant research, *Flora* includes papers dealing with plant structure (morphology and anatomy). *Flora* is the oldest continuously published scientific botanical journal. Frequently referred to as *Flora (Jena)*, *Flora*'s subtitle has varied and is currently listed as *Flora: Morphology, Distribution, Functional Ecology of Plants.*

*In Vitro Cellular and Developmental Biology-Plant.*
    See chapter 8 for full annotation. Articles cover research in cellular, molecular, and developmental biology involving *in vitro* grown or maintained organs, tissues, or cells.

*International Journal of Plant Sciences.*
    See chapter 2 for full annotation. Most issues include papers about plant development and structure.

506    *Phytomorphology: An International Journal of Plant Morphology*. Vol. 1– . Delhi, India: International Society of Plant Morphologists, 1951– . Quarterly. $120.00. ISSN 0031-9449.

This official organ of the International Society of Plant Morphologists publishes research on plant anatomy. It is particularly rich in research from the Indian subcontinent that focuses on tropical species.

# Dictionaries and Encyclopedias

507    Bell, Adrian D. *Plant Form: An Illustrated Guide to Flowering Plant Morphology*. New York: Oxford University Press, 1991. 341 p. $159.78. ISBN 0198542798; 0198542194 (paper).

This well-designed book can be used as either an illustrated dictionary for the experienced botanist or an introductory text for students new to the field. The first half of the book describes the major plant organs: shoots, roots, leaves, and both vegetative and floral reproductive structures; in the second part, meristematic tissues, including distinctive structures such as galls and nodules, are discussed. The text includes many color photos and line drawings, is well cross-referenced, and has a bibliography and a subject index.

508    Kremp, Gerhard O. W. *Morphologic Encyclopedia of Palynology: An International Collection of Definitions and Illustrations of Spores and Pollen*. Tucson, AZ: University of Arizona Press, 1965. 185 p. (University of Arizona Program in Geochronology series, contribution no. 100).

Comprehensive illustrated encyclopedia for spore and pollen terminology.

509    Linsbauer, K. *Handbuch der Pflanzenanatomie = Encyclopedia of Plant Anatomy = Traité d'Anatomie Végétale*. 2nd ed. Berlin: Gebrüder Borntraeger. 1934– . Multivolume. Price varies.

Designed to be a comprehensive treatise of plant anatomy, each volume in this series deals with specific aspects of plant anatomy. As of 2004 there were 30 volumes that were written in German, English, or French. Recent volumes in English have included *Pathological and Regenerative Plant Anatomy* (1999) and *Seed Anatomy* (1997). Earlier classic volumes have included Katherine Esau's *The Phloem* (1969) and Ingrid Roth's *Fruits of Angiosperms* (1977).

510a    *Plant Ontology Consortium*. URL: http://www.plantontology.org/index .html.

See chapter 8 for full annotation. This group aims to develop a standardized vocabulary that can be used by molecular biologists to describe plant structures and the developmental stages of plants.

## Handbooks and Methods

510b   Berlyn, Graeme P., and Jerome P. Miksche. *Botanical Microtechnique and Cytochemistry.* Ames, IA: Iowa State University Press, 1976. 326 p. $41.99. ISBN 0813802202.

This manual, which is a revision of the well-known *Botanical Microtechnique* by J. E. Sass, can be used to introduce teachers and researchers to the basic principles of microtechnique and cytochemistry. It is not an inventory of techniques but provides a good introduction to some of the methods of interest to botanists, in spite of its advanced age. Contains a good bibliography and an index.

511   Botanical Society of America. *Botanical Images Collection.* URL: http://images.botany.org/.

This Web site provides over 800 botanical images that are freely available for educational use. The images have been divided into 15 sets, several of which are relevant to plant structure and development, including plant morphology, phloem development, xylem development, floral ontogeny, organography, and plant anatomy.

512   Bowes, Bryan G. *A Color Atlas of Plant Structure.* Ames IA: Iowa State University Press, 1996. 192 p. $49.99 (paper). ISBN 081382687X; 0813826934 (paper).

Features over 360 illustrations of a wide range of plant structures, many in color. Examples include light micrographs of plant tissues, scanning electron micrographs of pollen grains, and diagrammatic drawings of cambium development. Includes a glossary and a brief bibliography.

513   Bracegirdle, Brian, and Patricia H. Miles. *An Atlas of Plant Structure.* London: Heinemann Educational, 1971—1973. 2 vol. ISBN 0435603124 (vol. 1); 0435603140 (vol. 2).

This set was developed to help students interpret their laboratory specimens, and to this end, each photomicrograph example is accompanied by an interpretive line drawing. Bacteria, algae, fungi, lichens, liverworts, mosses, and vascular plant tissues are included for examination and comparison. This source is unique and of great assistance in the classroom laboratory.

514   Centre for Plant Architecture Informatics. *Virtual Plants*. Queensland, Australia: The Centre at University of Queensland, 2001. URL: http://www.cpai .uq.edu.au/index.php?q=./our_research/virtual_plants.php.

This Web site offers an introduction to plant modeling and three-dimensional digitizing of plants. Includes virtual models and animations of cotton, beans, corn, weeds, trees, roots, and plant/insect interactions. Also has bibliographies and downloadable modeling software.

515   Dashek, William V., ed. *Methods in Plant Electron Microscopy and Cytochemistry*. Totowa, NJ: Humana, 2000. 312 p. $99.50. ISBN 0896038092.

Each of the 21 chapters in this book describes a particular technique, including radioautography, fluorescence microscopy, computer-assisted microphotometry, immunocytochemistry, dark-field microscopy, atomic force and scanning tunneling microscopy, and immunogold localization. For advanced undergraduate students, graduate students, and researchers.

516   Dykstra, Michael J. *Biological Electron Microscopy: Theory, Techniques and Troubleshooting*. New York: Plenum, 1992. 360 p. $54.50. ISBN 0306442779.

Originally designed as a text for a one-semester course on microscopy and specimen preparation, this book provides an introduction to the basic techniques used in transmission and scanning electron microscopy. Principles of fixation, specimen preparation, cryotechniques, and immunolabeling are explained.

517   Gunning, Brian E. S., and Martin W. Steer. *Plant Cell Biology: An Ultrastructural Approach*. Dublin: M. W. Steer, 1986. 104 p. ISBN 0901120952 (paper).

A total of 49 black-and-white micrographs provide excellent images of the ultrastructure of plant cells. Each plate is labeled and provides an extensive description. Specimens are viewed primarily with transmission electron microscopy and scanning electron microscopy, with specimen preparation briefly discussed. Reprinted from a larger work by the same authors published in 1975 under the title *Ultrastructure and the Biology of Plant Cells*.

518   Hakevy, A. H., ed. *CRC Handbook of Flowering*. Boca Raton, FL: CRC, 1985—1989. 6 vol. ISBN 0849339103 (set).

This reference aims to be comprehensive for information on the control and regulation of flowering. The set provides information encompassing over 5,000 species of plants with specific data on all aspects of flower development, sex expression, requirements for flower initiation and development, photoperiod, light density, vernalization, and other temperature effects and interactions. The set is useful in both applied and theoretical areas for a variety of students, researchers, scientists, laboratories, and libraries. All information is presented alphabetically for easy reference.

519  Hall, J. L., and C. R. Hawes, eds. *Electron Microscopy of Plant Cells.* San Diego, CA: Academic, 1991. 466 p. ISBN 0123188806.

Nine illustrated chapters written by authorities in the field discuss techniques for the preparation of botanical specimens for electron microscopy. Basic principles, useful applications, and full details of the procedures are provided. Each chapter serves as a comprehensive review and entry to the literature.

520  Hough, Romeyn B. *The Wood Book.* New York: Taschen, 2002. 863 p. $99.99. ISBN 3822817422.

Based on the original 15-volume set published by Hough between 1888 and 1928 that contained real wood samples, this new version features high-quality color plates instead. Transverse, radial, and tangential sections are provided for each of 350 different kinds of wood. The descriptive text for each wood is in English, German, and French.

Kelber, Klaus-Peter, comp. *Links for Palaeobotanists: Plant Anatomy.* URL: http://www.uni-wuerzburg.de/mineralogie/palbot/taxonomy/taxonomy.html.

This well-maintained site has gathered together many of the Web sites put up by university professors who are teaching plant anatomy. Includes image sources, lab guides, plant anatomy atlases, lecture notes, and more. See chapter 4 for complete annotation.

521  Metcalfe, C. Russell. *Anatomy of the Monocotyledons.* Oxford, England: Claredon, 1960–2002. 9 vol. Price varies.

This series is a collection of monographs that describe the anatomy of specific families of monocotyledons. Completed volumes are as follows: Volume 1, *Gramineae*, by C. R. Metcalfe; Volume 2, *Palmae*, by P. B. Tomlinson; Volume 3, *Commelinales-Zingiberales*, by P. B. Tomlinson; Volume 4. *Juncales*, by David F. Cutler; Volume 5, *Cyperaceae*, by C. Russell Metcalfe; Volume 6, *Dioscoraeles*, by E. S. Ayensu; Volume 7, *Helobiae (Alismatidae)* by P. B. Tomlinson; Volume 8, *Iridaceae*, by Paula Rudall; and Volume 9, *Acoraceae and Araceae*, by Richard C. Keating. Note: Volumes 8 and 9 are edited by David F. Cutler and Mary Gregory.

522  Metcalfe, Russell C., and Laurence Chalk. *Anatomy of the Dicotyledons.* 2nd ed. Oxford, England: Claredon, 1979-1988. 4 vol. ISBN 0198543832 (vol. 1), 0198545940 (vol. 2), 0198545932 (vol. 3), 0198547927 (vol. 4).

Companion to Metcalfe's series for the monocotyledons, above. Volumes include Volume 1, Systematic Anatomy of Leaf and Stem, with a Brief History of the

Subject; Volume 2, Wood Structure and Conclusion of the General Introduction; Volume 3, Magnoliales, Illiciales, and Laurales; and Volume 4, Saxifragales.

523   Perry, James W., and David Morton. *Photo Atlas for Botany*. Belmont, CA: Wadsworth, 1998. 141 p. $46.95 (paper). ISBN 0534529380 (paper).

Designed as an adjunct to plant biology courses, this atlas contains color photographs of all the major taxa of plants, with photomicrographic cross sections of the frequently studied anatomical features. Clear photomicrographs of the stages of cell division, specialized roots, leaves, stems, and wood are also included. A useful source for botanical photographs.

524   Prasad, B. K. *Staining Technique in Botany for Light Microscopy*. Dehra Dun, India: International Book Distributors, 1986. 107 p. ISBN 8170890810.

This primer for light microscopy staining is aimed at the student or lab worker. Beginning with cleaning lab glassware, the directions move on to actual techniques, dyes, sectioning for bryophytes, algae, fungi, lichens, and pollen grains. Includes a list of suggested readings, references, and a subject index.

525   Ruzin, Steven E. *Plant Microtechnique and Microscopy*. New York: Oxford University Press, 1999. 322 p. $54.95 (paper). ISBN 0195089561 (paper).

This is a very practical text covering an extensive array of techniques for the manipulation of plant tissue. These include traditional methods such as paraffin embedding to newer innovations such as *in situ* hybridization. Includes an extensive bibliography with over 550 references, a detailed subject index, and several practical appendixes.

# Textbooks and Treatises

526   Bold, Harold C., Constantine J. Alexopoulos and Theodore Delevoryas. *Morphology of Plants and Fungi*. 5th ed. New York: Harper and Row, 1987. 912 p. ISBN 006350197X.

Standard textbook used in undergraduate and graduate plant survey courses. Coverage includes algae, fungi, lichens, cryptogams, gymnosperms, and seed plants. Illustrations are black-and-white photomicrographs, drawings, and photographs. Includes a comprehensive glossary and bibliography.

527   Bowman, John, ed. *Arabidopsis: An Atlas of Morphology and Development*. New York: Springer-Verlag, 1994. 450 p. ISBN 0387940898.

This atlas documents the morphology and development of *Arabidopsis thaliana*, the primary model for research in plant genetics, biochemistry, development, and radiation biology. It is extensively illustrated and comprehensively covers the principal areas of embryogenesis, vegetative growth, root growth, reproductive structures, and host–pathogen interactions.

528   Crang, Richard, and Andrey E. Vassilyev. *Plant Anatomy*. Boston, MA: McGraw-Hill, 2003. 128 p. plus CD-ROM. $49.06. ISBN 0072510846.

From the flyer, "*Electronic Plant Anatomy* deals with the structural characteristics of mature and developing cells, tissues, and organs of seed plants. Anatomical structures of flowering plants are given special emphasis. It is intended to serve as a complete guide for beginning college/university students in plant anatomy, as well as a reference for advanced studies in various fields of plant biology." Includes a complete glossary. The supporting Web site is open to all, http://highered.mcgraw-hill.com/sites/0072510846/. Not seen.

529   Cronk, Quentin C. B., Richard M. Bateman, and Julie A. Hawkins, eds. *Developmental Genetics and Plant Evolution*. New York: Taylor and Francis, 2002. 539 p. (Systematics Association Special Volume Series, 65). $169.95; $69.95 (paper). ISBN 0415257905; 0415257913 (paper).

Describes how the plant genomic data provided by molecular genetic analysis are providing new tools for the study of plant morphology, systematics, and ecology. Twenty-five chapters written by experts in plant "evo-devo" describe some of the advances that have been made as a result of this paradigm shift.

530   Cutter, Elizabeth G. *Plant Anatomy: Cells and Tissues, Part 1*. 2nd ed. London: Edward Arnold, 1978. 315 p. 0713126386; 0713126396 (paper).

This is a revision of the original edition published in 1969. Focus is on the cell and tissue level of plant structure including different cell types—such as sclerenchyma and transfer cells—to tissue types such as xylem, phloem, and the vascular cambium. A well-written comprehensive text, including 750 references to the literature.

531   Cutter, Elizabeth G. *Plant Anatomy: Experiment and Interpretation, Part 2*. London: Edward Arnold, 1971. 343 p. ISBN 071312301X; 0713123028 (paper).

A companion volume to Cutter's *Plant Anatomy, Part 1*, above, this text describes and illustrates the root, stem (both primary and secondary growth), leaf, flower, fruits, and seeds and embryos of flowering plants. Connections between plant form and function, particularly growth and metabolism, are integrated throughout the text.

532   Dickison, William C. *Integrative Plant Anatomy*. San Diego, CA: Academic, 2000. 533 p. $78.95. ISBN 0122151704.

The aim of this book is to link the subject of plant anatomy to other fields of inquiry. A four-chapter overview of the anatomical foundations of higher plants is followed by chapters linking plant anatomy to the broad subjects of evolution, physiology, ecology, as well as economic and applied botany. Included are bibliographic references, a 14-page glossary of terms, and an index.

533    Esau, Katherine. *Plant Anatomy,* 2nd ed. New York: Wiley, 1965. 767 p.

This classic is still the standard by which other plant anatomy texts are measured in that it "emphasized the developmental aspects of plant anatomy and the significance of understanding development for interpreting function." Covers intracellular structure and cell types, as well as the anatomy and development of tissues, cell wall, wood structure, stems and roots, flower, seeds, and fruits. Illustrated with black-and-white photomicrographs and line drawings by the author. Esau's later book, *Anatomy of Seed Plants*, 2nd ed. (1977), revised some of the content of *Plant Anatomy*, digesting it for the undergrad, and included a comprehensive, detailed glossary.

534    Fahn, A. *Plant Anatomy*. 4th ed. New York: Pergamon, 1990. 588 p. ISBN 0080374905; 0080374913 (paper).

Widely used textbook for graduate-level plant anatomy courses, but less easily read than Mauseth's *Plant Anatomy,* below. Well illustrated with black-and-white photomicrographs, line drawings, and scanning electron micrographs. Each chapter has extensive references with a comprehensive author index at the end of the book. Includes an extensive glossary.

535    Gifford, E. M., and A. S. Foster. *Morphology and Evolution of Vascular Plants*. 3rd ed. New York: W. H. Freeman, 1989. 626 p. ISBN 0716719460.

Revised edition of *Comparative Morphology of Vascular Plants* by Adriance C. Foster and Ernest M. Gifford (2nd ed., 1974). For upper-level undergraduates and graduate students.

536    Gilbert, Scott F. *Developmental Biology*. 7th ed. Sunderland, MA: Sinauer Associates, 2003. 838 p. $109.95. ISBN 0878932585.

This is the most widely used textbook for courses in developmental biology. The 30-page chapter on plant development, written by Susan R. Singer, provides the basics on plant life cycles, gamete production, embryonic development, vegetative growth, and senescence.

537    Greyson, R. I. *The Development of Flowers*. New York: Oxford University Press, 1994. 314 p. $78.95. ISBN 019506688X.

This text focuses on the cellular and organismal aspects of floral development. Includes an extensive bibliography.

538   Howell, Stephen H. *Molecular Genetics of Plant Development*. New York: Cambridge University Press, 1998. 365 p. $50.00 (paper). ISBN 0521582555; 0521587840 (paper).

The purpose of this textbook is to discuss plant development in the context of gene discoveries that are elucidating the roles of hormones and other factors. Emphasis is on organ formation—the development of roots, shoots, leaves, seeds, and flowers. The primary focus is on the well-studied model systems, *Arabidopsis* and *Zea mays*.

539   Kurmann, M. H., and A. R. Hemsley, eds. *The Evolution of Plant Architecture*. London: Royal Botanic Gardens, Kew, 1999. 491 p. $99.00. ISBN 1900347725.

This book is based on papers presented at an international symposium held in 1995 and sponsored by the Linnean Society of London and the Royal Botanic Gardens, Kew. The papers discuss the origins of plant architecture, the architecture of vegetative and reproductive structures, and architecture as related to biomechanics. A taxonomic index is included.

540   Leyser, Ottoline, and Stephen Day. *Mechanisms in Plant Development*. Malden, MA: Blackwell, 2003. 241 p. $55.95 (paper). ISBN 0865427429 (paper).

Intended for undergraduate and graduate courses in plant development, this book is organized around the intrinsic and environmental mechanisms that determine how complex flowering plants develop. A final short chapter compares animal and plant development mechanisms. Well indexed; no glossary.

541   Mauseth, James D. *Plant Anatomy*. Menlo Park, CA: Benjamin/Cummings, 1988. 560 p. (Benjamin/Cummings Series in the Life Sciences). $29.99. ISBN 0805345701.

Presently the most extensively used textbook for plant anatomy courses, this successor to Esau's *Anatomy of Seed Plants* covers the anatomical and histological structure of the vegetative and reproductive plant organs at the cell, tissue, and organ level. Well illustrated with black-and-white photomicrographs and line drawings. Includes an extensive, clearly written glossary that is suitable for use as a plant anatomy dictionary.

542   McManus, Michael T., and Bruce E. Veit, eds. *Meristematic Tissues in Plant Growth and Development*. Boca Raton, FL: CRC, 2002. 301 p. $199.95. ISBN 0849397928.

This advanced text describes plant meristematic tissues in relation to plant growth and development. Molecular, physiological, and anatomical aspects are considered.

543   Nicklas, Karl J. *Plant Biomechanics: An Engineering Approach to Plant Form and Function.* Chicago, IL: University of Chicago Press, 1992. 607 p. $90.00; $47.00 (paper). ISBN 0226586308; 0226586316 (paper).

This book explores how plant biological processes and structures adhere to the physical laws of physics and chemistry. Topics include fluid mechanics, plant–water relations, the chemistry of cell walls, plant organ topography, and more.

544   Peterson, R. Larry, Hugues B. Massicotte, and Lewis H. Melville. *Mycorrhizas: Anatomy and Cell Biology.* Ottawa, Ontario, Canada: NRC Research, 2003. 173 p. $70.00 (paper). ISBN 0660190877; 0851999018 (paper).

Mycorrhizas are the result of the important symbiotic relationship between fungi and the roots of plants. Liberally illustrated with clear, colored line drawings as well as micrographs, this book is essential for all who would understand this relationship. Includes a glossary and appendixes that give the procedures for preparing mycorrhizal roots for microscopy.

545   Raghavan, Valayamghat. *Developmental Biology of Flowering Plants.* New York: Springer-Verlag, 2000. 354 p. $89.95. ISBN 0387987819.

This book is organized for use as a textbook in plant developmental biology. The five parts of the book are seed germination and growth; growth and differentiation of the shoots, leaves, and roots; reproduction; seed and fruit formation; and development under tissue culture regimes. Well illustrated and indexed.

546   Ritchie, Steven W., John J. Hanway, and Garren O. Benson. *How a Corn Plant Develops.* Ames, IA: Iowa State University of Science and Technology, Cooperative Extension Service, 1993. 21 p. (Special Report No. 48). URL: http:// maize.agron.iastate.edu/corngrows.html.

This Web site, a digital representation of a print pamphlet, describes the development of a corn plant from its germination and vegetative growth through its reproductive stages and the maturation of the corn kernels. Each stage of growth is well illustrated and described.

547   Romberger, John A., Zygmunt Hejnowicz, and Jane F. Hill. *Plant Structure: Function and Development: A Treatise on Anatomy and Vegetative Development, with Special Reference to Woody Plants.* New York: Springer-Verlag, 1993. 524 p. $64.95 (paper). ISBN 0387563059; 1930665954 (paper).

For graduate students and researchers already familiar with basic anatomy and development of plants. Emphasis is on woody plants.

548   Rudall, Paula. *Anatomy of Flowering Plants: An Introduction to Structure and Development.* 2nd ed. New York: Cambridge University Press, 1992. 110 p. ISBN 0521421543 (paper).

Concise introduction to plant anatomy, suitable for students in other plant disciplines who require some knowledge of basic anatomy.

549   Sattler, Rolf. *Organogenesis of Flowers: A Photographic Text-Atlas.* Toronto, Canada: University of Toronto Press, 1973. 207 p. ISBN 0802018645.

The floral organogenesis of 50 species of plants is described using text, line diagrams, and photomicrographs. Provides unique illustrations of the external form of developing flowers.

550   Srivastava, Lalit M. *Plant Growth and Development: Hormones and Environment.* Boston, MA: Academic, 2002. 772 p. $89.95. ISBN 012660570X.

A comprehensive textbook covering in 27 chapters all aspects of plant development including cell division, cell wall formation, embryogenesis, tissue differentiation, photoperception, and tropic responses. The major portion of the book is devoted to a discussion of the seven classes of plant hormones, including their physiological effects, intracellular transport, chemistry, and molecular basis of action. Several appendixes are embedded in the chapters including two on the research tools and protocols used by plant development biologists. Well illustrated, with references for further reading at the end of each chapter.

551   Steeves, Taylor A., and Ian M. Sussex. *Patterns in Plant Development.* 2nd ed. New York: Cambridge University Press, 1989. 388 p. $69.00; $40.00 (paper). ISBN 0521246881; 0521288959 (paper).

Documents the plant developmental process beginning with the zygote, through the formation of the embryo and the primary body, and on to the development of secondary growth. Illustrated, though not copiously.

552   Tryon, Alice F., and Bernard Lugardon. *Spores of the Pteridophyta.* New York: Springer-Verlag, 1991. 648 p. ISBN 0387972188.

Fascinating scanning electron micrograph photographs of over 230 genera of ferns. The accompanying text describes the general characteristics of the spores of each family. Well referenced and includes a glossary of the descriptive terms used to discuss fern spores.

553   Van De Graaff, Kent M., Samuel R. Rushforth, and John L. Crawley. *A Photographic Atlas for the Botany Laboratory.* 4th ed. Englewood, CO: Morton, 2004. 182 p. $29.95. ISBN 0895826143.

This full-color photographic atlas provides clear photographs and drawings of tissues and organs similar to specimens seen in a botany laboratory. It is designed to accompany any botany text or laboratory manual. Many photomicrographs, photos of living specimens, and herbarium collections are included. The fundamental organization is by group of plants, ranging from the bacteria, Archaea, algae, slime molds, and fungi to the gymnosperms and flowering plants. Includes a glossary of terms.

554   Wardlaw, Claude Wilson. *Morphogenesis in Plants: A Contemporary Study*. London: Methuen, 1968. 451 p.

This classic is still a standard reference for plant development due to the clarity of the drawings and for the historical background. Newer treatments are more current in regard to research concerning our understanding of the molecular controls of morphogenesis.

## Associations

Botanical Society of America (BSA)—Developmental and Structural Section. c/o Dr. Pamela Diggle, Department of EE Biology—Box 334, University of Colorado, Boulder, CO 80309-0334. Phone: 303-492-4860. Fax: 303-492-8699. E-mail: diggle@spot.colorado.edu. URL: http://www.botany.org/bsa/sections/devel/index.htm.

See chapter 2 for full annotation. The Botanical Society of America is the primary organization with which plant anatomists affiliate. The main goal of this section of the BSA is to stimulate interest in research and teaching in plant development and structure. The section offers several awards for graduate students in this field of inquiry.

Canadian Botanical Association/L'Association Botanique du Canada (CBA/ABC)—Structure and Development Section. c/o Dr. Arthur R. Davis, Department of Biology, University of Saskatchewan, Saskatoon, SK S7N 5E2 Canada. Phone: 306-966-4732. E-mail: davisa@duke.usask.ca. URL: http://www.cba-abc.ca/.

See chapter 2 for full annotation. This section holds regular meetings at the annual meeting of the Association.

555   International Society of Plant Morphologists (Societé Internationale des Morphologistes de la Vie Vegetale). Department of Botany, University of Delhi, New Delhi 110 007, Delhi, India. Phone: 91 11 27667830. Fax: 91 11 7257830.

Founded in 1950, this international society has over 400 members. Membership is open to those interested in plant morphology, anatomy, embryology, and histochemistry. Members receive a subscription to the Society journal, *Phytomorphology*.

# 8
# Genetics, Molecular Biology, and Biotechnology

Genetics and molecular biology are the foundation of the booming field of genomics (the study of genes and their functions) and the basis for the plant biotechnological advances that have recently been accomplished. Recently several plant scientists testified before the Senate Committee on Agriculture, Nutrition, and Forestry on the topic of the science of biotechnology and its potential applications to agriculture (United States Congress. Senate Committee on Agriculture, Nutrition, and Forestry, 2000). Professor Ohlrogge, from Michigan State University, testified that "genetic engineering will transform crop plants from their traditional role of providing low-cost food and fiber toward a much more diverse and profitable role of producing an array of higher-value products." Another indication of the importance of plant molecular biology came from the National Science Foundation (NSF). During the NSF's fiftieth anniversary celebration in 2000, it highlighted 50 research areas (the "Nifty 50") that it judged will have a great impact or influence on every American's life (National Science Foundation, 2000). Among these were four plant research areas, all of which fall within the area of genetics, molecular biology, or biotechnology: the *Arabidopsis* genome project; vaccinating people by feeding them fruits or vegetables that have been bioengineered to contain vaccines; using plants in tissue culture as biofactories to produce pharmaceuticals such as taxol; and bioengineering plants so they are resistant to the heavy metals or have greater salt tolerance, which will make more of the world's acres suitable for producing crops.

This chapter focuses on resources in classical genetics, modern molecular biology, and the plant tissue culture techniques that enable genetically engineered

**149**

plants to become biotechnological products. The reader is advised to refer to the resources listed in chapter 9 for plant physiology and biochemistry resources and chapter 7 for plant development materials.

The primary bibliographic databases for plant genetics, molecular biology, and biotechnology are *CAB Abstracts*, *Biological Abstracts*, and *AGRICOLA*. Interestingly, although *PubMed (MEDLINE)* is not considered a primary resource for plants, it is increasingly becoming the first place plant molecular biologists search for literature. These bibliographic resources have been thoroughly described in chapter 2.

# Databases, Abstracts, and Indexes

556 *Agricultural and Environmental Biotechnology Abstracts.* Vol. 1– . Bethesda, MD: Cambridge Scientific Abstracts, 1993– . Monthly. $415.00. ISSN 1063-1151. Available electronically.

Covers biotechnology for food industry, agriculture, and the environment, including plant genome studies and genetic engineering. Complete bibliographic information is provided for each abstract; subject and author indexes are provided for each issue with annual accumulations. This rather small resource, which currently indexes only 133 serials, is available online as a standalone database or as part of the *Biological Sciences Collection* (see chapter 2) or *CSA Environmental Sciences and Pollution Management* database. Supersedes, in part, *Biotechnology Research Abstracts*.

# Serials

## General Serials

557 *Genetics.* Vol. 1– . Austin, TX: Genetics Society of America. 1916– . Monthly. $770.00. ISSN 0016-6731. Available electronically.

558 *Genome Research.* Vol. 5– . Cold Spring Harbor, NY: Cold Spring Harbor Laboratory Press, 1995– . Monthly. $1,010.00. ISSN 1088-9051. Available electronically.

559 *The Journal of Applied Genetics.* Vol. 36– . Poznan, Poland: Institute of Plant Genetics, Polish Academy of Sciences, 1995– . Quarterly. $120.00. ISSN 1234-1983. Available electronically.

Formerly *Genetica Polonica (The Polish Journal of Genetics and Plant Breeding)*. Recent volumes available online for free at http://jay.au.poznan.pl/JAG/.

560   *Nucleic Acids Research.* Vol. 1– . Oxford, England: Oxford University Press, 1974– . Bimonthly. $2,855.00. ISSN 0305-1048. Available electronically.

## Botanical Serials

561   *Advances in Cellular and Molecular Biology of Plants.* Vol. 1– . Boston, MA: Kluwer Academic, 1994– . Irregular. Price varies.

Six volumes published as of 2004 with various editors. Representative of the series, the most recent volume, *DNA-Based Markers in Plants*, 2nd ed. (2001), focused on topics related to exploiting the molecular biology of plants.

562   *Fungal Genetics and Biology: FG & B.* Vol. 20– . New York: Elsevier, 1996– . Monthly. $548.00. ISSN 0147-5975. Available electronically.

Devoted to the publication of research relating to the structure, function, growth, reproduction, morphogenesis, and differentiation of fungi and their traditional allies. Includes studies at the molecular, cellular, and subcellular levels. Formerly *Experimental Mycology*.

563   *In Vitro Cellular and Developmental Biology-Plant.* Vol. 27P– . Cambridge, MA: CABI, 1991– . Bimonthly. $292.00. ISSN 1054-5476. Available electronically.

Published for the Society for *In Vitro* Biology's Plant Division (four issues per year) and the International Association for Plant Tissue Culture and Biotechnology (two issues per year). Articles cover cellular, molecular, and developmental biology research involving *in vitro* grown or maintained organs, tissues, or cells. Topics include physiology, morphogenesis, somatogenesis, metabolic engineering, micropropagation, molecular farming, and secondary metabolism. Formerly *In Vitro Cellular and Developmental Biology: Journal of the Tissue Culture Association. Plant.*

564   *Plant Biotechnology Journal.* Vol. 1– . Oxford, England: Blackwell Scientific, 2003– . Bimonthly. $744.00. ISSN 1467-7644. Available electronically.

Co-published with the Society for Experimental Biology and the Association of Applied Biologists. Publishes primary research and occasional articles in research involving applications of plant biotechnology and plant biology across all industrial sectors. Applications may involve agriculture, horticulture, food and food processing, paper, pulp and timber, pharmaceuticals, medical, phyto-remediation, marine applications, or nonfood uses of plants and industrial crops. It does not publish primary basic research unless it is likely to enhance the application of plant science in the above industries.

565    *Plant Cell.* Vol. 1– . Rockville, MD: American Society of Plant Biologists, 1989– . Monthly. $2,160.00. ISSN 1040-4651. Available electronically.

*Plant Cell* is the most highly ranked plant biology journal, according to ISI's *Journal Citation Reports.* Its aim is to publish the most cutting-edge research plant biology, to be a *Science* for plant research. Its focus is plant cellular biology, molecular biology, genetics, development, and molecular evolution. The review articles, as well as other nonresearch articles, are freely available online at http://www.plantcell.org/collected/index.shtml. Subscription is bundled with *Plant Physiology* (see chapter 9 for full annotation).

566    *Plant Cell, Tissue and Organ Culture.* Vol. 1– . Dordrecht, the Netherlands: Kluwer Academic, 1981– . Monthly. $2,135.00. ISSN 0167-6857. Available electronically.

This is an international journal that publishes original results of fundamental studies on the behavior of plant cells, tissues, and organs *in vitro.* Some topics covered include growth, development, and differentiation; genetics and breeding; physiology and biochemistry; protoplast, cell, and tissue culture; micropropagation and secondary metabolism; and biotechnology. A special issue, Volume 64 (2–3), 2001, was titled "Reviews of Plant Biotechnology and Applied Genetics."

567    *The Plant Journal: For Cell and Molecular Biology.* Vol. 1– . Oxford, England: Blackwell Scientific, 1991– . Semimonthly. $3,229.00. ISSN 0960-7412. Available electronically.

Published on behalf of the Society for Experimental Biology, this highly rated journal publishes research and protocols (termed technical advances) in the area of plant molecular biology. It is particularly strong in the area of *Arabidopsis* research. Occasionally review articles, short communications, and gene and mutant directories are also included.

568    *Plant Molecular Biology.* Vol. 1– . Dordrecht, the Netherlands: Kluwer Academic, 1981– . 18 times per year. $2,938.00. ISSN 0167-4412. Available electronically.

Published in cooperation with the International Society for Plant Molecular Biology, this journal publishes both basic and applied research concerned with plant molecular biology, biochemistry, and plant molecular genetics. Includes such topics as comparative genomics, functional genomics, proteomics, bioinformatics, computational biology, biochemical and regulatory networks, and biotechnology.

569  *Plant Molecular Biology Reporter.* Vol. 1– . Ottawa, Ontario, Canada: NRC Research, 1983– . Quarterly. $240.00. ISSN 0735-9640. Available electronically.

The official publication of the International Society for Plant Molecular Biology. The primary focus of this journal is to publish plant molecular biology protocols. In addition it provides a venue for news and commentary concerning the availability of DNA clones, upcoming meetings, and announcements for the membership.

570  *Sexual Plant Reproduction.* Vol. 1– . Berlin: Springer-Verlag, 1988– . Quarterly. $950.00. ISSN 0934-0882. Available electronically.

The journal covers the dynamics and mechanisms of sexual processes in plants, including seed and nonseed plants. Most articles use biochemical, cytochemical, molecular, biophysical, and immunological methods.

# Dictionaries and Encyclopedias

571  Bains, William. *Biotechnology from A to Z.* 3rd ed. New York: Oxford University Press, 2004. 413 p. $49.50 (paper). ISBN 0198524986 (paper).

In about 350 short essays arranged alphabetically, explains over 1,000 terms used in biotechnology and genetic engineering. Resembling an extended glossary or small encyclopedia more than a dictionary, this volume has all the definitions that a plant biologist working in biotechnology needs to know. Has an excellent index and good cross-references.

572  *Biotech Life Science Dictionary.* URL: http://biotech.icmb.utexas.edu/search/dict-search.html.

The University of Texas at Austin's Biotech Resources Web Project provides this freely accessible dictionary, originally developed at the Indiana Institute for Molecular and Cellular Biology, of more than 8,300 life science terms. The focus is biochemistry, biotechnology, botany, cell biology, and genetics. Site has not been recently updated but is cited by many.

573  Brenner, Sydney, and Jeffrey H. Miller, eds.-in-chief. *Encyclopedia of Genetics.* San Diego, CA: Academic, 2002. 4 vol. $1,044.95. ISBN 0122270800 (set).

This is a monumental reference work in the field of genetics, co-edited by Dr. Sydney Brenner, recipient of the 2002 Nobel Prize in Physiology or Medicine, and Professor Jeffrey H. Miller of UCLA. With over 1,700 entries by over 700 contributors, this is an invaluable reference work for anyone interested in any aspect of genetics. Entries do not include bibliographies, but they usually suggest further readings and entries of related interest and always note the author. Among the many specifically plant-related headings: *Arabidopsis thaliana*: The Premier Model Plant, Plant Embryogenesis, Plant Hormones, Seed Development, Transposable Elements in Plants, Transfer of Genetic Information from *Agrobacterium tumefaciens* to Plants, Genetics of Chloroplasts, and Mendel's Laws.

574    Brown, R. G. *Dictionary of Plant Tissue Culture.* Delhi, India: Ivy, 2004. 204 p. $20.00. ISBN 8178901013.

Includes over 1,500 plant tissue culture terms likely to be found in textbooks and research journals. From the jacket: "This dictionary is intended for the use of students at both undergraduate and post graduate levels, as well as those involved in commercial micropropagation and research programs."

575    International Board for Plant Genetic Resources, comp. *Elsevier's Dictionary of Plant Genetic Resources.* New York: Elsevier, 1991. 187 p. $91.00. ISBN 0444889590.

This English language dictionary contains over 1,800 terms specific to plant genetic resources. This is not a listing of plant genetic resources (i.e., germplasm banks), but instead offers definitions of plant genetic terms.

576    *Plant Ontology Consortium (POC).* URL: http://www.plantontology.org/index.html.

Funded by the National Science Foundation (NSF), this group aims to develop controlled vocabularies (ontologies) that describe plant structures and developmental stages, providing a semantic framework for meaningful cross-species queries across genomic databases. All of the major plant database resources are members or collaborators in this endeavor, including the Gramene database, the *Arabidopsis* Information Resource (TAIR), and the MaizeGDB. The Missouri Botanical Garden, the Open Biological Ontologies project (OBO), the Gene Ontology Consortium (GO), and the Deep Gene project are also collaborators.

577    Schlegel, Rolf H. J. *Encyclopedic Dictionary of Plant Breeding and Related Subjects.* New York: Food Products, 2003. 563 p. $89.95; $49.95 (paper). ISBN 1560229500; 1560229519 (paper).

This dictionary is a unique attempt to gather in a single volume the scientific and common terms associated with plant breeding and related disciplines, with many of the terms described in page-length detail. Extensive cross-references ensure easy access to related entries throughout the dictionary. Also included are a bibliography, supplementary tables and figures, and an extensive table of crop plants with their DNA content, genome constitution, and other genetic data.

# Handbooks and Methods

578  *ATTC: The Global Bioresource Center.* Manassas, VA: American Type Culture Collection (ATTC). URL: http://www.atcc.org/.

The American Type Culture Collection (ATCC) is a nonprofit, private organization that was established in 1925 to acquire, preserve, and distribute well-characterized biological cultures for the international research community. Culture types that would be of interest to plant biologists include algae, filamentous fungi, yeast, plant tissue cultures, plant seeds, algae, and plant viruses. Presently 75 plant cell cultures and over 400 strains of patented seeds are available.

579  Bartlett, John M. S., and David Stirling, eds. *PCR Protocols.* 2nd ed. Totowa, NJ: Humana, 2003. 545 p. (Methods in Molecular Biology, 226.) $135.00; $99.50 (spiral bound). ISBN 0869036421; 0896036278 (spiral bound).

Though not specific to plant protocols, this is an essential reference for any lab or researcher utilizing PCR (polymerase chain reaction) technology. With 71 chapters, most of them describing a specific protocol, this book tries to cover as many PCR techniques as possible with kit-free methods.

580  Biotechnology and Biological Sciences Research Council (BBSRC). *U. K. Cropnet (U. K. Crop Plant Bioinformatics Network.* Swindon, England: The Council, 1996. URL: http://ukcrop.net/.

This Web site makes available crop genome databases on *Arabidopsis thaliana,* barley, *Brassica* species, forage grasses, millet, tef, and nearly 200 U. K. crop species from British research institutions. Databases on sequenced plant gene nomenclature, plant uses, cereal pathogens, plant ESTs (expressed sequence tags), STSs (sequence tagged sites), and plant gene families are also hosted here. Analysis software is also available for download.

581  Brendel, Volker, and Carol Lushbough. *PlantGDB: Resources for Plant Comparative Genomics.* URL: http://www.plantgdb.org/.

*PlantGDB* is the home page for the NSF-funded project, PlantGDB–Plant Genome Database and Analysis Tools. Through the development and implementation of integrated databases and analytical tools, the goal of this project and Web site is to aid in the organization and interpretation of plant genome sequence data from three major sources: whole genome sequencing and assembly, genome survey sequencing, and expressed sequence tags (ESTs). The project also includes the development of the *BioExtract Server* prototype (http://www.bioextract.org/), which provides a distribution point for plant genome data stored in different local and external databases. The *Plant Genome Research Outreach Portal* (PGROP) (http://www.plantgdb.org/PGROP/pgrop.php) was also set up to provide a centralized repository of various NSF-sponsored Plant Genome Research outreach programs and activities for the public at large, undergraduates, high school students, and teachers. PGROP seeks to broaden participation of these user groups in plant genome research topics by making information on appropriate programs, materials, and guidance available.

582   Carnegie Institution of Washington, Department of Plant Biology, and National Center for Genome Resources. *TAIR, the Arabidopsis Information Resource.* URL: http://www.arabidopsis.org/home.html.

*TAIR* contains a comprehensive collection of information for the scientific community about the most widely used model flowering plant, *Arabidopsis thaliana,* which was the first plant sequenced, in 2000. *TAIR* consists of a searchable relational database that includes many different datatypes such as DNA sequences, genes, proteins, vectors, genetic markers, and citations to publications. It is in the process of transitioning from a genome-centric resource to one that focuses on all aspects of *Arabidopsis* biology. In July 2002, *TAIR* logged over 500,000 Web pages visits, making it the most widely used plant biology information resource worldwide.

583   Chawla, H. S. *Plant Biotechnology: A Practical Approach.* Enfield, NH: Science, 2003. 302 p. $39.50 (paper). ISBN 157808296X (paper).

This is basically a lab manual for those who need to bioengineer plants. Included are chapters on plant tissue culture (e.g., the micropropagation of embryos, cell suspension culture, and anther culture) and the molecular techniques that are used to transform or analyze bioengineered plants (e.g., DNA isolation, microsatellite analysis, biolistic transformation, and *Agrobacterium*-mediated transformation). Each chapter starts with a brief introduction, lists the materials required, and then clearly details the procedures. There are nearly 20 appendixes covering the composition of various types of media, troubleshooting tips for electrophoresis, and much more. Although the subtitle of this book is A Practical Approach, it is not part of Oxford University Press's *Practical Approach* series.

584   Christou, Paul, and Harry Klee, eds. *Handbook of Plant Biotechnology.* Hoboken, NJ: Wiley, 2004. 2 vol. $787.00 (set). ISBN 047185199X (set).

An international team of researchers from both industry and academia has pulled together a series of review articles on virtually every aspect involved in the bioengineering of plants. The first volume starts with an introduction to classical plant breeding techniques and describes several projects that have been possible only by the molecular approach. Thereafter, the chapters are technical in nature, covering the tools used for genetic modification and analysis. A significant portion of the book focuses on engineering crops and other plants for improved traits or for use as biofactories to produce pharmaceuticals. Nonscientific issues that surround plant biotechnology such as risk assessment, patents, and intellectual property rights, consumer interests, global impact, and the use of these crops in developing countries are also covered. Two appendixes provide in tabular form lists of plant biotechnology products and patents. A unified, comprehensive index at the end of Volume 2 simplifies finding information in both volumes.

585   Collin, Hamish A., and Sue Edwards. *Plant Cell Culture*. New York: Springer, 1998. 158 p. (Introduction to Biotechniques series). $44.95 (paper). ISBN 0387915087 (paper).

The basic steps for putting plant tissues into *in vitro* culture are described in enough depth to help a person new to the field select a suitable tissue, put it into culture, and maintain it in either an undifferentiated or partially differentiated form, and finally to redifferentiate it back into an intact plant. The techniques are described for both haploid and protoplast culture and the pitfalls of various techniques are explained. Genetic manipulation of plants is not a major focus.

586   Cresti, Mauro, Stephen Blackmore, and J. L. van Went. *Atlas of Sexual Reproduction in Flowering Plants*. New York: Springer-Verlag, 1992. 249 p. ISBN 0387549048.

Over 100 scanning transmission electron and light micrographs and 93 figures describe and document the processes of sexual reproduction in higher plants. Text is divided into sections for anther development, pistil development, the pregamic phase and fertilization. Each plate is fully annotated and referenced; there are plant and subject indexes. Provides a valuable introduction into plant reproductive cell structures for researchers in genetics, plant breeding, and cell biology.

587   *Current Protocols in Molecular Biology*. New York: Wiley, 1998. 3 vol. (loose-leaf). Updated quarterly. $775.00 (vol. 1); $425.00 (vol. 2 and 3). Available electronically for $5,500 per year. ISBN 047150338X.

The essential methods book found on many lab benches, this set gives the basic, accepted methods for DNA preparation and isolation, library screening, and sequencing; protein interactions; yeast manipulation; and phosphorylation analyses. Though not focused on plant molecular biology, a search on the term *Arabidopsis* yielded 17 references including references to RNA interference (RNAi), gene silencing, restriction-mediated differential display, and protein identification. The online version is updated frequently and, though very costly, is highly recommended.

Dashek, William V., ed. *Methods in Plant Biochemistry and Molecular Biology*.

See chapter 9 for full annotation. Provides an assemblage of research protocols and cited literature references.

588    Endress, Rudolf. *Plant Cell Biotechnology*. New York: Springer-Verlag, 1994. 353 p. $189.00. ISBN 0387569472.

This book describes methods and techniques for gaining highly productive cells and plants to produce secondary metabolites, enabling the production of plant products on an industrial scale independent of environmental influences and natural resources.

589    *Entrez: The Life Sciences Search Engine*. Bethesda, MD: National Center for Biotechnology Information, 1996. URL: http://www.ncbi.nlm.nih.gov/gquery/gquery.fcgi.

Newly redefined, *Entrez* provides an integrated search engine for nucleotide and protein sequence data from over 100,000 organisms, including thousands of plant species. Additionally *Entrez* searches 3-D protein structures, genomic mapping information, *PubMed (MEDLINE)* citations (see chapter 2 for full annotation), and more. *Entrez* can be searched with a wide variety of text terms such as author name, journal name, gene or protein name, organism, and other terms, depending on the database being searched. Although certainly not primarily a botanical resource, because plant sequence data are deposited in *GenBank* (see below) and other nucleotide databases, *Entrez* provides a valuable tool for accessing plant molecular biology resources and citations. For example, at the time of writing (2005), searching *Entrez* for the term *Arabidopis* brought up over 16,500 citations in *PubMed*, nearly two million nucleotide sequences, over 130,000 protein sequences, and over 260,000 GEO gene expression profiles. Formerly the *Entrez Browser*.

590    *Environmental Plant Biology Series*. Oxford, England: Bios Scientific, 1991. Irregular. Price varies.

Focus is on the interface between plant physiology and the environment. Recent titles have included *Biological Rhythms and Photoperiodism in Plants* (1998); *Embryogenesis: The Generation of a Plant* (1996); and *Plant Cuticles: An Integrated Functional Approach* (1996).

591    Evans, David E., J. Coleman, and A. Kearns. *Plant Cell Culture*. Oxford, England: BIOS Scientific, 2003. 256 p. $52.95 (paper). ISBN 185996320X (paper).

Provides over 40 step-by-step protocols for the culturing of plant callus, cell suspensions, protoplasts, haploid tissues, and embryos. An entire chapter is devoted to culturing bacteria frequently used as plant transformation agents, such as

*Agrobacterium tumefaciens.* Additionally, basic background and orientation material is supplied, such as how tissue culture is used in agriculture, genetic engineering, biotechnology, and industry. Includes a useful glossary as well as contact information for suppliers of chemicals, apparatus, and cell culture products.

592   Foster, Gary D., and David Twell, eds. *Plant Gene Isolation: Principles and Practice.* New York: Wiley, 1996. 426 p. ISBN 0471955388; 0471955396 (paper).

Lying somewhere between a textbook and a lab manual, this book attempts to provide the reader with enough background and details in order to make an informed decision about which of the many possible techniques for isolating genes from plants to use. Covers the generation of cDNA (genomic) libraries, gene screening, identification of genes, mutagenesis, PCR-based techniques, and automated sequencing of selected cDNA clones.

593   Gamborg, Oluf L., and Gregory C. Phillips, eds. *Plant Cell, Tissue and Organ Culture: Fundamental Methods.* New York: Springer, 1995. 358 p. (Springer Lab Manual). $98.00. ISBN 3540580689 (spiral bound).

Designed to be used as a benchtop companion in both research and the classroom lab. After a brief introduction, each chapter contains clear procedures in such techniques as the preparation of sterile media, plant regeneration techniques, somatic embryogenesis, the culture of meristems, anthers, microspores, and embryos, and transformation procedures. A myriad of microtechniques are also delineated, such as the electron microscopy of protoplasts, immunofluorescence techniques, chromosomal staining procedures, enzyme-linked immunosorbent assays (ELISA), and polymerase chain reaction (PCR) applications. Includes a generous glossary and is fully indexed.

594   *GenBank.* Bethesda, MD: National Center for Biotechnology Information. URL: http://www.ncbi.nlm.nih.gov/entrez/query.fcgi?db=Nucleotide.

*GenBank* is the major gene sequence database. It includes both animal and plant sequences and may be searched for no fee. *GenBank* is searchable from the *Entrez Nucleotide* search engine, where one simultaneously searches nucleotides deposited in *GenBank;, EMBL (European Molecular Biology Laboratory); DDBJ (DNA Data Bank of Japan); RefSeq (NCBI Reference Sequence); PIR (Protein Information Resource); PRF (Protein Research Foundation); Swiss-Prot Protein Knowledgebase;* and *PDB (RCSB Protein Data Bank).* Refer to the citation for *Entrez,* above, for additional details.

595   Gilmartin, Philip M., and Chris Bowler, eds. *Molecular Plant Biology: A Practical Approach.* Oxford, England: Oxford University Press, 2002. 2 vol. (Practical Approach Series, 258). $170.00 per volume; $59.50 per volume

(paper). ISBN 0199638764 (vol. 1); 0199638195 (vol. 2); 0199638756 (vol. 1, paper); 0199638187 (vol. 2, paper).

An essential laboratory companion for all plant researchers, these volumes provide up-to-date protocols and practical advice. The broad areas included are gene identification, gene organization, gene expression, and gene product analysis. Each protocol is complete, well illustrated, and fully referenced. Highly recommended.

596    Glick, Bernard R., and John E. Thompson, eds. *Methods in Plant Molecular Biology and Biotechnology*. Boca Raton, FL: CRC, 1993. 360 p. ISBN 0849351642.

Covers a wide range of methods with an emphasis on well-tested approaches by experienced practitioners. The book deals with various dimensions of recombinant DNA technology, the production and analysis of plant mutants, relevant computer software, DNA mapping and analysis of DNA polymorphism, and methods for the detection and characterization of plant pathogens. Though a bit dated, this book is still frequently cited and used.

597    Hall, Robert D., ed. *Plant Cell Culture Protocols*. Totowa, NJ: Humana, 1999. 421 p. (Methods in Molecular Biology, 111). $89.50. ISBN 0896035492.

A collection of dozens of frequently used techniques for plant cell and tissue culture including culture initiation, maintenance, manipulation, application, and long-term maintenance. The emphasis is on techniques for genetic modification and micropropagation such as callus initiation, somatic embryogenesis, transformation by *Agrobacterium*, PEG, electroporation, and silicon carbide whiskers.

598    Harding, Stephen E., ed. *Biotechnology and Genetic Engineering Reviews*. Vol. 1– . Andover, England: Intercept, 1984– . Annual. $200.00. ISSN 0264-8725.

Each volume contains approximately 13 to 17 original review articles covering developments in the industrial, agricultural, and medical applications of biotechnology in the widest sense. Particular emphasis is given to the genetic manipulation of the organisms concerned. Although the series is not specifically devoted to plants, a recent volume devoted three of fourteen articles to plant biotechnology including bioengineered rice, nitric oxide in plants, and viruses as vectors for transformation of plants.

599    Jackson, John F., and H. F. Linskens, eds. *Molecular Methods of Plant Analysis*. Vol. 21– . New York: Springer-Verlag, 2002– . Price varies.

This series details the molecular procedures that have been utilized to analyze plant components. Recent volumes have covered such techniques as genetic transformation, genetic markers, DNA microarrays, and antisense technology. Formerly *Modern Methods of Plant Analysis*.

600   Jauhar, Prem P. *Methods of Genome Analysis in Plants*. Boca Raton, FL: CRC, 1996. 386 p. ISBN 0849394376.

This book takes a new look at the classical techniques of cytogenetics and examines how they can be applied in the era of modern genome analysis. Methods revisited include the cytogenetic tools of chromosome counting, karyotyping, and meiotic analysis as well as the newer techniques of chromosome microdissection, plastome analysis, and *in situ* hybridization.

601   Johnston, John R., ed. *Molecular Genetics of Yeast: A Practical Approach*. New York: IRL Press at Oxford University Press, 1994. 275 p. (Practical Approach Series, 141). $55.00 (paper). ISBN 0199634300; 0199634297 (paper).

The yeast *Saccharomyces cerevisiae* is used extensively for research and by industry, and is one of the most important organisms for studies in molecular biology, genetics, and biotechnology. Experimental procedures for DNA isolation, cloning and expression vectors, construction and use of DNA libraries, high-efficiency transformation, and aspects of industrial strains are some of the topics covered in this comprehensive compendium of detailed protocols.

602   Koncz, Csaba, Nam-Hai Chua, and Jozef S. Schell, eds. *Methods in Arabidopsis Research*. River Edge, NJ: World Scientific, 1992. 482 p. $58.00; $48.00 (paper). ISBN 9810209045; 9810209053 (paper).

Discussion of the methods used to explore the *Arabidopsis* genome, the most widely used plant model system, which is useful for investigating the molecular mechanisms responsible for the physiological, cellular, and biochemical properties of plants. Still frequently cited more than 10 years after publication.

603   Lindsey, Keith, ed. *Plant Tissue Culture Manual: Fundamentals and Applications*. Boston, MA: Kluwer Academic, 1991. ISBN 0792311159 (ring bound).

Emphasis is placed on presenting step-by-step protocols for basic techniques including introductory text and practical lab bench information. The core of model procedures was updated by supplementary chapters and sections. Included in this work manual are *Supplements* 1–7, 1992–1997. Companion to the *Plant Molecular Biology Manual* (1989, not reviewed).

604   Maliga, Pal et al., eds. *Methods in Plant Molecular Biology: A Laboratory Course Manual*. Plainview, NY: Cold Spring Harbor Laboratory Press, 1995. 446

p. (A Cold Spring Harbor Laboratory Course Manual). ISBN 087969386X (hardcover spiral).

This manual is the outgrowth of the summer course, the Molecular and Developmental Biology of Plants, taught each summer since 1981 at the Cold Spring Harbor Laboratory. Organized into 18 sections with each section containing 5 to 10 clear, step-by-step laboratory protocols. Among the covered topics are PEG-mediated plant cell transformation, functional analysis, biolistic transformation, microinjection, tissue printing, *in situ* hybridization, *in vivo* genomic footprinting, YAC analysis, and much more. Each protocol is complete and written to stand alone.

605    *Methods in Molecular Biology.* Vol. 1– . Totowa, NJ: Humana, 1984– . Irregular. Price varies. ISSN 1064-3745.

Though this series is not specific to plant biology, several volumes have focused on plants or deal with topics and techniques of interest to plant biologists. See descriptions of Hall, Robert D., ed., *Plant Cell Culture Protocols*; and Bartlett, John M. S., and David Stirling, eds., *PCR Protocols.* Other recent volumes include Volume 286 (2004), *Transgenic Plants: Methods and Protocols*; Volume 274 (2004), *Photosynthesis Research Protocols*; and Volume 236 (2003), *Plant Functional Genomics: Methods and Protocols.* For online access, Humana is marketing *Methods in Molecular Biology* and *Methods in Molecular Medicine* together as *BioMedProtocols.com.* Publication frequency varies but currently about 50 volumes per year are produced in this series. Many volumes are available in hardback, paperback, and as e-books.

606    *Molecular Biology Database Collection*, published as a yearly special issue of *Nucleic Acids Research.*

Each year since 1991, *NAR* (see full citation, above) has devoted one issue to a review and listing of the key databases of value to the biologists interested in various aspects of molecular biology, biochemistry, and genetics. To be included, the database must be freely available to the public, as is the *Molecular Biology Database Collection*, itself. The 2004 issue (Volume 32, Database Issue) included the URLs and a brief description for 548 databases. Additionally there were over 100 articles detailing new or updated information for specific databases, at least 10 of which were devoted to plants. Online database issues are freely available at http://nar.oupjournals.org. For the past few years, the Database Issue has been the first issue of the year.

607    *Nature Biotechnology Directory.* London: Nature Publishing Group, 2003– . Annual. $315.00. ISBN 140392046X (paper). URL: http://www.guide.nature.com/.

Deals with the state of biotechnology worldwide. The directory is divided into three parts: profiles of commercial biotechnology companies, universities, institutes, and research organizations; a buyers' guide to over 16,000 products, equipment, and services; and contact information for government departments, trade or industry associations, details of available academic grants, and a translation guide to common biotech terms in French, German, and English. This comprehensive directory is exceptionally useful and recommended for a wide group of users and libraries. The directory is searchable and free online.

608  *PlaNet: A Network of European Plant Databases.* URL: http://www.euplant-genome.net/.

PlaNet is a distributed, shared effort among European bioinformatics groups and plant molecular biologists to establish a comprehensive integrated plant genome database for the systematic exploration of *Arabidopsis* and other plants. Current partners include bioinformatics and biotechnology groups from Germany, France, Belgium, the Netherlands, Great Britain, and Spain.

609  *Plant Genomes Central: Genome Projects in Progress.* Bethesda, MD: National Center for Biotechnology Information, 2003. URL: http://www.ncbi .nlm.nih.gov/genomes/PLANTS/PlantList.html.

Provides a graphical representation of chromosomes from a variety of plant genomes that can be viewed in their entirety or explored in progressively greater detail, with links to associated sequence data. Additionally, the site features a multiplant species genome search engine; a plant-customized BLAST search engine for determining similarities; links for species-specific project centers; resources for plant mitochondria and plastid genomes; and links for research centers specializing in plant genome sequencing and analysis.

610  *Plant Molecular Biology LABFAX.* Oxford, England: BIOS Scientific, 1993. 382 p. (LABFAX Series). $96.95. ISBN 1872748155 (spiral bound); 0121983706.

A compendium of essential information and accurate data for plant anatomy, nucleic acids, transformation and expression, vectors, PCR techniques, and so on. Although not recently updated, it still provides easy access to a lot of valuable data and many protocols. A companion to *Molecular Biology Labfax* (1991, not reviewed), but specifically for the plant sciences.

611  Sambrook, Joseph, and David W. Russell. *Molecular Cloning: A Laboratory Manual.* 3rd ed. Cold Spring Harbor, NY: Cold Spring Harbor Laboratory Press, 2001. 3 vol. $249.00 (set, paper). ISBN 0879695773 (set, paper).

Although not focused on plants, this highly regarded set includes techniques for a wide variety of molecular cloning methods, with their advantages and disadvantages. The appendixes are also valuable and include information on media, the preparation of reagents and buffers, properties of nucleic acids, and more. There are extensive references and numerous diagrams. Access to a supporting Web site (http://www.MolecularCloning.com) is provided to purchasers of the set.

612   Soh, Woong-Young, and Sant Saran Bhojwani, eds. *Morphogenesis in Plant Tissue Cultures.* Boston, MA: Kluwer Academic, 1999. 520 p. $291.00. ISBN 0792356829.

The bulk of this book is devoted to chapters that detail the regeneration of plants from various plant parts—from protoplasts, haploid cell cultures, somatic embryos, roots, shoots, floral parts, and so forth. Later chapters discuss some practical applications that tissue culture has been used for such as plant improvement and secondary metabolite production.

613   *Stadler Genetics Symposia Series.* New York: Kluwer Academic/Plenum, 1984– . Irregular. Price varies. ISSN 1568-1009.

This series publishes the proceedings of the Stadler Genetics Symposia held on the campus of the University of Missouri–Columbia every three to four years. This symposium started out with an emphasis on maize genetics; however, it has become one of the premier symposia covering all aspects of plant genetics. Recent symposia focused on plant genomes, gene conservation, gene manipulation for plant improvement, and chromosome structure.

614   Stein, Lincoln, et al. *Gramene: A Resource for Comparative Grass Genomics.* URL: http://www.gramene.org/.

*Gramene* is a relational database built on the genome sequence for rice that allows comparative genome exploration in grasses such as maize, barley, oat, wheat, sorghum, wild rice, and rice. The *Gramene* database provides information about genetic maps, sequence, genes, genetic markers, mutants, QTLs (quantitative trait loci), controlled vocabularies, and publications.

615   Taji, Acram, producer. *Basic Plant Tissue Culture* [videorecording]. Armidale, New South Wales: Media Resources Unit, University of New England, 1997. 45 minutes. $45.00. ISBN 1863894489.

According to an announcement for the video, the purpose "is to provide the theoretical as well as practical basis of plant tissue culture for the production of higher plants via *in vitro* techniques." It covers stock plant management, media preparation, aseptic procedures, and micropropagation. The intended audience is "teachers, researchers, students, nursery people, and other individuals who are interested in plant cell, tissue and organ culture, particularly in clonal propagation."

616   Trigiano, Robert N., and Dennis J. Gray, eds. *Plant Development and Biotechnology.* Boca Raton, FL: CRC, 2005. 341 p. $89.95. ISBN 0849316146.

Most of the chapters describes cell or tissue culture techniques that can be used to propagate plants either to study plant development or for crop improvement. Key concepts are succinctly summarized at the beginning of each chapter.

617   Vienne, Dominique de, ed. *Molecular Markers in Plant Genetics and Biotechnology.* Enfield, NH: Science, 2003. 235 p. $79.00. ISBN 1578082390.

Because they reveal polymorphism at the DNA level, molecular markers have become essential tools for genetic mapping, comparative genomics, and population genetics. This book not only presents the principal marker techniques but also details how they can be used in fields such as molecular biology and plant breeding.

618   Vinci, Victor A., and Sarad R. Parekh, eds. *Handbook of Industrial Cell Culture: Mammalian, Microbial, and Plant Cells.* Totowa, NJ: Humana, 2003. 536 p. $199.00. ISBN 1588290328.

Plant cells are increasingly being used as biofactories to produce various commercially important metabolic products and drugs. Over a third of this book is devoted to describing the requirements for successfully scaling up plant cell cultures from the lab to the industrial level, with a particular emphasis on the possible pitfalls.

619   Wilson, Zoe A., ed. *Arabidopsis: A Practical Approach.* New York: Oxford University Press, 2000. 275 p. (Practical Approach Series, 223.) $145.00; $59.50 (paper). ISBN 019963565X; 0199635641 (paper).

Concisely deals with the key techniques for conducting experiments with *Arabidopsis,* the most frequently used model organism for the analysis of development in higher plants. Included are the optimal growth conditions, maintenance, available genetic resources, and mapping using multimarker lines or recombinant inbreds. Other molecular techniques covered include the characterization of mutants by molecular cytogenetics and gene expression analysis, cloning techniques using transposons, t-DNA and physical map positions, and the use of bioinformatics tools in *Arabidopsis* research.

# Textbooks and Treatises

620   Allard, R. W. *Principles of Plant Breeding*. 2nd ed. New York: Wiley, 1999. 254 p. $110.00. ISBN 0471023094.

Much of plant breeding involves the genetics of plants, and thus this second edition of the classic overview of plant breeding, written by one of the world's leading authorities on this subject, must be included on the bookshelf of any plant geneticist. The book covers the classical roots of plant breeding, its biological foundations (plant genetics), and reviews the future of plant breeding, including the issue of plant breeding for low-impact agriculture. At least one reviewer of this book has faulted it as an unworthy successor to the first edition, so readers are advised to keep their first editions, too.

621   Chawla, H. S. *Introduction to Plant Biotechnology*. 2nd ed. Enfield, NH: Science, 2002. 528 p. $48.00 (paper). ISBN 1578082285 (paper).

Designed for use as a textbook for upper-level students studying biotechnology, this book details the various plant tissue culture techniques (sterilization, micropropagation, protoplast development, somaclonal variation, cryopreservation) as well as the techniques used in recombinant DNA technology (e.g., dot blotting, gene cloning, vectors, PCR, molecular markers, and bioinformatics tools). The book concludes with a chapter on intellectual property rights. Includes an extensive glossary.

622   Chrispeels, Maarten J., and David E. Sadava, eds. *Plants, Genes, and Crop Biotechnology*. 2nd ed. Boston, MA: Jones and Bartlett, 2003. 562 p. $94.95. ISBN 0763715867.

Written as a textbook for undergraduates, this book explains the biological underpinnings for the genetic engineering of plants while discussing the human factors that must be considered when manipulating plant genes. Thus, there are chapters on food security, global food productivity, green agriculture, plants as chemical factories, plants as solar energy harvesters, strategies for pest control, and urban myths and real concerns about genetically modified crops.

623   Cullis, Christopher A. *Plant Genomics and Proteomics*. Hoboken, NJ: Wiley, 2004. 214 p. $73.95. ISBN 0471373141; 0471488585 (electronic).

Starting with the fundamentals of plant chromosome and gene structure, this book provides an understanding of the laboratory and bioinformatics tools that are used to characterize the transcription and translation products of plants. No prior knowledge about genomics is assumed, making this appropriate for the advanced undergraduate as well as the research scientist. Even those with knowledge about nonplant genomics will find it interesting to read about the novel structures and regulatory features in plant genomes. The book is fully indexed, with references and Web sites listed at the end of most chapters.

624    DiCosmo, Frank, and Masanaru Misawa, eds. *Plant Cell Culture Secondary Metabolism: Toward Industrial Application.* Boca Raton, FL: CRC, 1996. 232 p. $189.00. ISBN 0849351359.

This book provides several examples of the successful use of cultured plant cells for the production of useful natural products, while pointing out the drawbacks encountered including the slow growth rate of plant cells, low productivity, and often expensive isolation procedures. The technological advances that are required to ramp up projects to the industrial level are described.

625    Francis, Dennis, ed. *The Plant Cell Cycle and Its Interfaces.* Boca Raton, FL: CRC, 2001. 220 p. (Sheffield Biological Sciences series). $159.95. ISBN 0849305047.

Plant cell division is under quite different control mechanisms than one finds for animal cells. This slim volume reviews some of the endogenous factors involved in the plant cell cycle.

626    Francis, Dennis, Dénes Dudits, and D. Inzé, eds. *Plant Cell Division.* London: Portland, 1998. 347 p. (Portland Press Research Monograph, 10). $85.00. ISBN 1855780895.

The 16 chapters in this volume review and explore all aspects of the plant cell cycle from the macro- and molecular control mechanisms that regulate it to the structural aspects of mitosis. Well illustrated, with a comprehensive index.

627    Germplasm Resources Information Network; National Germplasm Resources Laboratory (U. S.). *National Plant Germplasm System.* Beltsville, MD: National Germplasm Resources Laboratory, Database Management Unit, 1996. URL: http://www.ars-grin.gov/npgs/.

The *National Plant Germplasm System (NPGS)* holds the germplasms of grains, vegetables, fruits, ornamentals, and woody landscape plants. The *NPGS* Web site lists the repositories and their holdings, and provides a request form for specimens for research. *GRIN (Germplasm Resources Information Network)*, a database of stored cultivars, plant variety protection submissions, and crop registration, is available for searching.

628    Gribskov M. *PlantsT: Functional Genomics of Plant Transporters.* URL: http://plantst.sdsc.edu/.

*PlantsT*, funded by the National Science Foundation (NSF), strives to pull together the most current information necessary for researchers to conduct experiments on membrane transport proteins and genes. *PlantsT* allows researchers to submit their own annotated research discoveries to the site and then propagates this information onto databases such as *GenBank* (see Handbooks, above), *PIR (Protein Information Resource)*, or *Swiss-Prot*. Users can search by name or accession number to retrieve plant transporter gene data including protein sequences, annotation information, a transmembrane domain prediction graph, and related protein sequences. Other resources available include outreach program information, movies, genechip tools, and membrane protein family lists, sequence alignments, and phylogenetic trees.

629    Hammond, John, Peter McGarvey, and Vidadi Yusibov, eds. *Plant Biotechnology: New Products and Applications.* New York: Springer, 2000. 196 p. (Current Topics in Microbiology and Immunology, 240). $119.00; $54.00 (paper). ISBN 3540651047; 3540662650 (paper).

Describes the foundations and basic protocols for creating transgenic plants with a focus on the use of plants as biofactories for vaccines or therapeutics. This book is of interest due to its specialized focus on the medical potential of plant transformation.

630    Interagency Working Group on Plant Genomes. Committee on Science. National Science and Technology Council. *National Plant Genome Initiative: 2003–2008.* Washington: National Science and Technology Council, 2003. 26 p. URL: http://www.ostp.gov/NSTC/html/npgi2003-2008.pdf.

The National Plant Genome Initiative (NPGI) was established in 1998 as a coordinated national plant genome research program by the Interagency Working Group (IWG) on Plant Genomes with representatives from the Department of Agriculture (USDA); Department of Energy (DOE); National Institutes of Health (NIH); National Science Foundation (NSF); Office of Science and Technology Policy (OSTP); and Office of Management and Budget (OMB). In this report, the IWG describes the NPGI plan for the next five years (2003–2008). See also *The National Plant Genome Initiative Objectives for 2003–2008*, below.

631    Inzé, Dirk, ed. *The Plant Cell Cycle.* Boston, MA: Kluwer, 2000. 244 p. $118.00. ISBN 0792366786.

During the 1990s, plant cell cycle research (the life of a cell during the process of mitosis) experienced a boom time. Molecular techniques allowed the discovery of cell cycle genes, and through the use of mutants, links between cell cycle genes, growth, and development were better understood. The 18 articles in this book, which is a reprint of a supplement to *Plant Molecular Biology*, 43(5/6), 2000, capture the excitement of that research period.

632  Lineberger, R. Daniel. *Plant Tissue Culture Information Exchange*. URL: http://aggie-horticulture.tamu.edu/tisscult/tcintro.html.

The Plant Tissue Culture Information Exchange was established by Professor Dan Lineberger of the Department of Horticultural Sciences, Texas A&M University, as part of *Aggie Horticulture*. The site aims to provide researchers, teachers, and producers worldwide with rapid access to information about plant tissue culture. Resources are organized into sections: micropropagation, which is the most developed section of the Web site, chimeras, protoplasts, embryogenesis, and biotechnology.

633  *The National Plant Genome Initiative Objectives for 2003–2008*. Washington, DC: National Academies Press, 2002. 75 p. $18.00. ISBN 0309085217. URL: http://www.nap.edu/books/0309085217/html/.

The National Plant Genome Initiative (NPGI) was launched in 1998 as a long-term project to explore DNA structure and function in plants so that their useful properties could be understood and harnessed to address needs in agriculture, nutrition, energy, and waste reduction. For this report, U. S. plant biology experts were asked to make recommendations for the next five-year phase of the Initiative. Among their recommendations: to focus the NPGI portfolio on a small number of key plant species for in-depth development of genome-sequence data and development of functional-genomics tools; translate the basic findings into relevant crop species; use genomics tools to probe for evolutionary relationships; expand bioinformatics tools; and create postdoctoral training opportunities.

634  Nester, Eugene, Milton P. Gordon, and Allen Kerr, eds. *Agrobacterium tumefaciens: From Plant Pathology to Biotechnology*. St. Paul, MN: American Phytopathological Society, 2005. 336 p. $95.00. ISBN 0890543224.

An anthology of 38 papers on *Agrobacterium* that traces its progress during the past century from just a pest studied by plant pathologists to an invaluable tool used by biotechnologists to transform plants genetically. Much more than just the causative agent of crown gall disease (a so-called plant cancer), this bacterium may one day be used in plant gene therapy.

635  Oksman-Caldentey, Kirsi-Marja, and Wolfgang Barz, eds. *Plant Biotechnology and Transgenic Plants*. New York: M. Dekker, 2002. 719 p. (Books in Soils, Plants, and the Environment, 92). $195.00. ISBN 082470794X.

In over 25 chapters, experts discuss the latest transgenic research, with each chapter focusing on a particular product or goal including improving food quality, the production of secondary metabolites and chemicals, oil and fragrance improvement, the production of immunotherapeutic agents, and improved stress tolerance. Highly recommended text for those desirous of an overview of what plant biotechnology can accomplish.

636   *Plant Variety Protection Office.* URL: http://www.ams.usda.gov/science/ PVPO/PVPindex.htm.

The Plant Variety Protection Office (PVPO) administers the *Plant Variety Protection Act (PVPA)* by issuing Certificates of Protection in a timely manner. The Act provides legal intellectual property rights protection to developers of new varieties of plants that are sexually reproduced (by seed) or tuber-propagated. The PVPO Web site provides information on the kinds of plants that are eligible for protection, what is protected, exemptions, how to apply, and costs. This site also supplies printable application forms, federal regulations, and links to public databases of protected plant varieties. There are also links to other plant intellectual property organizations and seed industry organizations.

637   Quatrano, Ralph. *Plant Genomics: Emerging Tools.* Rockville, MD: American Society of Plant Biologists, 2001. 319 p. $25.00. ISBN 0943088429. URL: http://www.aspb.org/publications/plantcell/articles.cfm.

This collection of articles from the journal *Plant Cell* succinctly pulls together key or review articles on the topics of functional and comparative genomics.

638   Shahidi, Fereidoon, et al., eds. *Chemicals via Higher Plant Bioengineering.* New York: Kluwer Academic/Plenum, 1999. 280 p. (Advances in Experimental Medicine and Biology, 464). $171.00. ISBN 030646117X.

This volume emphasizes the processes by which plants may be transformed or manipulated to produce novel or important chemicals. It also discusses important areas in which plant bioengineering is making important strides such as in the production of salt-tolerant crops and in the production of plants that can fix nitrogen.

639   Shargool, Peter D., and That T. Ngo, eds. *Biotechnological Applications of Plant Cultures.* Boca Raton, FL: CRC, 1994. 214 p. (CRC Series of Current Topics in Plant Molecular Biology). $129.95. ISBN 0849382629.

Covers four broad areas in plant culture techniques: production of secondary plant metabolites, plant cell transformation techniques, breeding and micropropagation techniques, and plant cell and tissue bioreactor design.

640   Singh, Ram J. *Plant Cytogenetics.* 2nd ed. Boca Raton, FL: CRC, 2003. 463 p. $129.95. ISBN 0849323886.

This volume presents an encyclopedic review of plant cytogenetics, the study of the biology of chromosomes and their relation to the transmission of genetic information. Covers classical and modern techniques in the handling of chromosomes, karyotype analysis, and chromosome manipulation in plant research. The new edition includes chapters on genomic *in situ* hybridization and the molecular basis of heredity.

641    Slater, Adrian, Nigel W. Scott, and Mark R. Fowler. *Plant Biotechnology: The Genetic Manipulation of Plants.* New York: Oxford University Press, 2003. 346 p. $49.50 (paper). ISBN 0199254680 (paper).

The aim of this textbook, written by members of the Norman Borlaug Institute for Plant Science Research in Leicester, is to provide the reader with a sound knowledge of plant biotechnology. A third of the book is devoted to explaining the underlying science (the organization of genomes, plant tissue culture, plant transformation techniques), with the rest of the book providing a balanced view of the issues involved in producing genetically modified plants including the economic, social, moral and ethical considerations that surround the subject. Text and illustrations can be downloaded from the companion Web site, http://www.oup.com/uk/booksites/content/0199254680/.

642    Somerville, Chris, and Elliot Meyerowitz, eds. *The Arabidopsis Book (TAB).* Rockville, MD: American Society of Plant Biologists, 2002– . ISSN 1543-8120. URL: http://www.bioone.org/bioone/?request=get-toc&issn=1543-8120.

*The Arabidopsis Book* is an Open Access project that is creating an encyclopedic work on one of the most heavily studied model plant species, *Arabidopsis thaliana*, the first plant fully sequenced. Currently with 47 chapters, the book will eventually have over 100 invited chapters reviewing *Arabidopsis* cellular processes, development, genetics, environmental influences, metabolism, and regulatory processes. The chapter authors are committed to frequently update the materials, either by themselves or having others do so. With copious references and hyperlinks, *TAB* is a pioneer in what scholarly resources can be. BioOne freely provides both HTML and PDF versions of each chapter and has implemented a search interface.

643    Trigiano, Robert N., and Dennis J. Gray. *Plant Tissue Culture Concepts and Laboratory Exercises.* 2nd ed. Boca Raton, FL: CRC, 2000. 454 p. $89.95. ISBN 0849320291.

Meant to serve as a primary text for both introductory and advanced plant biotechnology and tissue culture courses, this book intersperses chapters on the basic concepts that underlie tissue culture with chapters devoted to the hands-on laboratory protocols for a particular procedure. Includes basic methods as well as propagation techniques such as shoot organogenesis, suspension cultures, somatic embryogenesis, and transformation technologies. Extensive and well written, this book is widely used by students as well as lay practitioners.

# Associations

American Society of Plant Biologists (ASPB).
See chapter 9 for full annotation. Publishes *Plant Cell*, the most prestigious journal devoted to plant molecular biology studies.

644    Donald Danforth Plant Science Center. 975 North Warson Road, St. Louis, Missouri 63132. Phone: 314-587-1000. URL: http://www.danforthcenter.org/.
Founded in 1998, the Donald Danforth Plant Science Center is a not-for-profit plant research institute composed of 14 laboratories with a mission to improve the human condition by enhancing the nutritional content of plants or to explore novel uses of plants. Current research areas include computational and structural biology, biochemistry, phytochemistry, physiology, genetics, cell biology, and root biology. Sponsors a weekly seminar series as well as an annual symposium.

645    European Plant Science Organization (EPSO). Technologiepark 927, B-9052 Gent, Belgium. Phone: 32 93 313 810. Fax: 32 93 313 811. E-mail: epso@psb.ugent.be. URL: http://www.epsoweb.org/.
EPSO is an independent body that represents 54 research institutions from 23 European countries. The group was set up in 2000, and its top priorities include facilitating an understanding of modern plant molecular biology, boosting funding for basic plant science and coordinating research activities on national, E. U. levels and beyond. It sponsors a biennial five-day conference.

646    Genetics Society of America. 9650 Rockville Pike, Bethesda, MD 20814-3998. Phone: 301-634-7300. Fax: 301-634-7079. E-mail: Elaine Strass, Executive Director, estrass@genetics-gsa.org. URL: http://www.genetics-gsa.org/.
Founded in 1931, the Genetics Society of America includes over 4,000 scientists and educators interested in the field of genetics. The Society publishes the journal *Genetics* and sponsors scientific meetings focused on key organisms widely used in genetic research, including a fungal conference.

647    Institute of Plant Sciences. Federal Institute of Technology LFW, Universitätsstrasse 2, CH-8092 Zürich, Switzerland. Phone: 41 0 1 632 11 11. Fax: 41 0 1 632 10 37. URL: http://www.ipw.ethz.ch/.
Established in 1986, this Swiss institute integrates basic research in the physiology, biochemistry and development of plants, and gene technology with modern agricultural concerns in the areas of plant biology, crop science, and phytomedicine. There are currently over 200 research and support staff at the Institute.

648    International Association for Plant Tissue Culture and Biotechnology. c/o Professor Zhi-hong Xu, President, Office of the President, Peking University, Beijing 100871 China. Phone: 86 10 6275 1200. Fax: 86 10 6275 1207. E-mail: xuzh@pku.edu.cn. URL: http://www.genetics.ac.cn/iaptcb.htm.

The primary activities of the Association have been to organize quadrennial congresses of plant tissue culture and biotechnology, and to publish a newsletter for its membership. Its news is reported as part of the *In Vitro Report*, published by the Society for *In Vitro* Biology. Formerly International Council for Plant Tissue Culture.

649    International Plant Genetics Resources Institute (IPGRI). IPGRI Headquarters, Via dei Tre Denari 472/a, 00057 MACCARESE (Fiumicino), Italy. Phone: 39 06 6118.1. Fax: 39 06 61979661. E-mail: ipgri@cgiar.org. URL: http://www.ipgri.cgiar.org/.

*IPGRI* is an international research institute that focuses on the conservation and use of genetic resources important to developing countries. Its publications such as *Geneflow, Descriptors for . . .* , proscribe how information about varieties should be gathered. It is a Centre of the Consultative Group on International Agricultural Research (CGIAR) and was founded in 1974 as the International Board for Plant Genetic Resources (IBPGR).

650    International Society for Plant Molecular Biology (ISPMB). University of Georgia, Biochemistry Department, Athens, GA 30602-7229. Phone: 706-542-3239. Fax: 706-542-2090. E-mail: ldure@arches.uga.edu. URL: http://www.uga.edu/~ispmb/.

Founded in 1982, *ISPMB* has about 1,850 members. Publishes *Plant Molecular Biology Reporter* and is affiliated with *Plant Molecular Biology*. Sponsors a triennial international congress.

651    John Innes Centre. Norwich Research Park, Colney, Norwich, NR4 7UH, U. K. Telephone: 44 0 1603 450000. FAX: 44 0 1603 450045. E-mail: sce.mail@bbsrc.ac.uk. URL: http://www.jic.bbsrc.ac.uk/.

The John Innes Centre, located on the Norwich Research Park (U. K.), is an international center for research in plant and microbial science. There are about 900 staff at the Centre, including over 150 Ph.D.-level research scientists. The scientific research at the Centre makes use of a wide range of disciplines in the biological and chemical sciences, including cell biology, biochemistry, chemistry, genetics and molecular biology, understanding and exploitation of plants and microbes, with special emphasis on yield and productivity, quality and valuable products, and environmental interactions.

652    Max Planck Institute of Molecular Plant Physiology (Max-Planck-Institut für Molekulare Pflanzenphysiologie). Am Mühlenberg 1, 14476 Potsdam-Golm, Germany. Phone: +49 (331) 567 80. Fax: +49 (331) 567 8408. E-mail: contact@mpimp-golm.mpg.de. URL: http://www.mpimp-golm.mpg.de/.

Established in 1992 as one of 18 new Max Planck Institutes created since German reunification, this Institute, composed of over 250 researchers, staff, and students, studies the dynamics of plant metabolism and physiology in the context of the plant system as a whole.

653    MSU-DOE Plant Research Lab. Michigan State University. East Lansing, MI 48824-1312. Phone: 517-353-2270. Fax: 517-353-9168. E-mail: prl@.msu.edu. URL: http://www.prl.msu.edu/.

Established in 1965 on the campus of Michigan State University with the objective of bringing together a group of experimental plant biologists to work cooperatively on long-term, multidisciplinary plant research problems. To provide stable research funding, the U. S. Department of Energy (DOE) provides a substantial amount of financial support to the PRL on a continuing basis. There are currently 11 faculty and over 80 research staff and students affiliated with the Lab.

654    Society for *In Vitro* Biology. 13000-F York Road, #304, Charlotte, NC 28278. Phone: 704-588-1923 or 888-588-1923. Fax: 704-588-5193. E-mail: sivb@sivb.org. URL: http://www.sivb.org/.

The mission of the Society for *In Vitro* Biology is to foster the exchange of knowledge of the *in vitro* biology of cells, tissues, and organs from both plants and animals (including humans), though the focus is decidedly in favor of non-plant culture. In addition to the usual organization information and online bookstore, the home page of the Society includes a library of films and videos for rental.

655    TIGR: The Institute for Genomic Research. Rockville, MD, 1999. URL: http://www.tigr.org/.

Founded in 1992, The Institute for Genomic Research (TIGR) is a nonprofit research institute whose primary research interests are in structural, functional, and comparative analysis of genomes and gene products from a wide variety of organisms including plants. Currently it has the primary *Arabidopsis thaliana* database, which provides access to genomic sequence data and annotations generated at TIGR and assemblies of *Arabidopsis* ESTs (expressed sequence tags) from worldwide sequencing projects. TIGR also has sequence and other databases for rice, potato, maize, loblolly pine, and *Medicago truncatula* (the model legume). Additionally, TIGR houses the Plant Repeat database. Besides the databases, TIGR also provides lists of publicly accessible microarray resources, free gene analysis software tools, protocols, and much more.

# References

National Science Foundation. 2000. Nifty 50. URL: http://www.nsf.gov/od/lpa/nsf50/nsfoutreach/htm/home.htm.

United States Congress. Senate Committee on Agriculture, Nutrition, and Forestry. 2000. *Agricultural research and development: Hearings before the Committee on Agriculture, Nutrition, and Forestry, United States Senate, One Hundred Sixth Congress, First Session ... October 6, 7, 1999.* Washington: U. S. Government Printing Office. URL: http://agriculture.senate.gov/Hearings/Hearings_1999/wit99106.htm.

# 9
# Plant Physiology and Phytochemistry

Plant physiology is the study of how plants function; that is, how they germinate, grow, develop, reproduce, and die. It is how they capture the sun's energy and use that energy to convert carbon dioxide into the organic compounds required by most other organisms on earth. It is the study of how plant hormones regulate plant development, how plants obtain nutrients and water from the soil and distribute these throughout the plants, how plants can survive the harshest environmental conditions, and much more. Plant physiologists have traditionally used the tools of biochemistry, cell biology, tissue culture, physics, and anatomy to study plants. Recently new research directions and experimental procedures have been created by the boom in genetic engineering and in particular with completion of the *Arabidopsis* (The Arabidopsis Genome Initiative, 2000) and rice (Goff et al., 2002, and Yu et al., 2002) genomic sequences. *Arabidopsis*, a small, mustard-like plant, is used to study the physiology and genetics of plants due to its short life cycle and its ability to be manipulated genetically. Although not well known outside of the scientific community, *Arabidopsis* is the model organism for plant research, and research findings based on its genome will be used to solve problems with many agronomically important plants.

The resources in this chapter have, by and large, been restricted to those that deal with nonagricultural plant physiology or biochemistry. Another body of literature exists about crop physiology, which includes plant pathology, and the reader is referred to the recent chapter on field crops (Clark, 2002) for additional resources of an agronomic nature. Similarly, for the most part phytochemical resources have been restricted to those that deal with the biochemistry of plants or with the unique phytochemicals that plants contain. No attempt has been made to review the pharmacological literature, though some of these resources may be found in chapter 5, Ethnobotany.

**177**

For related resources, the reader is advised to review the resources listed in chapter 8 that deal with molecular biology, plant tissue culture, and biotechnology. Additionally, the plant development titles listed in chapter 7 will be of interest.

The primary bibliographic databases for plant physiology and phytochemistry are *CAB Abstracts, Biological Abstracts,* and *AGRICOLA.* One will also find that Thompson ISI's *Web of Science (Science Citation Index Expanded)* covers this topic well. For the phytochemical references, one would also want to consult *Chemical Abstracts.* These bibliographic resources have been thoroughly described in chapter 2.

## Bibliographies and Guides to the Literature

656   *Lynn Index: A Bibliography of Phytochemistry.* Vol. 1–8. Various locations: various publishers, 1957–1974.

This bibliography covers the literature of phytochemistry from 1560 to the present and is based on the citation collection of Dr. Eldin V. Lynn. The materials are arranged taxonomically; each section includes botany descriptions, constituents, and references for each order or family. Volume 8 provides a cumulative index for orders and families. The bibliography was variously published by the Massachusetts College of Pharmacy, University of Pittsburgh, and University of Illinois College of Pharmacy.

657   Orr, Larry and Govindjee. *Photosynthesis and the Web: 2005.* URL: http://porphy.la.asu.edu/photosyn/photoweb/.

Originally published in *Photosynthesis Research* 68:1–28 (2001), this comprehensive, updated site pulls together photosynthesis sites on the Web. Among the key resources listed are Web sites for photosynthetic research groups, the history of photosynthesis and the Nobel Prizes related to it, chloroplasts and pigments, and bacterial photosynthesis. Particularly rich is the list of research sites related to the dark (carbon) and light reactions. Additionally resources are listed for K–12 including protocols for classroom experiments. Finally, key photosynthetic journals, book series, and societies are listed.

## Serials

### General Serials

658   *Biochimica et Biophysica Acta (BBA).* Vol. 1– . Amsterdam, the Netherlands: Elsevier, 1947– . Irregular. $15,599.00. ISSN 0006-3002. Available electronically.

659    *Journal of Biological Chemistry (JBC).* Vol. 1– . Bethesda, MD: American Society for Biochemistry and Molecular Biology, 1905– . Weekly. $4,175.00. ISSN 0021-9258. Available electronically.

660    *Journal of Natural Products.* Vol. 42– . Washington, DC: American Chemical Society and American Society of Pharmacognosy, 1979– . Monthly. $704.00. ISSN 0163-3864. Available electronically.
Formerly *Lloydia.*

661    *Journal of Photochemistry and Photobiology. B: Biology (JPP).* Vol. 1– . Amsterdam, the Netherlands: Elsevier, 1987– . Monthly. $3,008.00. ISSN 1011-1344. Available electronically.
Formerly part of the *Journal of Photochemistry.*

662    *Methods.* Vol. 1– . New York: Elsevier, 1990– . Monthly. $403.00. ISSN 1046-2023. Available electronically.
Formerly *Methods: A Companion to Methods in Enzymology.*

663    *Methods in Enzymology.* Vol. 1– . St. Louis, MO: Elsevier Health Science, 1955– . Irregular. Price varies. ISSN 0076-6879. Available electronically.

664    *Photochemistry and Photobiology.* Vol. 1– . Lawrence, KS: Allen Press for the American Society for Photobiology. 1962– . Monthly. $610.00. ISSN 0031-8655. Available electronically.

*Proceedings of the National Academy of Sciences of the United States of America (PNAS).*
See chapter 2 for full annotation.

## Botanical Serials

665    *Advances in Photosynthesis and Respiration.* Vol. 1– . Dordrecht, the Netherlands: Kluwer Academic, 1994– . Irregular. Price varies. ISSN 1572-0233.
Each volume of this comprehensive series focuses on some aspect of photosynthesis and respiration research. Recent volumes have included *Respiration in Archaea and Bacteria: Diversity of Prokaryotic Electron Transport Carriers*; *Photosynthesis in Algae; Light-harvesting Antennas in Photosynthesis;* and *Photosynthetic Nitrogen Assimilation and Associated Carbon and Respiratory Metabolism.* Series formerly titled *Advances in Photosynthesis.*

666    *Annual Plant Reviews.* Vol. 1– . Boca Raton, FL: CRC, 1998– . Irregular. Price varies. ISSN 1460-1494.

Each volume focuses on a specific topic in plant physiology, biochemistry, cell biology, or molecular biology. Recent volumes include Volume 8 (2003), *The Plant Cell Wall*; Volume 9 (2003), *Golgi Apparatus and the Plant Secretory Pathway*; Volume 10 (2004), *The Plant Cytoskeleton in Cell Differentiation and Development*; Volume 11 (2004), *Plant–Pathogen Interactions*; and Volume 12 (2004), *Polarity in Plants*.

667   *Annual Review of Plant Biology*. Vol. 53– . Palo Alto, CA: Annual Reviews, 2002– . Annual. $231.00. ISSN 1040-2519. Available electronically.

This series is addressed to the advanced student doing research in plant biochemistry, physiology, or molecular biology. There are subject and author indexes for each volume. All articles have extensive literature references. This series has the highest Impact Factor ranking in the plant sciences category in *Journal Citation Reports*. The first chapter in many volumes features a historical reminiscence by a preeminent researcher, often near the time of his or her retirement, and as such can be consulted as a historical source. The Web version has an image capture search, which allows one to search the *Annual Review* series for images that match given text. Formerly *Annual Review of Plant Physiology and Plant Molecular Biology*.

668   *Brazilian Journal of Plant Physiology*. Vol. 14– . Londrina, Brazil: Brazilian Society of Plant Physiology, 2002– . 3 times per year. $75.00. ISSN 1677-0420. Available electronically.

The official journal of the Brazilian Society of Plant Physiology, this journal publishes papers, short communications, and mini-reviews. Issued online for free as part of *SciELO* at http://www.scielo.br/scielo.php/. Formerly *Revista Brasileira de Fisiologia Vegetal*.

*Critical Reviews in Plant Sciences.*

See chapter 2 for full annotation. Provides substantive reviews in plant biochemistry, molecular biology, plant physiology, and other areas.

*Current Opinion in Plant Biology.*

See chapter 2 for full annotation. Includes review articles for physiology and metabolism, cell signaling and gene regulation, and cell biology. Often a single issue will be devoted to one of these areas.

*Environmental and Experimental Botany.*

See chapter 2 for full annotation. Publishes many articles dealing with the physiology of plant adaptation to environmental stressors.

669   *Functional Plant Biology, FPB*. Vol. 29– . East Melbourne, Australia: CSIRO, 2002– . Monthly. $1,135.00. ISSN 1445-4408. Available electronically.

A journal for research and review articles in plant biochemistry, biophysics, developmental biology, cell and molecular biology, and plantenvironment and plantmicrobe interactions. Formerly *Australian Journal of Plant Physiology.*

670   *Indian Journal of Plant Physiology: Official Publication of the Indian Society for Plant Physiology.* Vol. 1– . New Delhi, India: Indian Society for Plant Physiology, 1958– . Quarterly. $140.00. ISSN 0019-5502.

Publishes research in the fields of plant physiology, genetics, horticulture, biochemistry, agronomy, soil science, and other sciences that are of interest to plant physiology. Contributions are not dependent on membership in the Indian Society for Plant Physiology.

671   *Journal of Experimental Botany.* Vol. 1– . Oxford, England: Oxford University Press, 1950– . 14 times per year. $1,366.00. ISSN 0022-0957. Available electronically.

Published for the Society for Experimental Botany and designated as an official journal of the Federation of European Societies of Plant Biology. The journal acts as a medium for the publication of original papers and occasional review articles in the field of plant physiology, biochemistry, biophysics, and related topics. Book reviews form a part of each issue.

672   *Journal of Plant Biochemistry and Biotechnology.* Vol. 1– . New Delhi, India: Society for Plant Biochemistry and Biotechnology, Indian Agricultural Research Institute, 1992– . Semiannually. $250.00. ISSN 0971-7811.

Publishes primary research in all areas of plant biochemistry, mostly from the Indian subcontinent.

673   *Journal of Plant Growth Regulation.* Vol. 1– . New York: Springer-Verlag, 1982– . Quarterly. $588.00. ISSN 0721-7595. Available electronically.

Published in cooperation with the International Plant Growth Substances Association, this journal accepts research papers using hormonal, physiological, environmental, genetic, biophysical, developmental, or molecular approaches to the study of plant growth regulation. Beginning in 2000, each issue is devoted to a particular theme, with articles invited by the issue editor.

674   *Journal of Plant Physiology.* Vol. 115– . New York: Elsevier, 1984– . Monthly. $1,620.00. ISSN 0176-1617. Available electronically.

This international journal of plant physiology is published in affiliation with the Federation of European Societies of Plant Biology (FESPB), the Spanish Society of Plant Physiology, and the Portuguese Society of Plant Physiology. It publishes original articles, short communications, and reviews on all aspects of plant physiology, biochemistry, molecular biology, and the basic aspects of plant biotechnology. All articles are in English. Formerly *Zeitschrift für Pflanzen-physiologie,* 1909–1983, and incorporated *Biochemie und Physiologie der Pflanzen (BPP)* in 1993.

675   *Journal of Plant Research.* Vol. 106– . Tokyo, Japan: Springer-Verlag for the Botanical Society of Japan, 1993– . Bimonthly. $343.00. ISSN 0918-9440. Available electronically.

Publishes articles, short communications, and mini-reviews in all areas of the plant sciences, but most are in the area of plant physiology or biochemistry. Formerly *The Botanical Magazine, Tokyo.*

676   *Photosynthesis Research.* Vol. 1– . Dordrecht, the Netherlands: Kluwer Academic, 1980– . Monthly. $1,718.00. ISSN 0166-8595. Available electronically.

Published in conjunction with the International Society of Photosynthesis Research, this international journal publishes papers dealing with both basic and applied aspects of photosynthesis.

677   *Photosynthetica.* Vol. 1– . Dordrecht, the Netherlands: Kluwer Academic, 1967– . Quarterly. $868.00. ISSN 0300-3604. Available electronically.

Devoted to the biochemical, biophysical, and ecological investigation of photosynthesis in plants. Sponsored by the Institute of Experimental Biology of the Czechoslovak Academy of Sciences.

678   *Physiologia Plantarum.* Vol. 1– . Oxford, England: Blackwell, 1948– . Monthly. $909.00. ISSN 0031-9317. Available electronically.

An official journal of the Federation of European Societies of Plant Biology, this is published on behalf of the Scandinavian Society for Plant Physiology. The journal publishes papers in English on experimental plant biology research concerning the physiological, molecular, and ecological mechanisms that govern plant development and growth. Besides the standard research reports, it also has topical mini-reviews and technological focus papers.

679   *Phytochemical Analysis.* Vol. 1– . New York: Wiley, 1990– . Bimonthly. $1,400.00. ISSN 0958-0344. Available electronically.

Publishes articles on the utilization of analytical methodology in the plant sciences. The spectrum of coverage is broad, covering the analysis of whole plants, plant cells, tissues and organs, plant-derived extracts, and plant products. All forms of physical, chemical, biochemical, spectroscopic, and chromato-graphic investigations of plant products are included.

680   *Phytochemistry.* Vol. 1– . New York: Elsevier, 1961– . Semimonthly. $4,391.00. ISSN 0031-9422. Available electronically.

An international journal of plant biochemistry and an official organ of the Phytochemical Society of Europe and the Phytochemical Society of North America. This journal publishes research on all aspects of pure and applied plant biochemistry, especially that which leads to an understanding of the factors underlying the growth, development, and metabolism of plants and the chemistry of plant constituents. The journal is divided into eight sections: review articles, protein biochemistry, molecular genetics and genomics, metabolism, ecological biochemistry, chemotaxonomy, bioactive products, and chemistry (including macromolecules).

681   *Phytochemistry Reviews.* Vol. 1– . Dordrecht, the Netherlands: Kluwer Academic, 2002– . 3 times per year. $315.00. ISSN 1568-7767. Available electronically.

Publishes papers that result from meetings of the Phytochemical Society of Europe. Each issue is devoted to a particular topic dealing with some aspect of the biochemistry of plants, biosynthesis of compounds by plants, or the application of such knowledge in agriculture and industry. Recent issues have featured articles on topics such as isotopic methods for studying plant metabolism; methods used to find pharmacologically active compounds in plants; dietary phytochemicals; and use of plants as biochemical factories.

682   *Plant and Cell Physiology.* Vol. 1– . Oxford, England: Oxford University Press. 1959– . Monthly. $672.00. ISSN 0032-0781. Available electronically.

Published for the Japanese Society of Plant Physiologists, the scope of this international journal includes papers pertaining to the physiology, biochemistry, biophysics, chemistry, genetics, molecular biology, gene engineering, and cell engineering of plants and microorganisms. The text is in English. Besides regular papers, invited mini-reviews and rapid communications are also published.

683   *Plant and Soil.* Vol. 1– . Dordrecht, the Netherlands: Kluwer Academic, 1948– . 20 times per year. $4,285.00. ISSN 0032-079X. Available electronically.

Issued under the auspices of the Royal Netherlands Society of Agricultural Science. Contains original papers and solicited review articles dealing with the interface of plant biology and soil sciences including mineral nutrition, plant-water relations, symbiotic and pathogenic plantmicrobe interactions, root anatomy and morphology, soil biology, ecology, agrochemistry, and agrophysics.

*Plant Biology.*
See chapter 2 for full annotation. Publishes in all areas of plant biology including physiology, molecular biology, cell biology, development, and genetics.

684   *Plant, Cell and Environment.* Vol. 1– . Oxford, England: Blackwell, 1978– . Monthly. $3,100.00. ISSN 0140-7791. Available electronically.

Includes key papers that explore the ways that plants respond to their environment from the molecular to the community level. Covers plant biochemistry, molecular biology, biophysics, cell physiology, whole plant physiology, crop physiology, and physiological ecology, together with structural, genetic, pathological, and meteorological aspects as related to plant function.

685   *Plant Cell Reports.* Vol. 1– . New York: Springer-Verlag, 1981– . Monthly. $1,795.00. ISSN 0721-7714. Available electronically.

This journal presents original research results dealing with new advances in plant cell biology including morphogenesis, genetic transformation and hybridization, genetics, genomics, physiology, and biochemistry. Of particular interest is research dealing with stress tolerance mechanisms.

686   *Plant Growth Regulation.* Vol. 1– . Dordrecht, the Netherlands: Kluwer Academic, 1982– . 9 times per year. $908.00. ISSN 0167-6903. Available electronically.

Offers original research dealing with plant hormones; the chemical, molecular, and environmental regulation of plant growth and development; and plant responses to abiotic stressors such as high salinity.

687   *Plant Physiology.* Vol. 1– . Rockville, MD: American Society of Plant Biologists, 1926– . Monthly. $2160.00 ISSN 0032-0889. Available electronically.

Devoted to physiology, biochemistry, cellular and molecular biology, biophysics, and the environmental biology of plants. Full-length papers and short communications reporting research in all phases of plant physiology are considered for publication. Supplements to the journal record abstracts of papers presented at the annual meeting of the society. *Plant Physiology* is one of the oldest and most well-respected plant science journals. Price bundled with *Plant Cell* (see chapter 8 for full annotation).

688   *Plant Physiology and Biochemistry.* Vol. 25– . Amsterdam, the Netherlands: Elsevier, 1987– . Monthly. $740.00. ISSN 0981-9428. Available electronically.

An official journal of the Federation of European Societies of Plant Physiology and the French Society of Plant Physiology (Société Française de Physiologie Végétale), publishing research in physiology, biochemistry, molecular biology, biophysics, structure, and genetics at levels from the molecular to the whole plant and environment. Continues *Physiologie Végétale*.

689    *Plant Science*. Vol. 38– . Limerick, Ireland: Elsevier, 1985– . Monthly. $3,683.00. ISSN 0168-9452. Available electronically.

An international journal of experimental plant biology that quickly publishes papers in plant physiology, biochemistry, genetics, molecular biology, cell biology, and related areas, as well as fundamental work in these areas related to agriculture and phytopathology. Formerly *Plant Science Letters.*

*Planta.*

See chapter 2 for full annotation. This international journal publishes original articles and rapid communications in all aspects of plant biology but is especially rich is physiology papers.

690    *Recent Advances in Phytochemistry*. Vol. 1– . New York: Elsevier, 1968– . Irregular. Price varies. ISSN 0079-9920.

This monographic series contains papers from the annual meeting of the Phytochemical Society of North America. Each volume covers a different topic; for example, a recent meeting was devoted to genomics, resulting in Volume 36 (2002), *Phytochemistry in the Genomics and Post-Genomics Eras.*

691    *Tree Physiology*. Vol. 1– . Victoria, Canada: Heron, 1986– . 18 times per year. $1,224.00. ISSN 0829-318X. Available electronically.

International journal publishing research reports and technical reviews on all aspects of the physiology of trees. It is usually the most highly ranked forestry title, according to ISI's *Journal Citation Reports.*

*Trends in Plant Science.*

See chapter 2 for full annotation. Publishes short, authoritative review articles on basic research topics including physiology, genetics, and molecular biology. Other titles in the *Trends in . . .* series that are also of interest to physiologists and plant biochemists include *Trends in Biochemical Sciences, Trends in Biotechnology,* and *Trends in Cell Biology.*

# Dictionaries and Encyclopedias

692    *Encyclopedia of Plant Physiology, New Series*. New York: Springer-Verlag, 1975–1993. 20 vol. Price varies.

This monographic review series surveys all aspects of plant physiology such as photosynthesis, respiration, nutrition, hormones, photomorphogenesis, plant carbohydrates, physiological plant ecology, and secondary products, devoting one or more volumes to each topic. The volumes on nucleic acids and hormonal control are quite dated but the volumes on other topics still contain valuable information. The new series, in English, continues the older series, in German, *Handbuch der Pflanzenphysiologie*, Volume 1–18 (1955–1967). A General Index, Volume 20, covers both series.

693    Glasby, J. S. *Dictionary of Plants Containing Secondary Metabolites.* New York: Taylor and Francis, 1991. 488 p. ISBN 0850664233.

Plants that are known sources of organic chemicals are listed in this dictionary, along with the classes of compounds that have been extracted from them and references to the original reports. An index of the compounds is also included. The plants are listed by scientific name, with family given for some genera. The dictionary covers the literature up to 1987.

694    Harborne, Jeffrey B., Herbert Baxter, and Gerard P. Moss. *Phytochemical Dictionary: A Handbook of Bioactive Compounds from Plants.* 2nd ed. Philadelphia: Taylor and Francis, 1999. 976 p. $579.95. ISBN 0748406204.

This dictionary covers over 3,000 substances that occur in plants, both primary and secondary metabolites. Compounds include insect deterrents, carcinogens, phytoalexins, and many others. Information for each compound includes synonyms, structure, molecular weight and formula, natural occurrence, biological activity, and uses. The second edition has added Chemical Abstract Service Registry Numbers, which allows one to find specific references for entries.

# Handbooks and Methods

695    Blum, Abraham. *PlantStress.* URL: http://www.plantstress.com/.

Supported by the Rockefeller Foundation, *PlantStress* is focused on topics related to abiotic plant stressors such as drought, heat, mineral deficiency, salinity, cold, mineral toxicity, oxidation, and water logging. For each of the stressors, the physiological impact is described, agricultural management and plant resistance strategies are outlined, and references are given to recent research. Articles and links are available for genetic resources and for the genetic engineering of plant resistance traits. This site also offers a bibliographic reference database on plant stress. News, announcements, meeting information, and a bulletin board are also available.

696    Dashek, William V., ed. *Methods in Plant Biochemistry and Molecular Biology.* Boca Raton, FL: CRC, 1997. 457 p. $129.95. ISBN 0849394805.

Designed for the trained scientist performing research in a college or commercial laboratory, this manual provides an assemblage of research protocols and cited literature references. Included are such biochemical methods as how to isolate and analyze plant lipids, nucleic acids, phytochemicals, and hormones; physiological methods such as how to measure oxygen uptake or deduce hormone pathways; and molecular biology techniques such as constructing a cDNA library, performing plant transformations, and using antisense RNA to manipulate gene expression.

697   Ehrhardt, David. *Plant Cell Imaging*. Stanford, CA: Carnegie Institute of Washington, Department of Biology, Stanford University. URL: http:// deepgreen.stanford.edu/index.html.

This site offers images and videos of living plant cells and cell components using genetic fluorescent molecular tags and laser scanning confocal microscopy. Fluorescent tags have been developed for cell surfaces, vacuolar membranes, endoplasmic reticulum surfaces, nuclear structures, chromosomes, and more. The Web site also discusses the equipment and methods used when working with green fluorescent protein (GFP).

698   Harborne, Jeffrey B. *Phytochemical Methods: A Guide to Modern Techniques of Plant Analysis*. 3rd ed. New York: Chapman and Hall, 1998. 302 p. $173.00; $55.00 (paper). ISBN 0412572605; 0412572702 (paper).

This authoritative reference is intended for students and researchers as a guide to recommended phytochemical techniques. Chapters describe methods for identifying phenolic compounds, terpenoids, organic acids and related compounds, nitrogen compounds, endogenous growth regulators, sugars and their derivatives, and macromolecules. This edition includes modern methods such as HPLC and NMR, which are being used to screen for substances of pharmacological interest as well as of taxonomic interest. Appendixes provide a checklist of thin layer chromatography procedures for all classes of plant substances and a list of useful addresses for rare chemicals, chromatographic equipment, and spectrophotometers. It also includes an important bibliographic guide to specialized texts.

699   Hawes, C. R., and Béatrice Satiat-Jeunemaitre, eds. *Plant Cell Biology: A Practical Approach*. 2nd ed. New York: Oxford University Press, 2001. 338 p. (Practical Approach Series, 250). $49.50 (paper). ISBN 0199638667; 0199638659 (paper).

It is increasingly important to be able to localize intracellular proteins and macromolecules in plant cells. This second edition covers established techniques such as classical histochemistry and electron microscopy as well as newer methods such as the application of fluorescent probes, cytometry, expression systems, the use of green fluorescent protein, micromanipulation, and electrophysiological techniques. There are also chapters on the isolation of cytoplasmic organelles and macromolecular location procedures involving immunocyto-chemistry and *in situ* hybridization.

700    Keegstra, Kenneth, coord. *WallBioNet—Plant Cell Wall Biosynthesis Research Network*. URL: http://xyloglucan.prl.msu.edu/.

Developed at the MSU-DOE Plant Research Laboratory and funded by the National Science Foundation (NSF) as part of its research coordination program, the *WallBioNet* Web site was established to promote cooperation among researchers studying various aspects of plant cell wall biosynthetic genes and to define the roles of the cell wall in plant growth, development, and defense. The site includes a database with information on wall biosynthetic genes, wall component mutants and knockout lines, antibodies to wall components and biosynthetic proteins, and sugar nucleotide donors. See also *Plant Cell Walls*, from the Complex Carbohydrate Research Center, University of Georgia (http://www.ccrc.uga.edu/~mao/cellwall/main.htm), and *Cell Wall,* hosted by the Carnegie Institution of Washington (http://cellwall.stanford.edu/).

*Methods in Enzymology.*

See above, in General Serials, for full annotation. This valuable series frequently has volumes or chapters that deal with plant topics. The title is a misnomer, because the series deals with the whole of biochemistry, from molecular biology, nucleotides, and pigments to organellar isolation and photosynthesis. Indexed in *PubMed/MEDLINE.*

701    *Methods in Plant Biochemistry*. San Diego: Academic Press, 1989–1997. 11 vol. Price varies. ISSN 1059-7522.

Each volume of this series provides comprehensive, practical information on the assays and analytical techniques appropriate for a particular family of plant compounds.

702    Polya, Gideon Maxwell. *Biochemical Targets of Plant Bioactive Compounds: A Pharmacological Reference Guide to Sites of Action and Biological Effects*. New York: Taylor and Francis, 2003. 847 p. $199.95. ISBN 0415308291.

In this reference guide to the biochemical targets of plant defensive compounds, the author has categorized plant natural products into 14 broad biochemical target areas. Information on plant bioactive compounds and their producing organism has been collated from *PubMed; Biological Abstracts*; and major reference compendia such as the *Phytochemical Dictionary* (Harborne), the *Merck Index,* and *Dr. Duke's Phytochemical and Ethnobotanical Databases* (see chapter 5 for full annotation). With 500 pages of tables, it presents a mine of succinctly summarized information relating to the structures of bioactive compounds, plant sources, biochemical targets, and physiological effects that can be readily accessed via chemical compound, plant name (scientific and common), and subject indexes. The appendix has chemical line drawings of key parent compounds. It includes an extensive bibliography and comprehensive indexing.

703    Raffauf, Robert Francis. *A Handbook of Alkaloids and Alkaloid-Containing Plants.* New York: Wiley. 1970. 1 vol. ISBN 0471704784.

This reference is a compilation of data concerning plant alkaloids and their distribution. The body of the work is a set of tables giving the plant source, formulas, and physical properties of the known alkaloids arranged in alphabetical order of the plant families in which they occur. Data include name and structure, botanical family and genus of origin, molecular formula, molecular weight, melting point, optical rotation, and literature citation.

704    Sigee, David C., et al., eds. *X-Ray Microanalysis in Biology: Experimental Techniques and Applications.* New York: Cambridge University Press, 1993. 337 p. $110.00. ISBN 0521415306.

Up-to-date look at the use of X-ray microanalysis in biology with applications for plant cell physiology. Four main areas are discussed: detection and quantification of X-rays, associated techniques, specimen preparation, and applications.

705    Tucker, G. A., and J. A. Roberts. *Plant Hormone Protocols.* Totowa, NJ: Humana, 2000. 199 p. (Methods in Molecular Biology, 141). $99.50. ISBN 0896035778.

In 12 chapters, the focus of this book is on the tools used to study hormones in plants including how to measure them, how to detect them, and how to determine their mechanism of action. Step-by-step protocols are provided that are suitable for use by the experienced researcher. A basic list of references is provided for each chapter.

706    Walker, John C, Michael Gribskov, and Jeffery Harper. *PlantsP—Functional Genomics of Plant Phosphorylation.* URL: http://plantsp.sdsc.edu/.

*PlantsP* is a database of sequence and functional information for protein kinases and phosphatases in *Arabidopsis thaliana* and other plants. Because protein kinases and phosphatases control hundreds of processes in plants, it was felt that a genome-wide approach was needed to make advances in discovering the roles of these enzymes in the regulation of plant function. Information is searchable by keyword, species, NCBI protein ID, various protein sequence features, or via BLAST. The site also provides abstracts of recent papers on plant protein kinases and related topics.

# Textbooks and Treatises

707   Buchanan, Bob B., Wilhelm Gruissem, and Russell L. Jones, eds. *Biochemistry and Molecular Biology of Plants*. Rockville, MD: American Society of Plant Physiologists, 2000. 1367 p. $213.00; $148.00 (paper). ISBN 0943088372; 0943088399 (paper).

Without a doubt, this is currently the best, most comprehensive book on plant molecular biology and physiology. An essential reference and textbook for plant biologists, this book has integrated molecular biology, cell biology, and plant biochemistry in 24 chapters that are centered around the themes of cell compartmentation, cell reproduction, energetics, metabolism, development, and the responses of plants to environmental factors. Over 50 of the top researchers in their fields contributed to this worthy successor to Bonner and Varner's *Plant Biochemistry*, 3rd edition. Copiously illustrated with figures; online access to the images is available for a fee. There is also a CD-ROM of illustrations available for purchase.

708   Davies, Peter J., ed. *Plant Hormones: Biosynthesis, Signal Transduction, Action!* 3rd ed. New York: Springer, 2004. 700 p. $225.00; $95.00 (paper). ISBN 1402026846; 1402026854 (paper).

This book of 31 chapters, written by 52 international experts, is a summary of all that is known about plant hormones: how they are synthesized and metabolized, how they act at both the organismal and molecular levels, how we measure them, and descriptions of some of the roles they play in regulating plant growth and development. Prospects for the genetic engineering of hormone levels or responses in crop plants are also discussed. Recently updated from the highly acclaimed 1995 text, *Plant Hormones, Physiology, Biochemistry and Molecular Biology*, 2nd edition, it includes a table of genes; fully indexed.

709   De, Deepesh N. *Plant Cell Vacuoles: An Introduction*. Collingwood, Australia: CSIRO, 2000. 288 p. $65.00 (paper). ISBN 0643062548 (paper).

This book is included as one example of many books that focus on a particular plant organelle, detailing and synthesizing the current state of knowledge about the organelle. In this case, the vacuole, a central large sac of enzymes that is responsible for homeostatis and turgor in plant cells, is discussed; other books can be found that focus on the mitochondria, chloroplasts, nuclei, Golgi, cell walls, and more.

710   Dennis, David T., David B. Layzell, Daniel D. Lefebvre, and David H. Turpin, eds. *Plant Metabolism*. 2nd ed. Essex, England: Addison Wesley Longman, 1997. 631 p. ISBN 0582259061 (paper).

With contributions from over 60 research scientists, each chapter integrates what is known on a particular topic from the standpoint of plant biochemistry, molecular biology, and physiology. Topics include metabolism in the cytosol, mitochondria, and chloroplasts; lipid metabolism; and nitrogen metabolism. With the rise of plant metabolomics, a text such as this will provide a valuable frame of reference. The former edition was titled *Plant Physiology, Biochemistry and Molecular Biology*.

711   Dey, Prakash M., Jeffrey B. Harborne, and James F. Bonner, eds. *Plant Biochemistry*. San Diego: Academic, 1997. 554 p. $97.95. ISBN 0122146743.

Written as a replacement for the classic *Plant Biochemistry*, 3rd edition, by Bonner and Varner, and as a distillation and update of Conn and Stumpf's *Biochemistry of Plants*, this book covers the usual plant biochemistry topics such as photosynthesis, plant carbohydrates, plant lipids, gene regulation, and secondary compounds. In addition, it has chapters on biochemical plant pathology, biochemical plant ecology, and plant cell biotechnology.

712   Duke, James A. *Handbook of Biologically Active Phytochemicals and Their Activities*. Boca Raton, FL: CRC, 1992. 183 p. $199.95. ISBN 0849336708.

A compilation of data for 3,000 compounds. Available online, at least in part, as a searchable database as part of *Dr. Duke's Phytochemical and Ethnobotanical Databases* (see chapter 5 for full annotation). Information includes reported activity for each chemical, effective or inhibitory concentrations or doses, and reference sources.

713   Griffin, David H. *Fungal Physiology*. 2nd ed. New York: Wiley-Liss, 1996. 458 p. (Wiley Science Paperback Series). $89.95. ISBN 0471166154.

Integrates physiology and molecular genetics with the biochemistry and development of fungi. For the advanced student.

714   Hall, D. O., and K. K. Rao. *Photosynthesis*. 6th ed. New York: Cambridge University Press, 1999. 214 p. (Studies in Biology series). $24.99 (paper). ISBN 0521642574; 0521644976 (paper).

This highly readable text provides a good overall view of photosynthesis on both the macro- and molecular level. Generously illustrated with diagrams and figures.

715   Hangarter, Roger P. *Plants in Motion*. Bloomington, IN: Indiana University, Department of Biology, 2000. URL: http://sunflower.bio.indiana.edu/~rhangart/plantsinmotion.html.

The *Plants in Motion* Web site features a series of time-lapse movies of plant growth, movement, and behavior in response to various stimuli. Movie categories include germination, photomorphogenesis, phototropism, gravitropism, nastic movements, circadian responses, general growth, flowers, and cellular responses. *Arabidopsis*, morning glory, corn, sunflower, *Mimosa*, and Venus flytrap are among the plants represented in the movie collection.

716   Heldt, Hans-Walter, and Fiona Heldt. *Plant Biochemistry*. San Diego, CA: Elsevier, 2005. 630 p. $73.22. ISBN 0120883910.

Revised and expanded edition of the German text, *Pflanzenbiochemie*, published in 1997. Designed for use as a textbook, it covers the complete range of topics in plant biochemistry from photosynthesis to genetic engineering, including the commercial prospects for plant bioengineering.

717   Hemsley, Alan R., and Imogen Poole, eds. *The Evolution of Plant Physiology: From Whole Plants to Ecosystems*. Boston, MA: Elsevier, 2004. 492 p. (Linnean Society Symposium series, 21). $99.95. ISBN 0123395526.

This interesting book examines the evolution of how plants function as they do on the physical as well as biochemical or molecular level. For example, the evolution of stomata is considered, as is the evolution of strategies for dealing with stress, and much more. The authors use the term *palaeophytophysiology* to describe this type of approach.

718   Hooykaas, Paul J. J., M. A. Hall, and K. R. Libbenga. *Biochemistry and Molecular Biology of Plant Hormones*. New York: Elsevier, 1999. 541 p. (New Comprehensive Biochemistry, 33). $217.00. ISBN 0444898255.

Forty-four experts in plant hormonology wrote this volume that explains the methodologies used to study plant hormones, the current state of knowledge about how they are synthesized, and how they work at the cellular and whole-plant level.

719   Hopkins, William G., and Norman P. A. Hüner. *Introduction to Plant Physiology*. 3rd ed. Hoboken, NJ: Wiley, 2004. 560 p. $110.80. ISBN 0471389153.

This undergraduate textbook blends modern molecular approaches to plant physiology with traditional physiological, biochemical, and environmental plant physiology in order to understand how plants work. In addition to the standard index, it includes an Index of Genes referenced in the text.

Lambers, Hans, F. Stuart Chapin III, and Thijs L. Pons. *Plant Physiological Ecology*.

See chapter 6 for full annotation. Discusses the physiological basis for many plant responses to environmental factors.

Larcher, Walter. *Physiological Plant Ecology: Ecophysiology and Stress Physiology of Functional Groups.* 4th ed.

See chapter 6 for full annotation. Explains how the physiology of plants allows them to adapt to stressful environments such as drought, cold, and heat.

720    Lawlor, David W. *Photosynthesis.* 3rd ed. Oxford, England: BIOS, 2001. 386 p. $59.95; $54.95 (paper). ISBN 1859961576; 0387916075 (paper).

A balanced review of all the photosynthetic components including the electron transport reactions caused by light; the so-called "dark reactions" (the CAM, C3, and C4 chemical reactions); the molecular biology of chloroplasts; the influence of the environment on photosynthesis; and $CO_2$ chemistry. Suitable for advanced undergraduates as well as postgraduates desirous of obtaining an overview of this defining plant process.

721    Lea, Peter J., and Richard C. Leegood. *Plant Biochemistry and Molecular Biology.* 2nd ed. New York: Wiley, 1999. 364 p. $104.00; $74.00 (paper). ISBN 0471976822; 0471976830 (paper).

Frequently used as a resource book in biology, plant physiology, and plant biochemistry courses, this volume succinctly covers the primary plant biochemical topics including photosynthesis, carbohydrates, lipids, nitrogen metabolism, pigments, and secondary metabolism. Additional chapters are included on gene regulation, the molecular control of plant developmental processes such as fruit development and germination, and cell culture technology.

722    Mengel, Konrad, et al. *Principles of Plant Nutrition.* 5th ed. Boston, MA: Kluwer Academic, 2001. 849 p. $404.00. ISBN 079237150X.

A long overdue update (the previous edition was published in 1987), this is a comprehensive reference text for the discipline. Each of the 12 essential nutrients, from nitrogen to molybdenum, has its own chapter. Within each of these chapters, the full spectrum of basic processes and relevant relationships for the nutrient are covered from its availability in the soil, its uptake and movement within the plant, to its physiological and/or biochemical use in the plant. Also covered are deficiency and toxicity effects, where warranted. Well referenced and indexed.

Nicklas, Karl J. *Plant Biomechanics: An Engineering Approach to Plant Form and Function.*

See chapter 7 for full annotation. This book explores how plant biological processes and structures adhere to the physical laws of physics and chemistry.

723    Steward, F. C., ed. *Plant Physiology: A Treatise.* New York: Academic, 1959–1991. 10 vol. in 15.

The volumes in this series are primarily of historical interest. Covered topics include cellular organization, respiration, photosynthesis, nitrogen metabolism, growth and development, hormones, and water and solute movement. There is no overall index.

724　Stumpf, P. K., and E. E. Conn, eds. *The Biochemistry of Plants: A Comprehensive Treatise.* New York: Academic, 1980–1990. 16 vol.

Much of the information is out of date; still this classic series is worth consulting for fundamental plant biochemistry. Volumes include Volume 1, The plant cell; Volume 2, Metabolism and respiration; Volumes 3 and 14, Carbohydrates; Volumes 4 and 9, Lipids; Volume 5, Amino acids and derivatives; Volume 6, Proteins and nucleic acids; Volume 7, Secondary plant products; Volumes 8 and 10, Photosynthesis; Volume 11, Biochemistry of metabolism; Volume 12, Physiology of metabolism; Volume 13, Methodology; Volume 15, Molecular biology; and Volume 16, Intermediary nitrogen metabolism.

725　Taiz, Lincoln, and Eduardo Zeiger. *Plant Physiology.* 3rd ed. Sunderland, MA: Sinauer Associates, 2002. 690 p. $107.95. ISBN 0878938230.

The most frequently used plant physiology textbook for undergraduates; the concepts are clearly written and understandable. The three major parts of the book are devoted to transport and translocation of water and solutes, biochemistry and metabolism, and growth and development. A companion Web site is also available at http://www.plantphys.net/ that, among other things, contains frequently updated essays on emerging areas.

726　Waisel, Yoav, Amram Eshel, and Uzi Kafkafi, eds. *Plant Roots: The Hidden Half.* 3rd ed. New York: Marcel Dekker, 2002. 1,120 p. (Books in Soils, Plants, and the Environment). $250.00. ISBN 0824706315.

This reference presents the latest developments in the study of roots—their origin, structure, development, physiology, genetics, response to stress, soil interactions, and behavior during the production of useful pharmaceuticals and other chemicals. Over 100 specialists contributed chapters for this massive book. Fully indexed, with a separate index of organisms.

727　Willmer, Colin M., and Mark Fricker. *Stomata.* 2nd ed. New York: Chapman and Hall, 1996. 375 p. (Topics in Plant Functional Biology, 2). $239.00; $95.00 (paper). ISBN 0412725002; 0412574306 (paper).

Stomata, small apertures in leaves that regulate gas exchange between a plant and its environment, are highly studied as a key to drought and stress resistance in plants. Although a bit dated, this book synthesizes what was known about stomata and serves as a good starting point for understanding stomatal research.

# Associations

728   American Society for Photobiology (ASP). P. O. Box 1897, Lawrence, KS 66044. Phone: 785-843-1235. Fax: 785-843-1287. E-mail: phot@allenpress.com. URL: http://www.photobiology.org/.

According to its Web site, "The ASP promotes original research in photobiology, facilitates integration of different disciplines in the study of photobiology, promotes dissemination of knowledge of photobiology, and provides information on the photobiological aspects of national and international problems." Publishes *Photochemistry and Photobiology.*

729   American Society of Plant Biologists (ASPB). c/o ASPB, 15501 Monona Dr., Rockville, MD 20855-2768. Phone: 301-251-0560. Fax: 301-279-2996. E-mail: info@aspb.org. URL: http://www.aspb.org/.

The largest professional society of plant scientists interested in physiology, molecular biology, environmental biology, cell biology, and biophysics of plants, and other related matters. Publishes *ASPB Newsletter, Plant Cell,* and *Plant Physiology.* Formerly the American Society of Plant Physiologists.

730   Australian Society of Plant Scientists (ASPS). c/o Professor Hans Lambers, President, School of Plant Biology, Faculty of Natural and Agricultural Sciences, University of Western Australia, Nedlands, WA 6907, Australia. Phone: 61 8 93807381. Fax: 61 8 93801108. E-mail: secretary@plantsci.org.au. URL: http://www.plantsci.org.au/.

The focus of this group is to promote communication between teachers and researchers of plant physiology and molecular biology. An annual conference, ComBio, is organized jointly with one or more of the following societies: the Australian Society for Biochemistry and Molecular Biology, the Australia and New Zealand Society for Cell and Developmental Biology, the New Zealand Society for Biochemistry and Molecular Biology (NZSPP), and the New Zealand Society of Plant Physiologists. Publishes *Phytogen* and *Functional Plant Biology.* Formerly the Australian Society of Plant Physiologists.

731   Canadian Society of Plant Physiologists (CSPP). c/o Dr. Harold Weger, Treasurer, Department of Biology, University of Regina, 3737 Wascana Parkway, Regina SK S4S 0A2. Fax: 306-337-2410. E-mail: treasurer@cspp-scpv.ca. URL: http://cspp-scpv.ca/.

The members' research interests span a broad spectrum, including whole plant physiology, cell biology, metabolism, molecular biology, biotic interactions, plant defense mechanisms, and environmental physiology. The annual meeting is often held in conjunction with related societies such as the American Society of Plant Biologists, the Japanese Society of Plant Physiologists, and the Australian Society of Plant Scientists.

732    Federation of European Societies of Plant Biology (FESPB). c/o Professor Renate Scheibe, Treasurer, Lehrstuhl Pflanzenphysiologie, Fachbereich Biologie/ Chemie, Universität Osnabrück, Barbarastraße 11, D-49069 Osnabrück, Germany. Phone: +49 541 9692284. Fax: +48 541 9692265. E-mail: scheibe@ biologie.uni-osnabrueck.de. URL: http://www.fespb.org/.

The aims of FESPB are to advance research, education, and the exchange of information among plant biologists within Europe and beyond; and to support the publication of the results of research through its five affiliated international journals: *Journal of Experimental Botany, Journal of Plant Physiology, Plant Physiology and Biochemistry, Functional Plant Biology,* and *Physiologia Plantarum.* FESPB also publishes a newsletter, *FESPBAlert,* which is available at the Web site. Formerly Federation of European Societies of Plant Physiology.

733    International Association for Plant Physiology (IAPP). c/o Dr. Donald R. Ort, President, Plant Biology Department, University of Illinois, 190 ERML, 1201 W. Gregory Drive, Urbana, IL 61801-3838. E-mail: d-ort@life.uiuc.edu.

National and regional societies of plant physiologists. Publishes a newsletter.

734    International Society of Photosynthesis Research (ISPR). c/o Robert E. Blankenship, President, Department of Chemistry and Biochemistry, Arizona State University, Tempe, AZ 85287-1604. Phone: 1-480-965-4430. Fax: 1-480-965-2747. E-mail: Blankenship@asu.edu. URL: http://www .photosynthesisresearch.org.

The purposes of ISPR are to encourage and to promote the growth and development of photosynthesis as a pure and applied science and to facilitate publication of topics relating to the study of photosynthesis. Publishes *Photosynthesis Research.*

735    Japanese Society of Plant Physiologists (JSPP). c/o Shimotachiuri Ogawa-Higashi, Kamikyo-ku, Kyoto, 602-8048 Japan. Fax: +81-75-415-3662. E-mail: jspp@nacos.com. URL: http://www.jspp.org/eng/index.html.

Although its initial charter was to foster academic exchange in the area of plant physiology, it has become a more comprehensive society including those who research microbiology, biochemistry, molecular biology, cell biology, and genetics. Publishes *Plant and Cell Physiology.*

736    Phytochemical Society of Europe (PSE). c/o Dr. Simon Gibbons (Membership Secretary), University of London, the School of Pharmacy, Centre for

Pharmacognosy and Phytotherapy, 29-39 Brunswick Square, London WC1N 1AX, U. K. URL: http://www.phytochemicalsociety.org/.

Acts as a forum for specialists in plant chemistry, biochemistry, and biotechnology who are interested in applying their research findings to agriculture and industry. Publishes *Proceedings of the Phytochemical Society of Europe; Phytochemistry;* and *Phytochemistry Reviews.*

737   Phytochemical Society of North America (PSNA). c/o Clint Chapple, Department of Biochemistry, Purdue University, West Lafayette, IN 47907-1153. Phone: 765-494-0494. Fax: 765-496-7213. URL: http://www.ucalgary.ca/~dabird/psna/.

Primarily research scientists interested in all aspects of the chemistry of plants. Purpose is to promote phytochemical research and communication. An annual conference is held, often with another small, related group. Publishes *Recent Advances in Phytochemistry.*

738   Plant Growth Regulation Society of America (PGRSA*).* c/o Charles Hall, Executive Secretary, P.O. Box 2945, LaGrange, GA 30241. Phone: 706-845-9085. Fax: 706-883-8215. E-mail: assocgroup@mindspring.com. URL: http://www.griffin.peachnet.edu/pgrsa/.

The primary purpose is to disseminate information concerning regulation of plant growth that results in safe, environmentally sound, and efficient production of food, fiber, and ornamentals. Publishes *PGRSA Quarterly* and several books and handbooks on plant growth regulators.

739   Scandinavian Society for Plant Physiology (Societas Physiologia Plantarum Scandinavica, SPPS). SPPS Office, Department of Agricultural Sciences, Royal Veterinary and Agricultural University, DK-1871 Frederiksberg, Denmark. Phone: +45-35283458. Fax: +45-35283460. E-mail: spps@kvl.dk. URL: http://www.spps.kvl.dk.

Founded 1947, the SSPP has about 500 members of which about half come from the United States, Japan, Germany, and over 40 other non-Scandinavian countries. Works to further the development of the field of plant physiology by sponsoring courses, seminars, and symposia; an international conference is held biennially. Publishes *Physiologia Plantarum.* SPPS is affiliated with the Federation of European Societies of Plant Biology.

# References

The Arabidopsis Genome Initiative. 2000. Analysis of the genome sequence of the flowering plant *Arabidopsis thaliana. Nature* 408(6814): 796–815.

Clark, Kathleen A. 2002. Field crops. Chapter 8 in *Using the Agricultural, Environ-mental, and Food Literature,* edited by Barbara Hutchinson and Antoinette Paris Greider, pp. 241–279. New York: Marcel Dekker.

Goff, S. A., et al. 2002. A draft sequence of the rice genome (*Oryza sativa* L. ssp. *japonica*). *Science* 296(5565):92–100.

Yu, J., et al. 2002. A draft sequence of the rice genome (*Oryza sativa* L. ssp. *indica*). *Science* 296(5565):79–92.

# 10
# Systematics and Identification

This chapter includes resources for the closely related areas of systematics and identification. Systematics attempts to identify patterns in organisms and is sometimes used as a synonym for taxonomy, which is the theory and practice of classifying and naming organisms. Nomenclature is the system that describes how species and higher groups are to be named, including which names are valid and how to Latinize terms from other languages.

The literature of plant systematics is a difficult field to encompass. Taxonomists must trace species names and descriptions back to the first publication, which may have occurred any time since the publication of Linneaus's *Species Plantarum* in 1753. Plant groups have been described in a large variety of journals, bulletins, monographs, floras, circulars, pamphlets, and other often rare or hard-to-locate publications. As a result taxonomists still rely on a range of specialized finding tools. Large Web-accessible taxonomic databases such as the *Species Plantarum Project* and *Species 2000* (see descriptions in the Handbooks and Methods section, below) are being developed to pull together this dispersed data, but it will be a long time before they are completed. For the foreseeable future, taxonomists will have to continue using the existing fractured and paper-based system.

Plant taxonomists do not agree on the number of plant species that have been identified so far. Most previous estimates ranged from 230,000 to 270,000 known species, but recently two botanists have independently estimated that there are at least 422,000 described species (Bramwell, 2002; Govaerts, 2001). On the other hand, Scotland and Wortley (2003) still feel that these estimates are too high and place the number of species at around 223,300. Perhaps after the comprehensive

Web catalogs are completed, we may have a better idea of the true number of identified plant species.

There are two primary types of books that provide catalogs of plants. Floras catalog all the plants of a particular geographical region, regardless of their taxa. Monographs deal with only a specific taxon such as gymnosperms or orchids. Users looking for information on a particular species may find it in either type of catalog. This chapter also includes plant identification tools ranging from easy-to-use field guides to highly technical keys and manuals. The emphasis is on North American plants because covering the rest of the world would result in an impossibly long list. However, the chapter does include the major floras from around the world. See also the general resources such as plant name dictionaries listed in chapter 2, historical sources in chapter 3, and identification guides for edible or useful plants found in chapter 5.

## Bibliographies and Guides to the Literature

740    Chase, Agnes, and C. D. Niles, comps. *Index to Grass Species.* Boston, MA: G. K. Hall, 1970. 3 vol. ISBN 081610445X.

This index is a reproduction of a card index kept by the U. S. Department of Agriculture for many years. It is international in scope and lists names of the species of grasses described from 1763 to 1962. Information provided includes scientific name, authority with bibliographic citation to the publication in which it appeared, type locality, and country. This is useful in the same way as *Index Kewensis,* below, is, although it covers a different part of the Plant Kingdom.

741    Christensen, Carl. *Index Filicum: Sive, enumeratio omnium generum specierumque Filicum et Hydropteridum ab anno 1753 ad finem anii 1905 descriptorum, H. Hagerup, 1905–06.* 744 p. Königstein, Germany: Koeltz, 1973. $160.00. ISBN 3874290484. *Supplements* 1–7.

This lists in alphabetical order the names of ferns and fern allies from family to species published from 1753 on. It is to ferns what *Index Kewensis* is to the taxonomy of flowering plants. Reprint of 1906 edition.

742    Culberson, W. L., R. S. Egan, and T. L. Esslinger. 2004. *Recent Literature on Lichens.* URL: http://www.nhm.uio.no/botanisk/bot-mus/lav/sok_rll.htm.

"*Recent Literature on Lichens* is a series published in *The Bryologist,* a journal of The American Bryological and Lichenological Society. The series aims at listing all recently published papers in lichenology, with a complete bibliographic reference, keywords, and abstract—including mention of all new scientific names and combinations." The database can be searched by words from the citation or by scientific name, and results can be sorted and downloaded in several formats.

743    Farr, Ellen R., Jan H. Leussink, and Frans A. Stafleu, eds. *Index Nominum Genericorum (Plantarum)*. Utrecht, the Netherlands: International Bureau for Plant Taxonomy and Nomenclature, 1979. 3 vol. ISBN 9031303272 (set). (Regnum Vegetabile, vol. 100, 102, 103). *Supplementum I*, 1986. (Regnum Vegetabile, vol. 113).

This is a list of valid published scientific plant names of all genera, recent and fossil, and includes citations to authors, reference to the place and time of publication, homonymy, indications of taxonomic placement, and additional information on names. The index is now searchable from the Smithsonian Institute's Web site at http://rathbun.si.edu/botany/ing/.

744    Frodin, D. G. *Guide to Standard Floras of the World: An Annotated, Geographically Arranged Systematic Bibliography of the Principal Floras, Enumerations, Checklists, and Chorological Atlases of Different Areas*. 2nd ed. New York: Cambridge University Press, 2001. 1100 p. $250.00. ISBN 0521790778.

This massive work updates Blake's two-volume *Geographical Guide to Floras of the World* (originally published in 1942 and 1961) and presents a list of standard floras for all regions of the world. Introductory material discusses the history of floras and the scope of the guide, whereas the bulk of the guide consists of annotated descriptions of the floras arranged by geographical location. The geographical regions include narrow floras to states or regions within countries as well as country or continent-wide floras.

745    *Gray Herbarium Index: Harvard University*. Boston, MA: G. K. Hall, 1968. 10 vol. Supplement 1– . 1978–1992.

This is an index to the names of flowering plants of the Western Hemisphere with citations to their authority and publication history. It duplicates *Index Kewensis* in part but is especially useful for verifying the names of New World plants. Supplements from 1986 to 1992 were published in microfiche. The index was formerly available separately on the Web but has now been incorporated into the *International Plant Names Index* (see below).

746    Greene, Stanley W., and A. J. Harrington. *The Conspectus of Bryological Taxonomic Literature*. Berlin: J. Cramer, 1988–1989. 2 vol. (Bryophytorum Bibliotheca, bd. 35, 37). ISBN 3443620078 (vol. 1); 3443620094 (vol. 2).

These two volumes present a survey of the literature of bryophyte identification. The first volume, *Index to Monographs and Regional Review*, provides annotated references to regional or worldwide monographs, reviews, or revisions and is arranged in alphabetical order by order, family, or genus. The second volume, *Guide to National and Regional Literature*, covers material that has a geographical treatment such as floras, checklists, or bibliographies. It is arranged by geographical region.

747    *Index Hepaticarum.* 2nd ed. Vol. 1– . Vaduz, Liechtenstein: Lubrecht and Cramer, 1962– . Irregular.

This index presents nomenclatural, bibliographical, and systematic data for Hepaticae. It serves the same sort of function as does *Index Kewensis* (below), Christensen's *Index Filicum* (above), and Saccardo's *Sylloge Fungorum* (below), and is updated in *Taxon* (see Botanical Serials, below). Currently up to Volume 12, *Racemigemma to Zoopsis*, published in 1990.

748    *Index of Fungi.* Vol. 1– . Kew, England: Commonwealth Mycological Institute, 1940– . Semiannual. $315.00. ISSN 0019-3895.

"A list of names of new genera, species and varieties of fungi, new combinations and new names, compiled from world literature." This standard reference work contains 10-year cumulative indexes and some supplements. It supersedes Petrak's *Lists of New Species* (see below) to provide full bibliographic citations for fungi and lichens since 1971. It is searchable on the Web as part of Kirk et al.'s *IndexFungorum*, below.

749    *Index of Mosses.* St. Louis, MO: Missouri Botanical Garden, 1989– . Triennial. (Monographs in Systematic Botany from the Missouri Botanical Garden).

The *Index* is a guide to newly published nomenclature for mosses and supersedes *Index Muscorum*. The index is also available online as the *Index of Mosses ($W^3MOST$)*, at http://www.mobot.org/MOBOT/tropicos/most/iom.shtml, and includes information on the name of the bryophyte, its place of publication, type, specimen lists, and distribution, where available.

750    Kirk, P. M., et al. *IndexFungorum.* Wallingford, England: CAB International. URL: http://www.indexfungorum.org/.

This database contains over 345,000 names of fungi (including yeast, lichens, chromistan fungi, protozoan fungi, and fossil forms) at the species level and below. It is comprised of data taken from Saccardo's *Sylloge Fungorum* (below), Petrak's *Lists* (below), Saccardo's *Omissions*, Lamb's *Index*, Zahlbruckner's *Catalogue of Lichens* (not reviewed), and the *Index of Fungi* (above).

751   Mears, James A., comp. *Plant Taxonomic Literature: Bibliographic Guide.* Cambridge, England: Chadwyck-Healey, 1989. 177 p. ISBN 0859642178.

The volume lists a collection of rare and useful books listed in the second edition of *Taxonomic Literature* that are available on microfiche from UMI (originally Chadwyk-Healey). The collection includes 4,679 important plant taxonomy books and is available as a complete set on 13,047 fiches or as selected volumes by region.

752   Petrak, Franz. *List of New Species and Varieties of Fungi, New Combinations and New Names Published, 1920–1939.* Kew, England: Commonwealth Mycological Institute, 1950–1957.

This work covers the mycological literature from 1922 through 1935. It is superseded by *Index of Fungi,* above.

753   Pfister, Donald H., Jean R. Boise, and Marin A. Eifler. *A Bibliography of Taxonomic Mycological Literature 1753–1821.* Berlin: J. Cramer, published for the New York Botanical Garden in collaboration with the Mycological Society of America, 1990. 161 p. (Mycologia Memoir, no. 17). $55.00. ISBN 3443760074.

This bibliography is an account of taxonomic literature that appeared between 1753 and 1821 pertaining to fungi. This complete listing, anchored by Linnaeus's *Species Plantarum* and Fries's *Systema Mycologicum,* includes books and journal articles presenting wholly new binomials, use of names in nomenclaturally significant ways, or general or historically important treatments. A useful list of references of books and periodicals consulted is included.

754   Reveal, James T. *Systematic Botany Resources for Reference Librarians.* URL: http://www.life.umd.edu/emeritus/reveal/pbio/FindIT/brrl.html

Librarians aren't the only people who can find helpful information at this site, which includes Web sites and standard print resources on systematic botany and the history of botany.

755   Saccardo, Pier A. *Sylloge Fungorum Omnium Hoc Usque Cognitorum.* New York: Johnson, 1966. 25 vol. Volume 26. New York: Johnson, 1972. ISBN 0384528317 (set); 0384528309 (paper/set).

This catalog of names with Latin descriptions of fungi predates Petrak's *List* (see above) and is included in the online *IndexFungorum* at http://www.indexfungorum.org/. Both data sets can also be searched at the USDA's Systematic Botany and Mycology site at http://nt.ars-grin.gov/fungaldatabases/index.cfm. Reprint of the 1931 edition.

756   Solbrig, Otto Thomas, and T. W. J. Gadella, eds. *Biosystematic Literature: Contributions to a Biosystematic Literature Index (1945–1964)*. Utrecht, the Netherlands: International Bureau for Plant Taxonomy and Nomenclature, Tweede Transitorium, 1970. 566 p. (Regnum Vegetabile, vol. 69).

This is a source of references for use by people without the benefit of a large library at hand. It is not intended to be comprehensive, although it is international in scope for the years covered.

757   Stafleu, Frans A., and Richard S. Cowan. *Taxonomic Literature: A Selective Guide to Botanical Publications and Collections with Dates, Commentaries and Types*. 2nd ed. Utrecht, the Netherlands: Bohn, Scheltema and Holkema, 1976–1988. Vol. 1–7. ISBN 9031302244 (set). (Regnum Vegetabile no. 94, 98, 105, 110, 112, 115, 116). *Supplements* (Regnum Vegetabile, no. 125, 130, 132, 134, 135, 137, and continuing).

This is one of the most important guides to the taxonomic literature, and it contains a wealth of other pertinent information. Arranged alphabetically by author, data include brief biographical information, herbaria where collections are held, location of bibliography and biographical entries, composite works, eponymy, location of handwriting specimens, and an annotated list of authors' important publications with complete bibliographical details. There are name and title indexes for each volume. This highly specialized reference work is indispensable for the taxonomist/detective trying to locate elusive coauthors, titles, collections, and writings of significant botanists of the past.

758   Van Der Wijk, R., ed. *Index Muscorum*. Utrecht, the Netherlands: International Bureau for Plant Taxonomy and Nomenclature, 1959–1969. 5 vol. (Regnum Vegetabile, vol. 17, 26, 33, 48, 65).

This is a compendium setting forth the nomenclatural status of the mosses up to 1969. There is information concerning published names, valid or not, substitute names, and new combinations of names. *Index Muscorum* was superseded by *Index of Mosses* (see above).

759   *World Checklist and Bibliography Series*. Richmond, Surrey, England: Royal Botanic Gardens, Kew, 2000– . Rev. ed. Multivolume. URL: http://www.rbgkew.org.uk/wcb/.

This series presents global checklists of selected families of seed plants. To date, publications include *Araceae, Magnoliaceae, Fagales, Conifers, Euphorbiaceae*, and *Sapotaceae* with several other volumes planned. The families are chosen because of their interest to researchers at the Royal Botanic Gardens at Kew; in particular, families covered in the garden's database, *Survey of*

*Economic Plants for Arid and Semi-Arid Lands* (http://www.rbgkew.org.uk/ceb/sepasal/), which requires free registration.

# Databases, Abstracts, and Indexes

760    *Bibliography of Systematic Mycology.* Vol. 1– . Wallingford, England: CAB International, 1947– . Semiannual. $340.00. ISSN 0006-1573.

The bibliography covers the literature of the taxonomy, classification, nomenclature, and phylogeny of the fungi. Citations are arranged by systematic group, and there is an author index in each issue; books and book reviews are also included. A partial database covering citations beginning with 1986 but excluding the most recent five years is available for free at http://www.indexfungorum.org/BSM/bsm.htm.

*Excerpta Botanica. Sectio A: Taxonomica et Chorologia.*

See chapter 2 for full annotation. This section covers systematic botany.

761    *Index Kewensis Plantarum Phanerogamarum Nomina et Synonyma Omnium Generum et Specierum a Linnaeo Usque ad Annum MDCCCLXXXV Complectens Nomine Recepto Auctore Patria Unicuique Plantae Subjectis.* 2 vol. Königstein, Germany: Koeltz, 1977. ISBN 3874291170. *Supplementum.* 1886– . Vol. 1– . Priced separately.

Originally published in 1893 to 1895. "An enumeration of the genera and species of flowering plants from the time of Linnaeus to the year 1885 inclusive together with their authors' names, the works in which they were first published, their native countries and their synonyms." This is an indispensable reference. Although the earlier volumes, particularly Volumes 1 and 2 of the original set, contain many mistakes, the later supplements are reputed to be much more accurate. Supplements are issued every few years; Supplement 21, issued in 2002, covers 1996 to 2000. There is a cumulated microfiche index through supplement 16. *Index Kewensis* is also available on CD-ROM from Oxford University Press; version 2.0 covered all volumes to Supplement 20 on a single disc. Data from *Index Kewensis* was also included in the *International Plant Names Index* (see below).

762    *Index to Plant Chromosome Numbers.* 1956– . Various locations: Various publishers. Biennial. Price varies.

The *Index to Plant Chromosome Numbers* has variously been published as part of the Regnum Vegetabile series (Volumes 50, 55, 59, 68, 77, 84, 90, 91, 96, and 108) and the Missouri Botanical Garden's Monographs in Systematic Botany series (Volumes 5, 8, 13, 23, and 30). Entries are arranged alphabetically by family within these groupings: algae, fungi, bryophytes, pteridophytes, and spermatophytes; this is to provide references to the literature of plant chromosome number information for the period covered. These compilations provide a useful service for botanists and should be included in any botanical library; between compilations, chromosome number information is updated in the periodical, *Taxon* (see Botanical Serials, below). The most recent print compilation was published in 2000; data from 1984 to date can be viewed at http://mobot.mobot.org/W3T/Search/ipcn.html.

763    *Index to European Taxonomic Literature*. Königstein, Germany: Koeltz, 1965–1970. 5 vol. (Regnum Vegetabile, vol. 45, 53, 61, 70, 80). *Index to European Taxonomic Literature for 1970*. Kew, England: Bentham-Moxon Trustees, 1977. 215 p.

An index covering European literature, now superseded by *Kew Record of Taxonomic Literature*. Arranged by subject.

764    *The International Plant Names Index*. Plant Names Project, 1999– . URL: http://www.ipni.org/.

A database of the names and associated basic bibliographical details of 1.3 million names of seed plants. The database is a collaboration among the Royal Botanic Gardens, Kew, the Harvard University Herbaria, and the Australian National Herbarium. Data comes from *Index Kewensis* (IK), the *Gray Card Index* (GCI), the *Australian Plant Names Index* (APNI), and *Index Filicum*. It can be searched by scientific name, author, or publication. Common names are not included.

765    *Kew Record of Taxonomic Literature*. 1971–2001. London: Her Majesty's Stationery Office. Quarterly. ISSN 0307-2835.

This publication reported worldwide taxonomic literature of the flowering plants, gymnosperms and ferns in a systematic arrangement. It is comprehensive and includes all articles, books, and papers reporting new plant names with the exception of cultivars. Entries are arranged by subject, including systematics, bibliography, botanical institutions, chromosome surveys, anatomy, floristics, and so on. There are also author and genus indexes. The *Kew Record* was formerly an annual, but in 1987 it merged with the *Current Awareness List* and became a much more timely quarterly. It is no longer being printed but is being updated and made available for free on the Web at http://www.rbgkew.org.uk/bibliographies/KR/KRHomeExt.html.

766    *Taxonomic Index*. Vol. 1–19. Lancaster, PA: American Society of Plant Taxonomists, 1939–1956.

This index to botanical taxonomic literature was continued in *Brittonia* from 1957 to 1967 (see General Serials, below). The index was arranged by author within systematic categories.

# Serials

## General Serials

767   *Annual Review of Ecology, Evolution, and Systematics.* Vol. 34– . Palo Alto, CA: Annual Reviews, 2003– . Annual. $179.00. ISSN 1543-592X. Available electronically.
  Formerly *Annual Review of Ecology and Systematics.*

768   *Cladistics: The International Journal of the Willi Hennig Society.* Vol. 1– . New York: Blackwell, 1985– . Bimonthly. $440.00. ISSN 0748-3007. Available electronically.

769   *Systematic Biology.* Vol. 41– . Philadelphia, PA: Taylor and Francis, 1992– . Bimonthly. $173.00. ISSN 1063-5157. Available electronically.
  Formerly *Systematic Zoology.*

## Botanical Serials

770   *Annals of the Missouri Botanical Garden.* Vol. 1– . St. Louis, MO: Missouri Botanical Garden, 1914– . Quarterly. $140.00. ISSN 0026-6493.
  This journal publishes original papers, primarily in systematic botany, from the Missouri Botanical Garden, although outside articles will be considered. Contributions are accepted in English and Spanish. Only back issues are available electronically from JSTOR; current issues (a rolling five-year window) are not available electronically.

771   *Botanical Journal of the Linnean Society.* Vol. 1– . New York: Blackwell, 1855– . Monthly. $1,709.00. ISSN 0024-4074. Available electronically.
  The journal "publishes papers of relevance to, and reviews of, the taxonomy of all plant groups, including anatomy, biosystematics, cytology, ecology, electron microscopy, morphogenesis, paleobotany, palynology and phytochemistry." Published for the Linnean Society of London.

772   *Botanische Jahrbücher fur Systematik, Pflanzengeschichte und Pflanzengeographie.* Vol. 1– . Stuttgart, Germany: Schweizerbart, 1880– . 5 times per year. $122.40. ISSN 0006-8152. Available electronically.
  *Botanische Jahrbücher* (Botanical Yearbooks) publishes scholarly discussions and groundbreaking results in the field of systematics in the widest sense.

773   *Brittonia.* Vol. 1– . New York: New York Botanical Garden, 1931– . Quarterly. $105.00. ISSN 0007-196X. Available electronically.

This journal accepts research papers on systematic botany in the broadest sense, and includes relevant fields such as anatomy, botanical history, chemotaxonomy, cytology, ecology, morphology, paleobotany, palynology, phylogenetic systematics, and phytogeography. News, announcements, and book reviews are also included. Back issues are available electronically through JSTOR; current issues through BioOne.

774   *Fieldiana: Botany.* Vol. 1– . Chicago, IL: Field Museum of Natural History, 1895– . Irregular. ISSN 0015-0746.

Primarily a journal for Field Museum staff and research associates, although manuscripts from nonaffiliated authors are considered as space permits. The journal publishes field and systematic articles as well as floras with emphasis on biogeography and ecology.

775   *Journal of the Torrey Botanical Society.* Vol. 124– . Bronx, NY: Torrey Botanical Society, 1997– . Quarterly. $55.00. ISSN 0040-9618.

Each issue contains two parts: part I includes original research papers; part II, called Torreya, includes general, invited, review papers, and papers on local flora, field trip reports, obituaries, book reviews, notes, and short papers on conservation and environmental concerns. Continues the *Bulletin of the Torrey Botanical Club.* Only back issues are available electronically through JSTOR.

776   *Madroño: A West American Journal of Botany.* Vol. 1– . Berkeley, CA: California Botanical Society, 1916– . Quarterly. $60.00. ISSN 0024-9637.

Authors must be members of the California Botanical Society and works may be submitted in English or Spanish. This excellent regional journal favors systematic, field ecology, or biogeographic studies.

777   *Mycotaxon.* Vol. 1– . Ithaca, NY: Mycotaxon, 1974– . Quarterly. $165.00. ISSN 0093-4666.

Publishes articles on "all phases of the taxonomy and nomenclature of fungi (including lichens)." Papers may be in French or English.

778   *Novon: A Journal for Botanical Nomenclature.* Vol. 1– . St. Louis, MO: Missouri Botanical Garden, 1991– . Quarterly. ISSN 1055-3177.

Publishes "papers whose purpose is the establishment of new nomenclature in vascular plants and bryophytes." Subscription is included with *Annals of the Missouri Botanical Garden* (above).

779   *Plant Systematics and Evolution.* Vol. 123– . New York: Springer-Verlag, 1974– . Semimonthly. $2,915.00. ISSN 0378-2697. Available electronically.

"The journal is devoted to publishing original papers and reviews on plant systematics in the broadest sense, encompassing evolutionary, phylogenetic and biogeographical studies at the populational, specific, higher taxonomic levels. Taxonomic emphasis is on green plants." Continues *Österreichisches Botanisches Zeitschrift*.

780   *Rhodora: Journal of the New England Botanical Club.* Vol. 1– . Cambridge, MA: New England Botanical Club, 1899– . Quarterly. $80.00. ISSN 0035-4902.

The "journal is devoted primarily to the botany of North America and accepts manuscripts of scientific papers and notes relating to the systematics, floristics, ecology, paleobotany, or conservation biology of this or floristically related areas."

781   *Sida, Contributions to Botany.* Vol. 1– . Dallas, TX: BRIT Press, 1962– . Biannual. $60.00. ISSN 0036-1488.

"The journal publishes primary research papers in fields such as anatomy, biogeography, chemotaxonomy, ecology, evolution, floristics, genetics, paleobotany, palynology, and phylogenetic systematics." Articles may be written in English or Spanish; and the journal also publishes short communications, book reviews, and notices of new publications. The publisher, the Botanical Research Institute of Texas, also publishes *Sida, Botanical Miscellany*, a series of botanical monographs.

782   *Systematic Botany.* Vol. 1– . Lawrence, KS: American Society of Plant Taxonomists, 1976– . Quarterly. $135.00. ISSN 0363-6445. Available electronically.

Publishes "original articles pertinent to modern and traditional aspects of systematic botany, including theory as well as application. Papers longer than 50 printed pages, especially taxonomic monographs and revisions, appear in *Systematic Botany Monographs* published by ASPT."

783   *Taxon.* Vol. 1– . Utrecht, the Netherlands: International Bureau for Plant Taxonomy and Nomenclature, 1951– . Quarterly. $260.00. ISSN 0040-0262. Available electronically.

The journal is "devoted to systematic and evolutionary biology with emphasis on botany." Issues contain original articles, methods and techniques, nomenclature, proposals to conserve or reject, news, additions to *Index Herbariorum*, book reviews, and announcements. Published for the International Association for Plant Taxonomy.

# Dictionaries and Encyclopedias

784   Crosby, Marshall R., and Robert E. Magill. *A Dictionary of Mosses: An Alphabetical Listing of Genera Indicating Familial Disposition, Nomenclatural and Taxonomic Synonymy Together with a Systematic Arrangement of the Families of Mosses and a Catalogue of Family Names Used for Mosses.* 3rd printing, with corrections and additions. St. Louis, MO: Missouri Botanical Garden, 1981. 43 p. (Monographs in Systematic Botany from the Missouri Botanical Garden, vol. 3).

The subtitle of this dictionary nicely sums up its contents; it lists the family for each genus of mosses, including both valid and invalid names.

785   Harris, James G., and Melinda Woolf Harris. *Plant Identification Terminology: An Illustrated Glossary.* 2nd ed. Spring Lake, UT: Spring Lake, 2001. 206 p. $18.95 (paper). ISBN 0964022176; 0964022168 (paper).

A lavishly illustrated guide to terminology used in systematic botany, particularly terms used to describe plants in botanic keys. Part One is an alphabetical list of 2,400 terms. Part Two, designed for students, groups related terms for easier comprehension in areas such as roots, flowers, and so forth.

786   Hoen, Peter. *Glossary of Pollen and Spore Terminology.* 2nd rev. ed. Utrecht, the Netherlands: Laboratory of Palaeobotany and Palynology, 1999– . URL: http://www.biol.ruu.nl/~palaeo/glossary/glos-tin.htm.

The glossary is based on the publication by the same name printed by the Laboratory for Palaeobotany and Palynology in 1994. The terminology of palynology includes many esoteric terms for anatomical features of pollen and spores, so the fact that almost all definitions also include a diagrammatic illustration is a particularly nice feature of this highly hyperlinked glossary. The full glossary can also be downloaded for personal use.

787   Jaeger, Edmund C. *A Source-Book of Biological Names and Terms.* 3rd ed. Springfield, IL: C. C. Thomas, 1978. 360 p. $68.95. ISBN 0398009163; 0398061793 (paper).

This dictionary contains concise discussions on the building of words used in biological nomenclature, types of names considered, transliteration, Greek prefixes, the form of Latin nouns, and over 280 brief biographies of people commemorated in botanical and zoological generic names.

788   Kirk, P. M., P. F. Cannon, J. C. David, and J. A. Stalpers, eds. *Ainsworth and Bisby's Dictionary of the Fungi.* 9th ed. New York: CAB International, 2001. 655 p. $90.00. ISBN 085199377X.

The classic handbook for the fungi, this dictionary has been published for over 60 years. The dictionary includes both taxonomic names and definitions of terms used by mycologists, though the most detailed entries are for the names of genera. An attempt was made to include all known genera of fungi, including mushrooms, lichens, slime molds, water molds, and yeasts. The entries include the abbreviated names of the original author of the name, year of publication, number of species, distribution, and references. The editors include an appendix detailing the systematic arrangement used in the dictionary.

Lincoln, Roger J., Geoffrey Allan Boxshall, and P. F. Clark. *A Dictionary of Ecology, Evolution, and Systematics*. 2nd ed.

See chapter 2 for full annotation. Includes terms used in taxonomy and nomenclature and a chart showing the taxonomic hierarchy.

789   Mabberley, D. J. *The Plant-Book: A Portable Dictionary of the Vascular Plants*. 2nd ed., completely rev. New York: Cambridge University Press, 1997. 858 p. $52.95. ISBN 0521414210.

This invaluable dictionary contains over 20,000 entries, covering all currently accepted generic and family names as well as English common names for ferns and flowering plants. Generic entries include the family, number of species within the genus, distribution, and notes on use. Family entries include the number of genera and species within the family, a brief description of the plants, use, and common names. Common name entries refer to the proper scientific name. The author also includes appendixes listing the taxonomic system used in the book, references, and author name abbreviations. A vast amount of reliable data is compressed into this small dictionary. *The Plant-Book* is a replacement for J. C. Willis's classic *A Dictionary of the Flowering Plants and Ferns*, below.

790   Wielgorskaya, Tatiana. *Dictionary of Generic Names of Seed Plants*. New York: Columbia University Press, 1995. 570 p. $151.00. ISBN 0231078927.

Provides a comprehensive listing of all currently accepted generic names of seed plants and synonyms found in the modern literature. Contains more detailed information on distribution of the genera than the otherwise similar *Plant-Book* by Mabberley (above) and *Dictionary of the Flowering Plants* by Willis (below). The dictionary is in two parts: one listing alphabetically all families and the genera they contain and the other listing the generic names with their family, distribution, and date of first publication.

791   Willis, John Christopher. *A Dictionary of the Flowering Plants and Ferns*. 8th ed. Cambridge, England: Cambridge University Press, 1973. 1245 p. ISBN 052108699X.

Although this classic dictionary of plant names has been replaced by Mabberley's *The Plant-Book,* above, it is worth listing here because a number of other major works still reference it. Originally published as *A Manual and Dictionary of the Flowering Plants and Ferns.*

# Handbooks and Methods

**Taxonomy**

792   Anderson, Edward F. *The Cactus Family*. Portland, OR: Timber, 2001. 776 p. $99.95. ISBN 0881924989.

A lavishly illustrated guide to the cacti, this handbook provides extensive background information on the characteristics of the cactus family as well as the ethnobotany, conservation, cultivation, and classification of cacti. Much of the handbook consists of species accounts of most cacti, arranged alphabetically by genus. There are a number of color photographs illustrating the often lovely flowers and/or bizarre shapes of these fascinating plants.

793   Baranov, A. *Basic Latin for Plant Taxonomists*. Monticello, NY: Lubrecht and Cramer, 1971. 146 p. $45.00 (paper). ISBN 3768207277 (paper).

Although this is not as useful as Stearn's *Botanical Latin*, below, it does serve to instruct the plant taxonomist in preparing formal, Latin descriptions for new taxa. The guide is written from a practical point of view with emphasis on methods for writing plant descriptions, especially descriptions of species, and is intended for beginners in plant taxonomy. See also Jeffrey's *Biological Nomenclature* and Winston's *Describing Species*, both below. Reprint of the 1958 edition.

794   Bentham, George, and J. D. Hooker. *Genera Plantarum ad Exemplaria Imprimis in Herbariis Kewensibus Servata Definite*. London: Reeve, 1862–83. 3 vol.

Bentham and Hooker's taxonomic system treated dicotyledons, monocotyledons, and gymnosperms as distinct groups and included 202 families. The authors developed their own descriptions of each family that are still used, though their system has been superseded. It is still used to organize many major herbaria, however. Showing its age, the set is written in Latin (although even now, descriptions of new plant taxa must appear in Latin according to Greuter's 2000 *International Code of Botanical Nomenclature*, below).

*Bibliotheca Mycologica.*

See chapter 2 for full annotation. This monographic series includes books on fungal taxonomy.

795   Brickell, Christopher, et al., eds. *International Code of Nomenclature for Cultivated Plants: (I. C. N. C. P. or Cultivated Plant Code): Incorporating the Rules and Recommendations for Naming Plants in Cultivation.* 7th ed. Leuven, Belgium: International Society for Horticultural Science, 2004. 123 p. (Acta Horticulturae, no. 647; Regnum Vegetabile, vol. 144). $70.00. ISBN 9066055278.

"As well as containing the international rules for naming plants in cultivation, the Code also contains much ancillary information such as lists of special denomination classes, International Cultivar Registration Authorities (ICRAs), statutory registration authorities, and herbaria maintaining specimens that act as nomenclatural standards, together with a comprehensive glossary of terms used in nomenclature generally." Largely follows the rules set out in Greuter's *International Code of Botanical Nomenclature*, below, with the addition of allowing cultivar names for cultivated varieties.

796   Bridson, Diane, and Leonard Forman, eds. *The Herbarium Handbook.* 3rd ed. Kew, England: Royal Botanic Gardens, 1998. 334 p. ISBN 1900347431.

This new edition of the definitive and authoritative handbook on herbarium curation and management deals with the technical aspects of herbarium work; that is, preparation, housing, preservation, and organization of herbarium collections. Broader contexts concerning the relationship of the herbarium to economic botany, ecology, and conservation are included in a separate section.

797   Brodo, Irwin M., Sylvia Duran Sharnoff, and Stephen Sharnoff. *Lichens of North America.* New Haven, CT: Yale University Press, 2001. 795 p. $85.00. ISBN 0300082495.

This massive handbook is useful both as an introduction to lichenology and as an identification guide to some 3,600 species of lichens from North America. The identification section includes keys and species accounts with distribution maps, detailed descriptions including chemistry, habitat, and comments. Many species are illustrated with color photographs. Hale's *How to Know the Lichens* (see Identification section, below) is the only other identification guide to North American lichens, and where names have changed Hale's outdated terms are included in the present work for cross-referencing.

798   Brummitt, R. K. *Vascular Plant Families and Genera: A Listing of the Genera of Vascular Plants of the World According to Their Families, as Recognised in the Kew Herbarium, with an Analysis of Relationships of the Flowering Plant Families According to Eight Systems of Classification.* Kew, England: Royal Botanical Gardens, Kew, 1992. 804 p. $100.00. ISBN 0947643435.

The subtitle pretty much sums up the contents of this authoritative book. It is divided into three parts, consisting of an alphabetical list of all 14,000 generic names accepted at the Kew Gardens, a list of genera listed alphabetically by family, and a comparison of eight classification systems. The eight systems are Bentham and Hooker, De la Torre and Harms, Melchior, Thorne, Dahlgren, Young, Takhtadzhian (often spelled Takhtajan), and Cronquist. For more comparisons, see Swift's *Botanical Classifications* (below). The contents of the book are also available as a searchable database at the Kew Gardens site, http:// www.rbgkew.org.uk/data/vascplnt.html.

799    Brummitt, R. K., and C. E. Powell. *Authors of Plant Names: A List of Authors of Scientific Names of Plants, with Recommended Standard Forms of their Names, Including Abbreviations.* Kew, England: Royal Botanical Gardens, Kew, 1992. 732 p. $70.20. ISBN 0947643443.

As the title suggests, this is a list of authorities who have named plants, along with approved abbreviations. It is intended as a comprehensive checklist to be used to standardize names for future floras, databases, and other botanical works. The data included for each author includes full name, birth and death date where known, and recommended abbreviation to be used in nomenclature.

800    *Catalogue of New World Grasses (Poaceae).* Washington, DC: Department of Botany, National Museum of Natural History, 2000–2003. 4 vol. (Contributions from the United States National Herbarium, vol. 39, 41, 46, 48).

This is an ongoing project gathering together taxonomic and distributional information on North and South American grasses, including grasses from Greenland. The Web site at http://mobot.mobot.org/Pick/Search/nwgc.html is still being updated and is to be considered the most authoritative version of the project. On the Web, the species can be searched by scientific name or browsed using indexes to all taxa; accepted taxa; and suprageneric, generic, and subgeneric taxa.

801    Clayton, W. D., and S. A. Renvoize. *Genera Graminum: Grasses of the World.* London: H.M.S.O., 1986. 389 p. (Kew Bulletin Additional Series, no. 13). ISBN 0112500064 (paper).

The first major revision of the grasses since 1883, this guide allows users to key out over 650 genera of grasses from around the world, ranging from bamboos to corn. Each generic account includes information on distribution and number of species as well as a technical description.

802    Cronquist, Arthur. *The Evolution and Classification of Flowering Plants.* 2nd ed. Bronx, NY: New York Botanical Garden, 1988. 555 p. $42.00. ISBN 0893273325.

This text is based on the author's *Integrated System* (below) and provides a more compact version of his system of classification. It includes general information on taxonomy; species and speciation; the origin and evolution of flowering plants; and keys and a brief description of the subclasses, orders, and families of flowering plants.

803   Cronquist, Arthur. *An Integrated System of Classification of Flowering Plants*. New York: Columbia University Press, 1992. 1262 p. $267.00. ISBN 0231038801.

This is an indispensable work for botanical classification and an excellent compendium of information on the division, class, order, family, and basic features of 383 families in 83 orders of flowering plants. It was originally published in 1981. This reissue includes many corrections to the original. Cronquist has become the standard plant classification system, especially in the United States.

804   Cronquist, Arthur, et al. *Intermountain Flora: Vascular Plants of the Intermountain West, U.S.A.* New York: New York Botanical Garden, 1972– . Vol. 1, 3–6. ISBN 0231041209.

This set remains unfinished to date, with Volume 2, covering the Magnoliidae, Hamamelidae, Caryophyllidae, and Dilleniidae families, unpublished. The region covered includes the area from the Sierra Nevada to the Rocky Mountains, most or all of Utah and Nevada, and the southern portions of Oregon and Idaho.

805   Crum, Howard A., and Lewis E. Anderson. *Mosses of Eastern North America*. New York: Columbia University Press, 1981. 2 vol. $341.00. ISBN 0231045166.

This catalog provides detailed information on the mosses of North America west to Minnesota and south to the Gulf of Mexico. Because many bryophytes are widely distributed, the authors suggest that most of the mosses of the Rocky Mountains and the boreal forest are probably also included.

806   Dahlgren, R. M. T., H. T. Clifford, and P. F. Yeo. *The Families of the Monocotyledons: Structure, Evolution, and Taxonomy*. New York: Springer-Verlag, 1985. 520 p. ISBN 038713655X.

The authors provide extensive background information on the anatomy and evolution of the monocots as well as presenting a classification of the group down to the family level. Each family is described in detail. Dahlgren was also involved in Kubitzki's *Families and Genera of Vascular Plants*, below, which treats the monocot families in two volumes. Use this volume for general information on the evolution and morphology of the monocots, and use *Families and Genera of Vascular Plants* for family-level information.

807    Dressler, Robert L. *Phylogeny and Classification of the Orchid Family*. Portland, OR: Dioscorides, 1993. 314 p. $65.00. ISBN 0931146240.

There are between 17,000 and 35,000 species of orchids in the world. This book outlines their phylogeny and describes each of the many orchid subtribes. Information for each subtribe includes description, distribution, pollination, chromosome numbers, seed structure, number of species, names of genera included, general notes, and references. There are black-and-white illustrations, a glossary, key to major taxa, and an outline of the classification system.

808    Earle, Christopher J. *Gymnosperm Database*. 1997– . URL: http://www .conifers.org/index.htm.

The database provides basic information on each of the 1,000 species or higher taxa of gymnosperms. Most of the accounts include taxonomic notes, description, range, largest and oldest specimens, economic use, dendrochronology, remarks, bibliography, and photographs. Some obscure species have almost no information beyond the name and a citation. Species can be located by browsing through a taxonomic tree or can be searched by name. The author also provides several topical essays, for instance, on the gymnosperm flora of some regions or on dendrochronology.

809    *eFloras.org*. URL: http://www.efloras.org/index.aspx.

Provides access to the published family, genera, and species accounts from *Flora of China*; *Flora of Missouri, Flora of North America*; *Flora of Pakistan*; *Moss Flora of China*; and *Trees and Shrubs of the Andes of Ecuador*. Users can search within each flora or across all of them, and there are links to other databases such as Solomon's *W³Tropicos* (below) and *The International Plant Names Index* (above). The site also provides links to an English-to-Chinese botanical glossary and keys to plant families.

810    Eggli, Urs, Heidrun E. K. Hartmann, Focke Albers, and Ulrich Meve, eds. *Illustrated Handbook of Succulent Plants*. New York: Springer, 20012003. 6 vol. ISBN 3540416927 (vol. 1); 3540419667 (vol. 2); 3540416919 (vol. 3); 3540417230 (vol. 4); 3540419640 (vol. 5); 3540419659 (vol. 6).

The handbook provides details on 9,000 taxa of succulents, excluding the cacti. There are range maps and color photographs for many of the species.

811    Engler, Adolf. *Syllabus der Pflanzenfamilien, mit besonderer Berückcksichtigung der Nutzpflanzen nebst einer Übersicht über die Florenreiche und Florengebiete der Erde*. 12., völlig neugestaltete Aufl. Berlin-Nikolassee, Germany: Gebr. Borntraeger, 1954-64. 2 vol.

This latest edition of Engler's classic syllabus was edited by Hans Melchior and Erich Werdermann and is often cited with Melchior as the author. This outline of plant systematics is still often used. Volume 1 covers the bacteria through the gymnosperms whereas Volume 2 covers the angiosperms.

812   Engler, Adolf, and Karl Anton Eugen Prantl. *Die Natürlichen Pflanzen-familien nebst ihren Gattungen und wichtigeren Arten, insbesondere den Nutzpflanzen, unter Mitwirkung zahlreicher hervorragender Fachgelehrten begründet.* Leipzig: W. Engelmann, 1887–1909. 32 vol. in 17.

This massive handbook featured the first attempt to include phylogenetics in plant systematics, though it assumed that simple equaled primitive. Up to about 1980 this was the standard taxonomic system; and although modern taxonomists tend to use the Cronquist system, many herbaria still use Engler and Prantl to organize their collections. The handbook has a standard format, with keys to families, detailed descriptions of families, and less detailed information on genera of plants from around the world. There are numerous illustrations. A second edition was begun in 1942 but remains unfinished.

813   Expert Center for Taxonomic Identification. *World Taxonomist Database.* Amsterdam, the Netherlands: ETI, 1995. URL: http://www.eti.uva.nl/tools/wtd.php.

This database, set up to expedite contact between taxonomists, contained information on over 4,000 individuals at the time of viewing. It can be searched by name, institution, country, or specialty. Entries for each taxonomist include contact information and areas of interest. The *Plant Specialists Index* (see below) offers similar information.

814   *Flora Mesoamericana.* Vol. 1– . St. Louis, MO: Missouri Botanical Garden, 1994– . Multivolume. $85.00 (vol. 1); $85.00 (vol. 6). ISBN 9683647006 (vol. 1); 9683633102 (vol. 6).

A major new series covering the vascular plants from southern Mexico to Panama, this flora provides the basic information expected in a flora: scientific and common names, technical description, keys, and distribution. The series will be published out of sequence, with seven volumes expected, all in Spanish. As of late 2005, Volumes 1 and 6 had been published. The flora's Web site at http://www.mobot.org/MOBOT/fm/welcome.html contains the data from the published volumes.

815   *Flora Neotropica.* Monograph no. 1– . New York: New York Botanical Garden, 1964– . Irregular. Price varies. ISSN 0071-5794.

This important series (currently up to number 98) of taxonomic accounts of plant groups or families growing spontaneously in the Americas between the Tropics of Cancer and Capricorn is the official publication of the Organization for Flora Neotropica. The pagination for each monograph varies from a few pages to several hundred; data include ecology, cytology, anatomy, morphology, chemistry, economic importance, bibliography, and citation of specimens.

816    *Flora of Australia.* Vol. 1– . Canberra, Australia: Australian Government Publishing Service, 1981– . Multivolume. Irregular. Price varies. ISSN 0726-3449.

The massive *Flora of Australia* will cover all vascular and nonvascular plants of Australia. Volume 1 is an introduction with background information on the project, a key to flowering plant families, and a glossary. Volumes 2 through 48 cover the 20,000 species of vascular plants; Volumes 49 through 50 will cover several islands; Volumes 51 through 53 the bryophytes; and Volumes 54 through 58 the lichens. The algae and fungi are expected to require another 20 to 30 volumes. The flora is also available online at http://www.deh.gov.au/biodiversity/ abrs/online-resources/abif/flora/main/ in three separate sections covering Australia proper (Volumes 2 through 48 and 51 and continue), Norfolk and Lord Howe Islands (Volume 49), and other Oceanic islands (Volume 50).

817    *Flora of China.* Vol. 1– . St. Louis, MO: Missouri Botanical Garden, 1994– . Multivolume. Price varies.

Another of the Missouri Botanical Garden's flora projects, this will cover all of the vascular plants of China in a projected 25 volumes over a period of 15 years. Information will include brief descriptions, keys, synonymy, distribution, and indexes to Chinese and scientific names. *Flora of China* is an English language revision of the *Flora Republicae Popularis Sinicae.* The project's home page can be found at http://flora.huh.harvard.edu/china/ and contains information about the flora, the full text of published volumes, and more.

818    *Flora of China: Illustrations.* St. Louis, MO: Missouri Botanical Garden, 1999– . Multivolume. ISBN 0915279347 (set). Price varies.

Contains full-page line drawings illustrating the plants covered in the main *Flora of China* volumes. Like the main set, it is expected to consist of 25 volumes when complete.

819    *Flora of North America, North of Mexico.* New York: Oxford University Press, 1993– . Multivolume. Price varies.

This is the first comprehensive, modern flora discussing all of the vascular plants of North America. It is intended to be published in 30 volumes covering 20,000 species. Volume 1 contains the introduction; Volume 2 covers the ferns and gymnosperms; Volumes 3 through 26 will cover the vascular plants; Volumes 27 and 29 will cover the bryophytes; and Volume 30 will contain an index. The project's Web site at http://www.fna.org/FNA/ provides information on the project, full text of published volumes, and other information. As of late 2004, eight volumes had been published out of sequence. For another project with similar aims, see the monographic series *North American Flora*, below.

820   *Flora of Southern Africa*. Pretoria, South Africa: Department of Agricultural Technical Services, 1963– . Multivolume.

This flora covers the 24,000 species of vascular and nonvascular plants from Botswana, Lesotho, Namibia, South Africa, and Swaziland. It includes descriptions, synonyms, drawings, and maps for each species covered. The series is published out of sequence and is expected to comprise 33 volumes when complete.

821   *Flora of Tropical Africa*. London: L. Reeve, 1868–1937. 10 vol.

The first three volumes of this flora were edited by D. Oliver, whereas W. T. Thistleton-Dyer edited the remaining volumes. Publication was suspended after World War II, leaving the coverage of the Graminae incomplete.

822   Fosberg, Francis Raymond, and Marie-Hélène Sachet. *Manual for Tropical Herbaria*. Utrecht, the Netherlands: International Bureau for Plant Taxonomy and Nomenclature, 1965. 132 p. (Regnum Vegetabile, vol. 39).

This slim volume provides information for tropical herbaria, covering everything from functions of an herbarium to administration to the construction of specimen cabinets. It also includes instructions for collecting and preserving specimens. Savile's *Collection and Care of Botanical Specimens*, below, is written for more temperate climes.

Francki, R. I. B., Robert G. Milne, and T. Hatta. *Atlas of Plant Viruses*.

See chapter 2 for full annotation.

823   *Genera Orchidacearum*. New York: Oxford University Press, 1999– . Multivolume. $120.00 (vol. 1); $120.00 (vol. 2); $150.00 (vol. 3). ISBN 0198505132 (vol. 1); 0198507100 (vol. 2); 0198507119 (vol. 3).

This series is intended to provide a modern classification of the orchids. It will consist of five volumes, with Volume 1 including an introduction and the small families Apostasioideae and Cypripedioideae, Volumes 2 and 3 covering the Orchidoideae and Vanilloideae. Volumes 4 and 5 will cover the Epidendroideae and provide a summary and final classification system. The orchids are covered to the level of the genus, with each account including synonymy, etymology, description, distribution (including map), anatomy, palynology, cytogenetics, phytochemistry, phylogenetics, ecology, pollination, uses, cultivation, and references.

824   The Great Plains Flora Association. *Flora of the Great Plains*. Lawrence, KS: University Press of Kansas, 1986. 1392 p. $55.00. ISBN 070060295X.

This massive work provides keys, descriptions, and nomenclature for 3,000 taxa of vascular plants occurring in the Great Plains region of North America. A glossary and index by scientific and common names are also included.

825   Greuter, Werner, ed. *Family Names in Current Use for Vascular Plants, Bryophytes, and Fungi.* Königstein, Germany: Koeltz, 1993. 95 p. (NCU 1; Regnum Vegetabile, vol. 126). ISBN 1878762427 (paper).

An inventory of currently used family names (NCU) for all plants and fungi exclusive of algae and extinct families of plants. The intent is simply to list names in use, not proscribe which are correct. The author and original publication of each name is also included. Similar inventories have been published for species names in select families and all accepted generic names (see titles under *Names in Current Use . . .*, below). Updated and corrected on the *Vascular Plant Family Nomenclature: Names in Current Use* Web page at www.life.umd.edu/emeritus/reveal/pbio/fam/ncu.html.

826   Greuter, Werner, ed. *Names in Current Use in the Families Trichocomaceae, Pinaceae, and Lemnaceae.* Königstein, Germany: Koeltz, 1993. 150 p. (NCU 2; Regnum Vegetabile, vol. 128). ISBN 1878762443.

The purpose of this volume is similar to that of the above list of current names, except that this work is concerned with species and subspecies names in use in selected plant families.

827   Greuter, Werner, et al., eds. *International Code of Botanical Nomenclature: Saint Louis Code.* Königstein, Germany: Koeltz Scientific Books, 2000. (Regnum Vegetabile, vol. 138). 474 p. ISBN 3904144227.

Botanical nomenclature is governed by the *International Code* as adopted by each International Botanical Congress held about every six years. The *Code* aims at the provision of a stable method of naming taxonomic groups of plants (including fungi), avoiding and rejecting the use of names that may cause error, ambiguity, or confusion. Updates to the *Code* may be found in *Taxon* or *Mycotaxon*. This code also governs the use of scientific or Latin names for plants whether they are cultivated or wild; see the *International Code of Nomenclature for Cultivated Plants*, which is revised after each new *International Code of Botanical Nomenclature* appears. The full text of the St. Louis code is also available at http://www.bgbm.org/iapt/nomenclature/code/SaintLouis/0000St.Luistitle.htm. An attempt is being made to combine all five biological nomenclatural codes into a single code; the *Draft Biocode* was developed in 1997 and is available online at http://www.rom.on.ca/biodiversity/biocode/biocode1997.html

828   Greuter, Werner, et al., eds. *Names in Current Use for Extant Plant Genera.* Königstein, Germany: Koeltz, 1993. 1464 p. $398.00. ISBN 1878762486. (NCU 3; Regnum Vegetabile, vol. 129).

Lists 28,041 generic names in current use for extant plants, including algae and fungi as well as the higher plants. This list includes the original citation for the generic name and is intended to stabilize plant nomenclature. The data are searchable on the Web at the *NCU-3e. Names in Current Use for Extant Plant Genera* page at http://www.bgbm.fu-berlin.de/iapt/ncu/genera/.

829   Guiry, M. D., and E. Nic Dhonncha. *AlgaeBase.* Version 2.1. Galway, Ireland: National University of Ireland, 2004. URL: http://www.algaebase.org.

A taxonomic database covering the algae of the world. At the time of viewing, the amount of information on each species varied, with the marine species more complete. Full records include photograph, synonymy, publication details, etymology, common names, references, GenBank link, and classification hierarchy. The database can be searched by common name, genus, and species.

830   Hassler, Michael, and Brian Swale. *Checklist of World Ferns.* 2001. URL: http://homepages.caverock.net.nz/~bj/fern/.

This site provides a browseable checklist of the ferns. Most genera are listed with taxonomic hierarchy, synonymy, original publication, and distribution.

831   Hickman, James C., ed. *The Jepson Manual: Higher Plants of California.* Berkeley, CA: University of California Press, 1993. 1400 p. $85.00. ISBN 0520082559.

An updated version of Willis Jepson's *Manual of Higher Plants of California,* originally published in 1951. Unusual among floras, this manual is intended for use by both amateurs and professional botanists. Therefore, although there are the usual dichotomous keys and technical descriptions, the manual also includes horticultural information, an illustrated glossary, and a chapter on the geological history of California. There are line drawings of most of the over 4,000 taxa. The checklist and distribution maps for the plants can be found at http://ucjeps .berkeley.edu/jeps-list.html.

832   Hill, Ken. *The Cycad Pages.* Sydney, Australia: Royal Botanic Gardens, Sydney. URL: http://plantnet.rbgsyd.nsw.gov.au/PlantNet/cycad/index.html.

Based on the World List of Cycads originally published in *Encephalartos,* the journal of the Cycad Society of South Africa, in 1985 and subsequently updated, this site provides a searchable and browseable list of cycads with descriptions and taxonomic information for each species as well as several articles covering cycad ecology, physiology, and cultivation.

833    Hitchcock, Charles Leo, et al. *Vascular Plants of the Pacific Northwest.* Seattle, WA: University of Washington Press, 19551969. 5 vol. (University of Washington Publications in Biology, vol. 17).

Covers all of Washington, the northern part of Oregon, and parts of Idaho, Montana, and southern British Columbia. The catalog includes keys, distribution, description, synonymy, and original publication. There are line drawings of some plants.

834    Holmes, Sandra. *Outline of Plant Classification.* New York: Longman, 1983. 181 p. ISBN 0582446481.

This clear and comprehensive guide to the classification of the Plant Kingdom is useful for the amateur botanist as well as the professional biological writer, although some of the details are outdated. It is still useful for its brief descriptions of plant classes and orders, including prokaryotes, algae, and fungi. The appendix provides flowcharts of plant life cycles for alternation of generations.

835    Holmgren, Patricia K., et al., eds. *Index Herbariorum. Part I: The Herbaria of the World.* 8th ed. Bronx, NY: New York Botanical Garden, 1990. 693 p. (Regnum Vegetabile, vol. 120) $35.00. ISBN 0893273589.

Detailed directory of the public herbaria of the world. Herbaria are arranged alphabetically by country and alphabetically by city. Data include address; correspondent(s); telephone number; status; date established; names of herbarium, director, and curators; staff names and specialties; associated gardens and institutions; publications; and remarks. Appendixes include tables and lists of herbaria by size, age, importance, and so on. Both parts 1 and 2 (*Plant Specialists Index*, below) are also available on the Web at http://www.nybg.org/bsci/ih/ih.html. The database can be searched by herbarium acronym, institution name and location, and personal name and research specialty.

836    Holmgren, Patricia K. and Noel H. Holmgren. *Plant Specialists Index: Index to Specialists in the Systematics of Plants and Fungi, Based on Data from Index Herbariorum (Herbaria), Edition 8.* Königstein, Germany: Koeltz Scientific, 1992. 394 p. (Regnum Vegetabile, vol. 124). ISBN 187876232X.

This index, although dated, is still useful. It is arranged in various sections, including taxonomic, subject, geographical region, herbarium address, and specialists' names. It can also be searched on the Web as part of *Index Herbariorum*, above. The Expert Center for Taxonomic Identification's *World Taxonomist Database* (above) provides similar information on taxonomists.

837    Hutchinson, John. *The Genera of Flowering Plants: Angiospermae.* Oxford, England: Clarendon Press, 1964–1967. 2 vol.

Only two volumes covering the dicotyledons were ever finished in this major work. Although Hutchinson's taxonomy has been revised, his descriptions of genera are still used. The work is based on Bentham and Hooker's *Generum Plantarum*. Volume 1 covers Magnoliales through Leguminales, whereas Volume 2 covers Cunoniales through Malpighiales.

838    Hutchinson, John. *The Families of Flowering Plants: Arranged According to a System Based on Their Probable Phylogeny*. 3rd ed. Königstein, Germany: Koeltz, 1979. 968 p. $170.00. ISBN 0198543778.

Even though Hutchinson's division of dicotyledons into woody and herbaceous plants is no longer considered valid, his system was highly influential. It has been largely replaced by Cronquist's *Integrated System* (above).

839    *Integrated Taxonomic Information System: ITIS*. Washington, DC: U. S. Department of Agriculture, 1990s– . URL: http://www.itis.usda.gov/.

Provides authoritative information on plants, fungi, animals, and microbes of North America and the world. The database includes the authority (author and date), taxonomic rank, associated synonyms and common names, and references.

840    International Organization for Plant Information (IOPI). *Provisional Global Plant Checklist*. URL: http://www.biologie.uni-hamburg.de/b-online/ibc99/iopi/default.htm.

This database provides basic nomenclatural information (original reference, status, and synonyms). At the time of viewing in September 2005, the database contained 201,397 different plant names taken from six major databases. The checklist is designed as a tool for authors working on the *Species Plantarum* project (see below).

841    Jarvis, C. E., et al., comps. *A List of Linnaean Generic Names and Their Types*. Königstein, Germany: Published for the International Association for Plant Taxonomy by Koeltz, 1993. 100 p. (Regnum Vegetabile, vol. 127). ISBN 1878762435 (paper).

A list of the 1,313 generic names first published by Linnaeus and still accepted, along with the type specimen in most cases. The intent is to provide a list of protected names to stabilize nomenclature.

842    Jeffrey, Charles. *Biological Nomenclature*. 3rd ed. London: Edward Arnold, 1989. 86 p. ISBN 0713129832 (paper).

Though hardly large enough to notice on the shelf, this slim little volume does an excellent job of elucidating the complexities and technicalities of biological nomenclature. Although it covers all three major taxonomic divisions (bacteriological, botanical, and zoological), the author is a botanist and the volume is thus of particular use to botanists.

843    Kartesz, John T., Hugh D. Wilson, and Erich Schneider. *A Synonymized Checklist of the Vascular Flora of the United States, Puerto Rico, and the Virgin Islands.* Chapel Hill, NC: BONAP; College Station, TX: TAMU-BWG, 1998. URL: http://www.csdl.tamu.edu/FLORA/b98/check98.htm.

The data for this checklist came primarily from John Kartesz and the Biota of North America Program (BONAP). The checklist includes nomenclature and geographical distribution maps for the United States, Puerto Rico, and the Virgin Islands and can be browsed by family name, genus, or common name. The entries may include links to illustrations or information from other Web floras.

844    Komarov, V. L., ed. *Flora of the U. S. S. R.* Königstein, Germany: Koeltz Scientific, 1985– . Reprint of 1963–1977 series.

This is a major regional flora. The English translation was originally done by the Israel Program for Scientific Translation, under the sponsorship of the National Science Foundation and the Smithsonian Institution. The reprint series is now up to Volume 25. Translation of *Flora SSSR* (Moscow: Akademiia Nauk SSSR, 1934–1960. 30 vol. and index).

845    Kubitzki, K., ed. *The Families and Genera of Vascular Plants.* New York: Springer-Verlag, 1990– . Multivolume. ISBN 0387517944 (vol. 1); 0387555099 (vol. 2); 3540640606 (vol. 3); 3540640614 (vol. 4); 3540428739 (vol. 5); 3540065121 (vol. 6); 3540405933 (vol. 7).

This set covers all genera of vascular plants. The families are arranged alphabetically within each order, and accounts include author and citation to original description, information on the morphology, seeds or spores, karyology, reproduction, ecology, and taxonomy of each family, along with a key to genera. Generic descriptions are briefer and include many drawings and photographs. Volumes published to date include Volume 1, Pteridophytes and gymnosperms; Volume 2, Flowering plants, Dicotyledons: Magnoliid, Hammelid and Caryophyllid families; Volumes 3 through 7, Flowering plants, monocotyledons.

846    Kurtzman, C. P., and Jack W. Fell. *The Yeasts: A Taxonomic Study.* 4th ed. New York: Elsevier, 2000. 1055 p. $439.00. ISBN 0444813128.

This revision, which provides the criteria and methods for classification and identification of yeasts, follows the format of the successful earlier editions: introductory chapters discuss classification, importance of yeasts; ultrastructural and biochemical properties; and methods for isolation, maintenance, classification, and identification. The remaining chapters present keys for each genus and a standard description of each species including recognized varieties within a genus. A glossary, a bibliography, and an index of taxa are provided. This and Barnett's *Yeasts* (see Identification section, below) are worthy competitors.

847   Large, Mark F., and John E. Braggins. *Tree Ferns.* Portland: Timber, 2004. 359 p. $39.95. ISBN 0881926302.

Designed for both botanists and horticulturalists, this guide surveys the families, genera, and species of tree ferns. It provides taxonomical information, detailed descriptions, and extensive cultivation assistance.

848   Liesner, R. *Field Techniques Used by Missouri Botanical Garden.* St. Louis, MO: Missouri Botanical Garden, 1995. URL: http://www.mobot.org/ MOBOT/Research/Library/liesner/tpage.html.

This Web site outlines the best practices for collecting plant specimens as used by the Missouri Botanical Garden. The techniques are recommended for use in other herbaria as well. The site is available in English, French, and Spanish and includes a list of recommended readings.

849   Linneaus, Carolus. *Genera Plantarum: Eorumque Characteres Naturales Secundum Numerum, Figuram, Situm, et Proportionem Omnium Fructificationis Partium.* 5th ed. Stockholm, Sweden: Impensis Laurentii Salvii, 1754.

Linneaus was primarily a botanist. In this book, he outlined his system of classifying plants largely according to the number of stamens and pistils in the flower. Although this system has been discarded in favor of a phylogenetic relationship, *Genera Plantarum* still forms the basis of modern plant taxonomy. It has been reprinted a number of times.

850   Linneaus, Carolus. *Species Plantarum: Exhibentes Plantas Rite Cognitas, ad Genera Relatas, cum Differentiis Specificis, Nominibus Trivialibus, Synonymis Selectis, Locis Natalibus, Secundum Systema Sexuale Digestas.* 2 vol. Stockholm, Sweden: Impensis Laurentii Salvii, 1753.

*Species Plantarum* is considered the starting point for binomial nomenclature for plants. Linneaus established names for about 8,000 species of plants in this book, many of which are still used. The book is available in a number of reprint editions.

851   MacFarlane, Ruth B. Alford. *Collecting and Preserving Plants.* New York: Dover, 1994. 184 p. $7.95. ISBN 0486282813.

Unlike the other guides to plant collection listed in this chapter, this book is aimed at the amateur rather than the professional botanist. It covers the usual topics in collecting, preserving, mounting, and storing plant specimens but also discusses urban botanizing and ornamental uses of preserved plants. Originally published in 1985.

852    Maddison, D. R., and W. P. Maddison. *The Tree of Life: A Multi-Authored, Distributed Internet Project Containing Information About Phylogeny and Bio-diversity.* 1998– . URL: http://tolweb.org/tree/.

Although still a work in progress, *The Tree of Life* provides phylogenies for all groups of organisms, living and extinct, and is designed for researchers and advanced students. The treatments include extensive bibliographies dealing with the systematics of that group, and most also include photos or drawings of representative species, plus links to other Web sites dealing with the taxon. Some groups are treated in more detail than others depending on the availability of volunteer authors. See the University of California, Berkeley's *Phylogeny of Life* site, below, for a similar Web survey of phylogenies.

853    Maire, René. *Flore de l'Afrique du Nord (Maroc, Algérie, Tunisie, Tripo-litaine, Cyrénaïque et Sahara).* Paris: P. Lechevalier, 1952–1987. (Encyclopédie Biologique, vol. 33, 45, 48, 53–54, 57–60, 62–63, 67–68, 70, 72–73). ISSN 0301-4274.

Twenty volumes are planned for this flora of North Africa, though to date only 16 have been published, leaving part of the Leguminosae incomplete. The vol-umes include line drawings of selected plants and keys as well as species ac-counts.

854    Metsger, Deborah A., and Sheila C. Byers, eds. *Managing the Modern Herbarium: An Inter-Disciplinary Approach.* Vancouver, Canada: Elton-Wolf, 1999. 384 p. ISBN 0963547623.

Based on a 1995 workshop by the same name, this handbook provides detailed guidelines and protocols for a wide range of topics. It is arranged in three main sections covering preventive conservation, contemporary issues facing herbaria, and a section containing short papers from the workshop. The handbook includes both case studies and detailed protocols for temperate and tropical herbaria.

855    Nimsch, Hubertus. *A Reference Guide to the Gymnosperms of the World: An Introduction to Their History, Systematics, Distribution, and Significance.* Champaign, IL: Koeltz Scientific, 1995. 99 p. ISBN 1878762524.

This survey of gymnosperm diversity includes information on fossil gymno-sperms as well as living genera. The descriptions include original author and citation, etymology, distribution, and general descriptions. There are black-and-white photographs and line drawings as well as an illustrated key to genus.

856    *North American Flora.* Series I and II. New York: New York Botanical Garden, 1905–1990. Series I, pt. 1–94, 1905–49; ser., II, pt. 1–13, 1954–1990. ISSN 0078-1312.

The purpose of this series is to provide keys and descriptions of all plants growing spontaneously in North America, Central America, and the West Indies (excluding those islands whose flora is essentially South American). Each part is devoted to an order, family, or smaller group, complete with bibliography and index.

857   Pichi-Sermolli, Rodolfo E. G. *Authors of Scientific Names in Pteridophyta: A List of Authors of Names of Ferns and Fern Allies with Recommended Standard Forms of Their Names Including Abbreviations*. London: Royal Botanic Gardens, Kew, 1996. 78 p. ISBN 0947643907 (paper).

Contains nearly 400 names not found in Brummitt's *Authors of Plant Names*, above, with additional information on nearly 500 extra authors.

858   Reveal, James L. *Vascular Plant Family Nomenclature*. College Park, MD: University of Maryland, 1996. URL: http://www.life.umd.edu/emeritus/reveal/pbio/fam/revfam.html.

Reveal's Web site provides a list of valid plant family names as well as links to a number of other plant nomenclature databases, an essay on nomenclature above the genus level, and more.

859   Rose, Carolyn L., Catharine A. Hawks, Hugh H. Genoways, and Amparo R. de Torres, eds. *Storage of Natural History Collections*. 2 vol. Washington, DC: Society for the Preservation of Natural History Collections, 1995. ISBN 0963547615 (vol. 1); 0963547607 (vol. 2).

This set provides ideas and practical solutions for the storage of a complete range of natural history collections, including those for anthropology, herbaria, taxidermy, microscopy, living cells, and so on. Volume 1 covers preventive strategies whereas Volume 2 lists practical tips.

860   Savile, Douglas Barton Osborne. *Collection and Care of Botanical Specimens*. Ottawa, Canada: Research Branch, Canada Department of Agriculture, 1962. 124 p. (Canada. Department of Agriculture, Publication 1113).

Although some of the advice in this manual is dated (great advances in cold-weather clothing have been made since 1962, for instance), this is still a classic especially for those dealing with cold weather and Arctic conditions. The author discusses handling vascular plants, fungi, mosses and liverworts, lichens, and algae.

861   Scoggan, H. J. *Flora of Canada*. Ottawa, Canada: National Museum of Natural Sciences, 1978–79. 4 vol. (National Museum of Natural Sciences Publications in Botany, no. 7).

This flora covers 4,153 species, 3,218 of them native to Canada. It includes keys for identifying the plants and information on their ecology and distribution, but very little description. Volume 1 is a general survey, including an introduction, glossary and references. The remaining three volumes cover the plant species. There is a cumulative index to Latin names of families, genera, and species.

862    Slack, Adrian, and Jane Gate. *Carnivorous Plants*. Cambridge, MA: MIT Press, 2000. 240 p. ISBN 0262690896 (paper).

Discusses the genera of carnivorous plants from around the world. Each genus is described in layman's terms with interesting tidbits of its natural history and ethnobotany. Some individual species are also described. The authors also provide extensive information on the cultivation of carnivorous plants. There are a number of color photographs and black-and-white illustrations, making this a highly attractive book. See also Juniper's book by the same name in chapter 2 for information on the biology of carnivorous plants.

863    Small, John Kunkel. *Manual of the Southeastern Flora; Being Descriptions of the Seed Plants Growing Naturally in Florida, Alabama, Mississippi, Eastern Louisiana, Tennessee, North Carolina, South Carolina and Georgia*. New York: The author, 1933. 1554 p.

A classic flora, and one of the few comprehensive floras to cover the southeastern states. There are analytical keys and a descriptive flora that includes line drawings of representative species from most genera. Small followed Engler and Prantl's taxonomic system (above).

864    Solomon, Jim. *W³Tropicos*. Rev. 1.7. St. Louis, MO: Missouri Botanical Garden, 2000– . URL: http://mobot.mobot.org/W3T/Search/vast.html.

This search engine provides access to the Missouri Botanical Garden's VAST (VAScular Tropicos) nomenclatural database and associated authority files for vascular plants and bryophytes. The database includes information on the plant name and authors, original publication, synonymy and higher taxa, as well as references.

865    Soltis, Douglas E., Pamela S. Soltis, and Jeff J. Doyle, eds. *Molecular Systematics of Plants II: DNA Sequencing*. Boston, MA: Kluwer Academic, 1998. 574 p. $234.00; $108.00 (paper). ISBN 0412111217; 0412111314 (paper).

Covering both theoretical and practical aspects of plant systematics, this volume updates *Molecular Systematics of Plants*, published in 1992 by the same editors. In addition to providing information on techniques for various types of research, the text also surveys the recent studies on the systematics of algae and ferns.

866    *Species 2000*. International Union of Biological Sciences, 2000– . URL: http://www.sp2000.org/.

According to its Web site, "Species 2000 has the objective of enumerating all known species of organisms on Earth (animals, plants, fungi and microbes) as the baseline dataset for studies of global biodiversity." The database consists of checklists and nomenclatural information taken from several other major databases and projects, including the *Global Plant Checklist*; *International Plant Name Index*; *Plant Fossil Record*; *Moss/TROPICOS*; *Species Fungorum*; and *World Database of Legumes*. More names and databases are added continually.

867   *Species Plantarum: Flora of the World.* Canberra, Australia: Australian Biological Resources Study, 1999– . Irregular. ISSN 1441-1393. Available electronically.

This flora has the rather optimistic (not to mention ambitious) goal of covering all species of vascular plants in the world. The most recent attempt at a comprehensive flora prior to *Species Plantarum* was Engler's *Das Pflanzenreich* (see above). The flora is issued in a number of small parts and as of late 2003 was up to 10 parts. Nomenclatural and distributional data from the series will be available as part of the *Global Plant Checklist* at http://bgbm3.bgbm.fu-berlin.de/iopi/gpc/default.asp.

868   Stearn, William T. *Botanical Latin: History, Grammar, Syntax, Terminology, and Vocabulary.* 4th ed. Portland, OR: Timber, 1995. 546 p. $44.95. ISBN 0881923214.

A "... guide to the special kind of Latin internationally used by botanists for the description and naming of plants." This guide traces the development of botanical Latin terminology and introduces the Latin alphabet, pronunciation, grammar, and usage to the uninitiated. This is an authoritative, scholarly treatment.

869   Stebbins, G. Ledyard. *Flowering Plants: Evolution above the Species Level.* Cambridge, MA: Harvard University Press, 1974. 399 p. ISBN 0674306856.

Stebbins discusses evolutionary trends in angiosperm evolution and the factors that determine them. An appendix lists the orders and families of angiosperms according to Stebbins's system, which is basically a synthesis of Cronquist's *The Evolution and Classification of Flowering Plants*, above, and Takhtadzhian's *Diversity and Classification of Flowering Plants*, below.

870   Stevens, P. F. *Angiosperm Phylogeny Website.* 2001– . Version 5. May 2004. URL: http://www.mobot.org/MOBOT/research/APweb/.

Designed as an angiosperm phylogeny teaching aid, this site describes all families and orders of angiosperms as well as some higher and lower clades. The descriptions are quite technical, and the site includes phylogenetic trees, descriptions of the characters used to determine the phylogenies, references, glossary, and a search function.

871    Swift, Lloyd H. *Botanical Classification: A Comparison of Eight Systems of Angiosperm Classification*. Hamden, CT: Archon, 1974. 374 p. ISBN 0208014551.

Comparisons are made between the classification systems proposed by Endlicher, Bentham and Hooker, Eichlar, Engler and Prantl, Bessey, Hutchinson, Melchior, and Cronquist. See Brummitt's *Vascular Plant Families and Genera*, above, for additional comparisons.

872    Takhtadzhian, A. L. *Diversity and Classification of Flowering Plants*. New York: Columbia University Press, 1997. 643 p. $113.00. ISBN 0231100981.

Takhtadzhian presents a phyletic classification of plants to the family level. There are descriptive keys to families within each order and extensive references. Takhtadzhian's system closely resembles Cronquist's. The author's name was formerly transliterated as Takhtajan and may still be found under this spelling.

873    Thorne, Robert F., and James L. Reveal. *An Updated Classification of the Class Angiospermae*. University of Maryland, 1999. URL: http://www.rsabg.org/research/Angiosperms.htm.

Thorne's classification system is one of the standard alternatives. It was originally published in 1992 as an article in the journal *Botanical Review*. This Web site gives access to the system, along with some additional information provided by Reveal.

874    Tryon, Rolla Milton, and Alice F. Tryon. *Ferns and Allied Plants: With Special Reference to Tropical America*. New York: Springer-Verlag, 1981. 857 p. ISBN 038790672X.

The standard reference for the systematics of the ferns and fern allies, this handbook emphasizes New World species, as the title suggests, but also includes information on Old World species that are in genera that are found in the Americas. Each genus account includes synonymy, description, systematics, a list of tropical American species, ecology, geography, spores, cytology, and literature cited. There are maps and photographs and illustrations of ferns and spores as well.

875    Tutin, T. G., et al., eds. *Flora Europaea*. New York: Cambridge University Press, 1964–1980. 5 vol. plus CD-ROM. $1,150.00 (set). ISBN 0521805708 (set); 2nd ed. Vol. 1, 1993 (ISBN 052141007X).

*Flora Europaea* presents a synthesis of all the national and regional floras of Europe, based on critical reviews of existing literature and on studies in herbaria and in the field. The first edition was published from 1964 to 1980; a second edition of Volume 1 was published in 1993, but no further volumes of the second edition have been completed. The CD-ROM and all individual volumes are available separately. The data from *Flora Europaea* are also searchable on the Web at http://rbg-web2.rbge.org.uk/FE/fe.html. The information available on the Web site includes family, genus, species, original citation, synonymy, and distribution within Europe. Note: the search engine is case-sensitive!

U.S. Department of Agriculture, Agriculture Research Service, National Genetic Resources Program. *GRIN (Germplasm Resources Information Network) Taxonomy.*

See chapter 8 for full annotation under the title *National Plant Germplasm System*. This taxonomic authority file contains records for over 40,000 taxa, including 14,000 genera. The amount of data varies by name, but may include original citation, common name(s), economic importance, range, references, other databases to search, images, and whether germplasm has been deposited.

876   University of California, Berkeley. Museum of Paleontology. *Phylogeny of Life*. URL: http://www.ucmp.berkeley.edu/exhibit/phylogeny.html.

This Web site provides an introduction to almost all higher taxa of organisms, both extinct and living. The information for most taxa include a brief introduction to the taxonomy, ecology, and life history of organisms in the group plus illustrations, short lists of Web sites for further research, information on the paleontology of the taxa, and links to an online glossary. An excellent resource for information on even the most obscure group of plants. See also Maddison's *Tree of Life* Web site, above, for a similar guide to phylogeny on the Web.

877   *Vascular Flora of the Southeastern United States*. Chapel Hill, NC: University of North Carolina Press, 1980– . Multivolume. $59.95 (vol. 3, pt. 2). ISBN 0807849413 (vol. 1); 080781900X (vol. 3, pt. 2).

This unfinished series is projected to contain five volumes when complete. It covers the forested region of the southeastern United States from Delaware in the north to Florida in the south and west to Louisiana. Contents will include Volume 1, Asteraceae; Volume 2, Ferns, Gymnosperms, Magnoliidae; Volume 3, part 1, Rosidae and Asteridae; Volume 3, part 2, Leguminosae; and Volume 4, Liliopsida. Until this series is finished, Small's *Manual of the Southeastern Flora*, above, is still the most complete for this region.

878   Watson, L., and M. J. Dallwitz. *The Families of Flowering Plants: Descriptions, Illustrations, Identification, and Information Retrieval*. 1992– . Version 14. December 2000. URL: http://delta-intkey.com/angio/.

All families of flowering plants are included in this Web site. The descriptions are written in very technical language and include taxonomic information on both lower and higher taxa for each family. Many families also include information on use, technical drawings, and even some poetry. The same information was also published on CD-ROM by CSIRO in 1993–1994 under the same title.

879   Watson, L., and M. J. Dallwitz. *The Grass Genera of the World.* Wallingford, England: CAB International, 1992. 1038 p. $205.00. ISBN 0851988024.

Covers 10,000 species of Poaceae and Gramineae. The information provided for each species includes detailed description of each plant part, cytology, taxonomy and synonymy, distribution, economic importance, rusts and smuts, and more.

880   Welsh, Stanley L. *Anderson's Flora of Alaska and Adjacent Parts of Canada.* Provo, UT: Brigham Young University Press, 1974. 724 p. ISBN 0842507051.

Based on the work of Jacob Anderson, this flora covers the plants of Alaska, the Yukon, and parts of British Columbia. There are keys to family, genus, and species and line drawings of selected species.

881   Winston, Judith E. *Describing Species: Practical Taxonomic Procedure for Biologists.* New York: Columbia University Press, 1999. 518 p. $78.00; $40.00 (paper). ISBN 0231068247; 0231068255 (paper).

Everything you ever needed to know about describing and publishing valid species descriptions, from library and museum research through the actual naming, writing, illustrating, and publishing.

882   Womersley, J. S. *Plant Collecting and Herbarium Development: A Manual.* Rome: Food and Agriculture Organization of the United Nations, 1981. (FAO Plant Production and Protection Paper, 33). 137 p. ISBN 9251011443.

Womersley discusses practical information for the beginner, as well as specialized techniques for the more experienced botanist with chapters on field collecting, preservation, identification, function and organization of the herbarium, processing of herbarium collections, herbarium curation, and ancillary services.

**Identification**

883   Arora, David. *Mushrooms Demystified: A Comprehensive Guide to the Fleshy Fungi.* 2nd ed. Berkeley, CA: Ten Speed, 1986. 959 p. $39.95 (paper). ISBN 0898151708; 0898151716 (deluxe); 0898151694 (paper).

This hefty guide to mushrooms covers over 2,000 species of the United States, far more than most other field guides. The coverage is best for the author's home territory of California but is valuable for other parts of the country as well. There are keys, detailed descriptions with information on habitat and edibility, and black-and-white photographs of most species. A separate section of color plates illustrates the more gaudy species. There are also chapters on mushroom cookery, toxins, and etymology of scientific names as well as a glossary, bibliography, and general index.

### Audubon Society Field Guides

This highly regarded series is useful for all levels of interest. Unlike most other field guides, the Audubon guides are illustrated with color photographs rather than drawings. Some users do not like identifying plants or animals from photographs, but others may prefer it. See also *eNature.com*, below, for a Web version of most of the guides.

884   Lincoff, Gary. *The Audubon Society Field Guide to North American Mushrooms*. New York: Knopf, 1981. 926 p. $19.95. ISBN 0394519922.

Includes detailed information on 700 species with many more mentioned. It is organized by color and shape and includes a spore print chart along with information on eating mushrooms.

885   Little, Elbert L. *The Audubon Society Field Guide to North American Trees: Eastern Region*. New York: Knopf, 1980. 714 p. $19.95. ISBN 0394507606.

Covering North America east of the Rockies, this photographic guide identifies about 400 species. It is arranged visually by features such as type of leaf, flower, and/or fall coloration.

886   Little, Elbert L. *The Audubon Society Field Guide to North American Trees: Western Region*. New York: Knopf, 1980. 639 p. $19.95. ISBN 0394507614.

Companion to the author's eastern tree guide, above, the western guide covers the area from the Rocky Mountains to the Pacific Ocean and includes about 350 species.

887   Spellenberg, Richard. *The Audubon Society Field Guide to North American Wildflowers: Western Region*. Rev. ed. New York: Knopf, 2001. 896 p. $19.95. ISBN 0375402330.

Like its eastern companion, below, this guide covers about 600 species in detail and another 400 species briefly.

888    Thieret, John W., William A. Niering, and Nancy C. Olmstead. *The Audubon Society Field Guide to North American Wildflowers: Eastern Region*. Rev. ed. New York: Knopf, 2001. 879 p. $19.95. ISBN 0375402322.

Covers about 600 species in detail, with another 400 briefly described. Arranged by flower color.

889    Barnett, Horace L., and Barry B. Hunter. *Illustrated Genera of Imperfect Fungi*. 4th ed. Edina, MN: Burgess, 1987. 218 p. $48.00 (spiral-bound). ISBN 0808749773; 0890541922 (spiral-bound); 0023063955 (paper).

This identification manual is useful for work with a most difficult plant group.

890    Barnett, J. A., R. W. Payne, and D. Yarrow. *Yeasts: Characteristics and Identification*. 3rd ed. New York: Cambridge University Press, 2000. 1139 p. $350.00. ISBN 0521573963.

This massive reference provides commonly used procedures for yeast identification and gives detailed descriptions for all 678 known yeast species. There are identification keys, physiological tests, excellent photomicrographs, an extensive bibliography, and a section containing specific epithets and yeast names. *Yeasts* is accurate, authoritative, and a very important resource for yeast taxonomy.

891    Batson, Wade T. *Genera of the Western Plants: A Guide to the Genera of Native and Commonly Introduced Ferns and Seed Plants of North America, West of About the 98th Meridian and North of Mexico*. Columbia, SC: University of South Carolina Press, 1984. 210 p. ISBN 0872494519 (paper).

This field guide and its companion to the eastern plants, below, are compact publications describing the genera of the plants of North America. They provide keys for identification; drawings; and information on name authority, common names, synonyms, characteristics, habitat, and range.

892    Batson, Wade T. *Guide to the Genera of the Plants of Eastern North America*. 3rd ed., rev. Columbia, SC: University of South Carolina Press, 1984. 203 p. ISBN 0872494500.

See the author's *Genera of the Western Plants*, above.

893    Baumgardt, John Philip. *How to Identify Flowering Plant Families: A Practical Guide for Horticulturists and Plant Lovers*. Portland, OR: Timber, 1982. 269 p. $22.95. ISBN 0917304217 (paper).

As the title suggests, this book is designed for the nonprofessional but is still very useful for students. The author describes over 100 North American plant families and includes line drawings of typical members of each family. Although the descriptions are fairly technical, the glossary should clarify unknown terms, and there is an extensive opening discussion of how to identify plants, how to understand floral formulae (formulae describing the relationship of flower parts), and descriptions of flower anatomy. Very similar in aim to Hickey and King's handbooks, below, but briefer and on a less technical level.

894   Benson, Lyman David, and Robert Arthur Darrow. *Trees and Shrubs of the Southwestern Deserts.* 3rd ed., rev. and expanded. Tucson: University of Arizona Press, 1981. 416 p. ISBN 0816505918.

This manual covers the desert regions from about Palm Springs, California, to El Paso, Texas. The authors include extensive background information on the desert and plant classification as well as keys and species accounts. There are distribution maps and black-and-white photographs of most species.

895   Bessette, Alan, Arleen Rainis Bessette, and David W. Fischer. *Mushrooms of Northeastern North America.* Syracuse, NY: Syracuse University Press, 1997. 582 p. $95.00; $45.00 (paper). ISBN 0815627076; 0815603886 (paper).

This identification guide covers eastern Canada west to Manitoba and the United States west to the Dakotas and south to Tennessee. It includes nearly 1,500 species, arranged by appearance. A color key identifies the major groups of mushrooms, leading to the species account with detailed description of cap, gills, stalk, spore print, and microscopic features; the fruiting period and type and edibility are also included, as well as comments. Appendixes cover eating mushrooms, microscopic examination, chemical identification, and mushroom classification. Suitable for both professionals and amateurs.

896   Brown, Lauren. *Grasses: An Identification Guide.* Boston, MA: Houghton Mifflin, 1992. 240 p. (Peterson Nature Library). $16.00 (paper). ISBN 0395628814 (paper).

This field guide to the grasses of the northeastern United States is easy to use and includes a very basic key, description, and drawing of about 150 common plants. Unfortunately, it does not cover the prairie states, although many of the species covered will also be found farther west.

897   Brown, Lauren. *Weeds in Winter.* New York: Norton, 1986. 252 p. ISBN 0393303489 (paper).

This guide to dried weedy plants in the winter has a similar format to the previous volume and covers the same area. Identification is mostly made on the basis of the fruits or seedheads remaining on the stalks of winter plants.

898   Cody, William J., and Donald M. Britton. *Ferns and Fern Allies of Canada.* Ottawa, Canada: Research Branch, Agriculture Canada, 1989. 430 p. (Publication, Research Canada, 1829). ISBN 0660131021 (paper).

Issued also in French as *Les Fougeres et les Plantes Alliees du Canada*. This is the first comprehensive guide to the ferns of Canada and was written for amateurs and professionals alike. The authors supply keys, descriptions, illustrations, and distribution information for Canadian ferns. The range maps cover only Canada, but the descriptive material includes information on the United States, so this volume is useful for the northern United States as well as Canada.

899    Cullen, James, and Peter Hadland Davis. *The Identification of Flowering Plant Families: Including a Key to Those Native and Cultivated in North Temperate Regions*. 4th ed., completely rev. and edited. New York: Cambridge University Press, 1997. 215 p. $25.00 (paper). ISBN 052158485X; 0521585503 (paper).

The introductory chapters discuss usage of terms and how to examine the plant for identification purposes. There are keys followed by brief descriptions of each family. The guide is suitable for amateurs or professional botanists to identify all flowering plant families found wild or cultivated in both the East and West Hemispheres above 30 degrees north.

900    Elias, Thomas S. *Field Guide to North American Trees*. Rev. ed. Danbury, CT: Grolier Book Clubs, 1989. 948 p. ISBN 1556540493; 155654037X (paper).

The purpose of this classic guide is to help identify any of over 750 native and introduced North American trees. It is appropriate for both the specialist and the amateur and includes a diversity of information on trees of North America. The keys and descriptions are clear, useful, and easy to use. Only leaves and seeds are illustrated. Originally published as *The Complete Trees of North America*.

901    *eNature.com*. San Francisco, CA: ENature.com, 2000– . URL: http://www .enature.com.

A Web guide to over 4,800 plants and animals of North America taken from the Audubon Society Field Guide series (see above) and includes pictures and descriptions taken from the books. The plant section includes Audubon guides to trees and wildflowers as well as material taken from the Lady Bird Johnson Wildflower Center's *Native Plant Guide*. Users can search by name or by region, leaf type, color, bloom period, habitat, and other characteristics. The site is sponsored by the National Wildlife Federation.

902    Gleason, Henry A., and Arthur Cronquist. *Manual of Vascular Plants of Northeastern United States and Adjacent Canada*. 2nd ed. New York: New York Botanical Garden, 1991. 910 p. $69.00. ISBN 0893273651.

This work is based on the classic *New Britton and Brown Illustrated Flora of the Northeastern United States and Canada*. The second edition is far smaller and lacks illustrations but has a lengthy glossary, updated taxonomy, and extensive keys. The region covered is as far west as Minnesota and as far south as Kentucky. This is not a field guide for the casual layperson but is an important, definitive manual for the serious student or researcher. See Holmgren's *Illustrated Companion,* below, for a companion volume containing the original illustrations from the *Illustrated Flora.*

### Golden Field Guides

Each field guide in this series covers all of North America, in contrast to most field guides that cover a smaller area. They are well organized, with descriptions, illustrations, and maps of each flower or tree on the same two-page spread.

903   Brockman, C. Frank. *Trees of North America: A Field Guide to the Major Native and Introduced Species North of Mexico.* Rev. and updated ed. New York: St. Martin's, 2001. 280 p. $14.95 (paper). ISBN 1582380929 (paper).
Covers over 600 native and introduced species.

904   Venning, Frank D. *Wildflowers of North America: A Guide to Field Identification.* New York: St. Martin's, 1984. 340 p. $14.95 (paper). ISBN 0307470075; 0307136647.
Over 1,550 species are included, arranged by family.

905   Gray, Asa. *Gray's Manual of Botany: A Handbook of the Flowering Plants and Ferns of the Central and Northeastern United States and Canada.* 8th (Centennial) ed. New York: American Book, 1950. 1632 p. ISBN 0931146097.
"A handbook of the flowering plants and ferns of the central and northeastern United States and adjacent Canada." As with most floras, *Gray's* provides a key, synopsis of the classification system used, and authors' names in addition to the plant descriptions. There are also indexes to Latin, English, and French-Canadian names. This is a standard, and time honored, reference source for the names and descriptions of plants. This edition was revised and expanded by Merritt Lyndon Fernald.

906   Harrington, Harold Davis. *How to Identify Grasses and Grasslike Plants (Sedges and Rushes).* Chicago, IL: Swallow, 1977. 142 p. $11.95 (paper). ISBN 0804007462 (paper).
Written by a professional botanist, this clear, concise, well-organized manual gives practical information for identifying grasses. There are 500 drawings and illustrations, and a section listing manuals and floras appropriate to the subject.

907   Hickey, Michael, and Clive King. *100 Families of Flowering Plants.* 2nd ed. New York: Cambridge University Press, 1988. ISBN 0521337003; 0521330491 (paper).

Designed to acquaint the student of botany with members of 100 typical plant families. Each family is discussed in one to two pages, followed by a detailed description of a member of that family. There are numerous line drawings of flower, bud, and seed structure. This could equally well be placed in the textbook section and covers more families than the authors' *Common Families of Flowering Plants* (below).

908    Hickey, Michael, and Clive King. *Common Families of Flowering Plants.* New York: Cambridge University Press, 1997. 212 p. $28.00 (paper). ISBN 0521572819; 0521576091 (paper).

Provides an introduction for students to 25 common plant families, including plants of economic, ecological, and ornamental importance. The information for each family includes distribution, vegetative characteristics, floral formula, pollination, and description of the flower and inflorescence. There are several line drawings of plant parts for each family as well.

909    Holmgren, Noel H. *Illustrated Companion to Gleason and Cronquist's Manual: Illustrations of the Vascular Plants of Northeastern United States and Adjacent Canada.* Bronx, NY: New York Botanical Garden, 1998. 937 p. $125.00. ISBN 0893273996.

The latest (1991) edition of the *Manual of the Vascular Plants of Northeastern United States and Adjacent Canada,* above, lacked illustrations so that it could be published as a small field manual. This volume takes the more than 1,000 illustrations from the original 1963 edition and updates and corrects them.

910    Hutchinson, John. *Key to the Families of Flowering Plants of the World.* Oxford, England: Clarendon, 1967. $37.00. 117 p. ISBN 3874291618.

Revised and enlarged for use as a supplement to the author's *Genera of Flowering Plants* (see Taxonomy section, above). This is one of the best-known keys to the flowering plants and one of the few to include plants worldwide. Although Hutchinson's taxonomic system is outdated, family names are largely stable so the key is still valuable. Illustrations and a glossary were added to assist the botanical novice, although this key and Thonner's *Analytical Key* are more appropriate for the serious student than the amateur.

911    Keller, Roland. *Identification of Tropical Woody Plants in the Absence of Flowers: A Field Guide.* 2nd ed. Boston, MA: Birkhauser Verlag, 2004. 294 p. $79.95. ISBN 376436453X (paper).

Allows users to key out woody plants from tropical regions around the world down to the family level. There are many line drawings and some color photographs. The key is designed for the use of ecologists and tropical botanists.

912 Knobel, Edward. *Field Guide to the Grasses, Sedges and Rushes of the United States.* New York: Dover, 1977. 83 p. $4.95 (paper). ISBN 048623505X.

The small guide outlines a key to over 370 of the most common species of grasses, sedges, and rushes. It is easy to carry and an excellent companion in the field. There are 500 line drawings with concise, accurate descriptions.

913 Lellinger, David B. *A Field Manual of the Ferns and Fern-Allies of the United States and Canada.* Washington, DC: Smithsonian Institution Press, 1985. 389 p. ISBN 0874746027; 0874746035 (paper).

Written for the professional, amateur botanist, and horticulturist, this lavishly illustrated guide by an associate curator of botany at the Smithsonian Institution presents descriptions and keys for 406 native and naturalized species, subspecies, and important varieties of ferns and fern allies.

914 Miller, Orson K., Jr. *Mushrooms of North America.* Rev. ed. New York: Dutton, 1979. 359 p. ISBN 0525482261 (paper).

This guide covers about 680 species of the United States and Canada, and includes keys, glossary, bibliography, and index. The general introductory material is interesting, and the guide is written for the amateur as well as the student of botany. This book is more appropriate for comparing specimens in the laboratory or at home; its size is not conducive to field work.

915 Newcomb, Lawrence. *Newcomb's Wildflower Guide: An Ingenious New Key System for Quick, Positive Field Identification of the Wildflowers, Flowering Shrubs and Vines of Northeastern and North Central North America.* Boston, MA: Little, Brown, 1977. 490 p. $19.95 (paper). ISBN 0316604410; 0316604429 (paper).

This has been written for those with no formal botanical training and discusses 1,375 wildflowers, shrubs, and vines of the northeastern United States. The Newcomb system is based on answering five basic questions on flower, plant, and leaf type for diagnostic identification, and relies on easily seen features that are unique to the species in question. There are black-and-white illustrations.

### Peterson Field Guide Series

This may be the best-known and most highly regarded field guide series, and it includes field guides covering almost every group of plants in almost every part of North America.

916 Cobb, Boughton. *A Field Guide to the Ferns and Their Families: Northeastern and Central North America with a Section on Species also Found in the*

*British Isles and Western Europe.* Boston, MA: Houghton Mifflin, 1963. 288 p. $18.00 (paper). ISBN 0395975123 (paper).

Covers 500 species of ferns found as far north as Maine and southern Ontario, as far west as central Wisconsin, and as far south as northern Tennessee.

917   Craighead, John J., Frank C. Craighead, Jr. and Ray J. Davis. *A Field Guide to Rocky Mountain Wildflowers from Northern Arizona and New Mexico to British Columbia.* Boston, MA: Houghton Mifflin, 1963. 288 p. $21.00 (paper). ISBN 0395936136 (paper).

Includes 590 species found in the Rocky Mountain region; includes color photographs as well as color and black-and-white illustrations.

Foster, Steven, and James A. Duke. *A Field Guide to Medicinal Plants and Herbs of Eastern and Central North America.* 2nd ed.
See chapter 5 for full annotation.

Foster, Steven, and Christopher Hobbs. *A Field Guide to Western Medicinal Plants and Herbs.*
See chapter 5 for full annotation.

918   McKnight, Kent H., and Vera B. McKnight. *A Field Guide to Mushrooms, North America.* Boston, MA: Houghton Mifflin, 1987. 429 p. $21.00 (paper). ISBN 0395910900 (paper).

Includes 1,000 species of mushrooms from North America north of Mexico.

919   Niehaus, Theodore F. *A Field Guide to Pacific States Wildflowers: Field Marks of Species Found in Washington, Oregon, California, and Adjacent States.* Boston, MA: Houghton Mifflin, 1976. 432 p. $19.00 (paper). ISBN 0395910951 (paper).

Covers over 1,400 species found in the Pacific Coast states along with Nevada, part of Utah, far southern British Columbia, and the northern section of Baja California.

920   Niehaus, Theodore F. *A Field Guide to Southwestern and Texas Wildflowers.* Boston, MA: Houghton Mifflin, 1984. 464 p. $21.00 (paper). ISBN 0395936128 (paper).

Covers over 1,500 species of flowers found in Arizona, New Mexico, Colorado, and Texas; arranged by flower color and shape. Includes cacti.

Peterson, Lee. *A Field Guide to Edible Wild Plants of Eastern and Central North America.*
See chapter 5 for full annotation.

921  Peterson, Roger Tory, and Margaret McKenny. *A Field Guide to Wildflowers of Northeastern and North-Central North America*. Boston, MA: Houghton Mifflin, 1968. 480 p. $19.00 (paper). ISBN 0395911729 (paper).

Includes about 1,300 species of flowers as far west as Minnesota and as far south as Kentucky, including southern Ontario. It is arranged by flower color and appearance.

922  Petrides, George A. *A Field Guide to Trees and Shrubs: Field Marks of All Trees, Shrubs, and Woody Vines That Grow Wild in the Northeastern and North-Central United States and in Southeastern and South-Central Canada*. 2nd ed. Boston, MA: Houghton Mifflin, 1972. 448 p. $19.00 (paper). ISBN 039535370X (paper).

Includes about 650 species of trees, shrubs, and vines found in northeastern United States and southeast Canada. Petrides's *A Field Guide to Eastern Trees*, below, has partly superseded this guide, but does not include shrubs and vines.

923  Petrides, George A. *A Field Guide to Eastern Trees: Eastern United States and Canada, Including the Midwest*. 1st ed., expanded. Boston, MA: Houghton Mifflin, 1998. 441 p. $19.00 (paper). ISBN 0395904552 (paper).

About 445 trees from the eastern half of North America are included in this field guide. The expanded edition includes some color photographs as well as the usual high-quality illustrations.

924  Petrides, George A. *A Field Guide to Western Trees: Western United States and Canada*. 1st ed, expanded. Boston, MA: Houghton Mifflin, 1998. 428 p. $20.00 (paper). ISBN 0395904544 (paper).

Covers nearly 400 species of trees found as far east as the Dakotas; trees are grouped by visual similarities. This edition includes color photographs as well as color illustrations.

925  Phillips, Roger. *Trees of North America and Europe*. New York: Random House, 1978. $29.95 (paper). ISBN 0394502590; 0394735412 (paper).

This beautifully illustrated book is a photographic guide to the major species of trees that grow in temperate climates. It consists of a pictorial key to the species, arranged by leaf shape, and descriptions and photographs of the trees, arranged by scientific name. As in the previous book, the photographs are excellent and include shots of the bark and, where applicable, the cone, flowers, and fruit of each species as well as a drawing of the tree shape.

926  Phillips, Roger. *Mushrooms of North America*. Boston, MA: Little, Brown, 1991. 319 p. ISBN 0316706124, 0316706132 (paper).

Unlike most identification guides, this book features studio photographs of mushrooms rather than photographs of mushrooms in the field. It includes a visual key to major genera for beginners as well as the usual discussion of edible and poisonous species. The species accounts of 1,000 common mushrooms include brief, rather technical descriptions, habitat, season, edibility, and comments.

### Pictured Key Series

All of the volumes in this very successful series present introductory discussions on how to look, where to look, how to collect, and how to use dichotomous keys. Although written for the amateur botanist or student, the Pictured Key guides are more technical than most guides and cover "oddball" groups of plants that other field guide series avoid. Each volume includes glossaries, indexes, and numerous illustrations. Most are still in print.

927    Abbott, Isabella A., and E. Yale Dawson. *How to Know the Seaweeds*. 2nd ed. Dubuque, IA: William C. Brown, 1978. 141 p. (Pictured Key Nature Series). $47.25 (spiral-bound). ISBN 0697048950; 0697048926 (spiral-bound).

Covers 175 genera of common or conspicuous seaweeds found along the Atlantic, Gulf, and Pacific coasts of North America. Some of the plants are identified to the species, but most are only to the genus.

928    Conard, Henry Shoemaker, and Paul L. Redfearn, Jr. *How to Know the Mosses and Liverworts*. 2nd ed. Dubuque, IA: William C. Brown, 1979. 275 p. $31.25 (spiral-bound). ISBN 0697047695; 0697047687 (spiral-bound).

This second edition includes extensive taxonomic revisions and additional species.

929    Cronquist, Arthur. *How to Know the Seed Plants*. Dubuque, IA: William C. Brown, 1979. 250 p. $47.25. ISBN 0697047601; 069704761X (spiral-bound).

Keys out most plant families, with emphasis on plants from the United States.

930    Dawson, Elmer Yale. *How to Know the Cacti*. Dubuque, IA: William C. Brown, 1963. 158 p.

Identifies 170 species of cacti.

931    Hale, Mason E. *How to Know the Lichens*. 2nd ed. Dubuque, IA: William C. Brown, 1979. 246 p. $47.25. ISBN 0697047628; 0697047636 (spiral-bound).

Keys out 427 species of lichens, exclusive of crustose forms. *Brodo's Lichens of North America*, in the Taxonomy section above, is the only other identification resource for North American lichens and provides updated nomenclature.

932   Kapp, Ronald O., Owen K. Davis, and James E. King. *Ronald O. Kapp's Pollen and Spores*. 2nd ed. Dallas, TX: American Association of Stratigraphic Palynologists Foundation, 2000. 279 p. ISBN 931871050 (paper).

Originally titled *How to Know Pollen and Spores*, this guide has been extensively revised with an extended introduction. The guide identifies pollen of common North American plants, primarily wind-blown pollen from vascular plants, although some moss and fungal spores are also included. Most of the identification is to the species, although some difficult examples are only to the genus or family. This new edition includes a systematic list of the pollen and spores covered in the book as well as a glossary, bibliography, and index.

933   Mickel, John T. *How to Know the Ferns and Fern Allies*. Dubuque, IA: William C. Brown, 1979. 250 p. $31.25 (spiral-bound). ISBN 0697047717 (spiral-bound).

Illustrated keys to 400 species of North American ferns.

934   Pohl, Richard Walter. *How to Know the Grasses*. 3rd ed. Dubuque, IA: William C. Brown, 1978. 200 p. $30.00 (spiral-bound). ISBN 0697048772; 0697048764 (spiral-bound).

Provides illustrated keys to 324 out of the 1,400 grass species in North America.

935   Prescott, Gerald Webber. *How to Know the Aquatic Plants*. 2nd ed. Dubuque, IA: William C. Brown, 1980. 158 p. $47.25 (spiral-bound). ISBN 0697047741; 069704775X (spiral-bound).

Keys to 165 common genera of aquatic plants.

936   Preston, Richard J., Jr., and Richard R. Braham. *North American Trees*. 5th ed. Ames, IA: Iowa State Press, 2002. 520 p. $49.99 (paper). ISBN 0813815266 (paper).

The guide covers all trees known to occur spontaneously (native or naturalized) in North America north of Mexico and tropical Florida. The primary means of identification is by keys, although there are illustrations of leaves, twigs, and fruits as well. Each account includes description of each part of the tree (form, leaves, bark, etc.), natural history, and a range map. The language is fairly technical, although there is a glossary.

937   Sargent, Charles S. *Manual of the Trees of North America (Exclusive of Mexico)*. 2nd corrected ed. New York: Dover, 1965. 2 vol. $13.95 (paper, vol. 1); $13.95 (paper, vol. 2). ISBN 0486202771 (paper, vol. 1); 048620278X (paper, vol. 2).

This is the monumental work of a great dendrologist. It is comprehensive, authoritative, and the standard reference for native American trees. There are synoptic and analytical keys plus 100 other keys; 783 illustrations are included for 66 families with 185 genera and 717 species. This edition is a reprint of the 1922 edition of the work first published in 1905.

938    Schnell, Donald E. *Carnivorous Plants of the United States and Canada.* 2nd ed. Portland, OR: Timber, 2002. 468 p. $39.95. ISBN 0881925403.

This guide to carnivorous green plants is appropriate for the beginning botanist. The author discusses the biology, ecology, and cultivation of carnivorous plants in the introduction, and then provides detailed accounts of each North American species. The accounts include taxonomic information, detailed description, flowering season, distribution, habitat, biology, and cultural notes. There are many color photographs as well.

939    Smith, Alexander H., and Nancy S. Weber. *The Mushroom Hunter's Field Guide: All Color and Enlarged.* Ann Arbor, MI: University of Michigan Press, 1980. 316 p. $24.95. ISBN 0472856103.

This is a standard beginner's field guide to mushrooms that is accurate and dependable, including simple keys, good illustrations, and authoritative descriptions. The coverage emphasizes the Northeast, Great Lakes region, the Rocky Mountains, and the Pacific Northwest. It is not as comprehensive as Miller's *Mushrooms of North America*, above, but is, perhaps, easier to use.

940    Symonds, George W. D. *The Tree Identification Book: A New Method for the Practical Identification and Recognition of Trees.* New York: Morrow, 1958. 272 p. $20.00 (paper). ISBN 0688050395 (paper).

A companion volume to *The Shrub Identification Book*, below. Like its companion, this volume covers trees of the eastern United States, westward to North Dakota, and south to Texas. It contains keys to growth characteristics, thorns, leaves, flowers, fruit, twigs and buds, and bark, which lead to brief descriptions. There are ample photographs of all parts of the trees.

941    Symonds, George W. D. *The Shrub Identification Book: The Visual Method for the Practical Identification of Shrubs, Including Woody Vines and Ground Covers.* New York: Morrow, 1963. 379 p. $22.00 (paper). ISBN 0688050409 (paper).

Still in print, this classic identification guide has obviously proved its usefulness over the years. Its subtitle accurately reflects its purpose. It is easy to use and includes separate keys to the thorns, leaves, flowers, fruit, twigs, and bark of the shrubs. The descriptions are brief but include flowering season and distribution, and there are black-and-white photographs of all parts of the shrub (flowers, twigs, leaves, fruit, and bark).

942   Taylor, Ronald J. *Desert Wildflowers of North America*. Missoula, MT: Mountain, 1998. 349 p. $24.00. ISBN 0878423761.

A highly attractive field guide to more than 500 species of wildflowers and cacti of the Great Basin, Mojave, Painted, and Sonoran deserts, as well as the northernmost parts of the Chihuahuan Desert. It is arranged by family, with color photographs and distribution maps for each species. There is also a key to family, glossary, and introduction to desert ecology and geography.

943   Thonner, Franz. *Thonner's Analytical Key to the Families of Flowering Plants*. Boston, MA: Leiden University Press, 1981. 231 p. ISBN 9060214617; 906021479X (paper).

A translation of the classic *Anleitung zum Bestimmung der Familien der Blutenpflanzen (Phanerrogames)*, 2nd ed., 1917. This is one of the few keys to all families of flowering plants, and can be substituted, in some respects, for Hutchinson and Newcomb. It has been translated from the German and brought up to date so that it may be used with Willis's *Dictionary of the Flowering Plants and Ferns*, 8th edition, and Hutchinson's *Families of Flowering Plants,* 3rd edition. Thonner self-published his key at the beginning of the twentieth century and it was ignored for a long time, but it has since been acknowledged as one of the best worldwide keys available. The key is also available on the Web at http://home.iae.nl/users/linea/index.html.

944   Trelease, William. *Winter Botany*. New York: Dover, 1967. 393 p. $14.95 (paper). ISBN 0486218007 (paper).

Most tree field guides identify plants by their leaves; what to do during the winter when there are no leaves? This classic key to over 1,000 common trees and shrubs without foliage covers the northern United States and a few southern species. Trelease may be used in conjunction with Brown's *Weeds in Winter*. Reprint of the 3rd revised edition published in 1931.

# Textbooks and Treatises

945   Alexopoulos, Constantine John, C. W. Mims, and M. Blackwell. *Introductory Mycology*. 4th ed. New York: Wiley, 1996. 868 p. $110.95. ISBN 0471522295.

This text surveys the fungal kingdom in systematic order. Each taxonomic chapter covers a phylum or order, discussing the biology and general characteristics of the taxa as well as describing each order and genus.

946    Bell, Peter R., and Alan R. Hemsley. *Green Plants: Their Origin and Diversity*. 2nd ed. New York: Cambridge University Press, 2000. 349 p. $38.00 (paper). ISBN 0521641098; 0521646731 (paper).

Surveys the diversity of plant forms, from prokaryotes to angiosperms. It is arranged taxonomically and includes extensive information on the evolution and phylogenetic relationships of the plants.

947    Jeffrey, Charles. *An Introduction to Plant Taxonomy*. 2nd ed. Cambridge, England: Cambridge University Press, 1982. 154 p. ISBN 0521245427; 0521287758 (paper).

This book discusses the fundamentals and process of classification, taxonomic hierarchy, naming of plants, systems of classification, and includes an outline of plant classification and an index. It is suitable as an understandable overview of taxonomy for beginning students and the general public.

948    Judd, Walter S., et. al. *Plant Systematics: A Phylogenetic Approach*. 2nd ed. Sunderland, MA: Sinauer Associates, 2002. 576 p. plus CD-ROM. $92.95. ISBN 0878934030; 0878934022 (CD-ROM).

An undergraduate-level text based on the tree of life. The bulk of the text consists of detailed descriptions of plant families, but there are also sections on general and molecular systematics, classification, and evolution. Appendixes cover nomenclature and specimen preparation and identification. The accompanying CD-ROM, *Photo Gallery of Vascular Plants*, includes 2,200 photos, a glossary, and PDF files listing plant families according to three taxonomic systems.

949    Kitching, Ian J., Peter L. Forey, Christopher J. Humphries, and David M. Williams. *Cladistics: The Theory and Practice of Parsimony Analysis*. 2nd ed. New York: Oxford University Press, 1998. 228 p. (Systematics Association Publication, no. 11). $44.50 (paper). ISBN 0198501390; 0198501382 (paper).

Written by practicing cladists, this text leads readers through the process of cladistic analysis and tree development. It is aimed at advanced students.

950    Moore, Peter D., J. A. Webb, and Margaret E. Collinson. *Pollen Analysis*. 2nd ed. Malden, MA: Blackwell Science, 1991. 216 p. ISBN 0865428956; 0632021764 (paper).

The first edition of this textbook was published in 1978 as *Illustrated Guide to Pollen Analysis*. The authors describe the uses of palynology (the study of pollen and spores), how to collect and treat samples, the anatomy of pollen and spores, and assembling and interpreting data as well as providing a lengthy illustrated key. Most of the taxa included come from North America, northwestern Europe, and the Mediterranean region.

951   Pearson, Lorentz C. *The Diversity and Evolution of Plants*. Boca Raton, FL: CRC, 1995. 646 p. ISBN 0849324831 (paper).

This text is divided by taxonomy into "The Red Line," "The Brown Line," and "The Green Line," plus an introductory section. In contrast to many taxonomic surveys that describe each taxa in detail, the text emphasizes the biology of the plants and their ecological, economic, and research uses.

952   Radford, Albert E. *Fundamentals of Plant Systematics*. New York: Harper and Row, 1986. 498 p. ISBN 0060453052.

Includes information on plant systematics, identification, nomenclature, and speciation as well as extensive information on the botanical literature, herbaria, and botanical gardens. The focus is on the practice of plant systematics rather than on surveying the plant kingdom.

953   Radford, Albert E., W. C. Dickison, J. R. Massey, and C. R. Bell. *Vascular Plant Systematics*. New York: Harper and Row, 1974. 891 p. ISBN 0060453087; 0060453095.

A classic text outlining how to do plant systematics. In addition to discussion of methods, the authors provide extensive lists of the classic taxonomic literature and how to deal with it. Although some of the details are outdated, the text is still valuable.

954   Schuh, Randall T. *Biological Systematics: Principles and Applications*. Ithaca, NY: Cornell University Press, 2000. 236 p. $55.00. ISBN 0801436753.

Although Schuh himself is an entomologist rather than a botanist, this text nicely explains concepts and issues relating to plant cladistic taxonomy as well as animal taxonomy.

955   Singh, Gurcharan. *Plant Systematics*. Enfield, NH: Science, 1999. 258 p. $65.00; $39.50 (paper). ISBN 1578080819; 1578080770 (paper).

The text concentrates on the science of plant taxonomy, with extensive discussion of the history of plant systematics, nomenclature, identification, phylogeny, and taxonomic evidence. There are no descriptions of plant families.

956   Stace, Clive A. *Plant Taxonomy and Biosystematics*. 2nd ed. London: Edward Arnold, 1989. 264 p. ISBN 0713129557.

An introductory text to the theory and practice of plant taxonomy, Stace covers topics such as this history of plant taxonomy, sources of taxonomic information, and the practice of taxonomy. Also includes information on libraries and herbaria, but less extensive than either of Radford's texts, above. Does not describe plant families.

957    Stuessy, Tod F. *Plant Taxonomy: The Systematic Evaluation of Comparative Data.* New York: Columbia University Press, 1990. 514 p. $97.00. ISBN 0231067844.

This textbook, designed for upper-level undergraduate or graduate students, covers the theoretical aspects of plant taxonomy. Data collection and handling is given prominent coverage.

958    Walters, Dirk R., and David J. Keil. *Vascular Plant Taxonomy.* 4th ed., updated version. Dubuque, IA: Kendall/Hunt, 1996. 608 p. $62.95 (paper). ISBN 0787221082 (paper).

Introductory text covering both experimental methods in plant taxonomy and plant diversity, including a survey of plant families. Each chapter has selected references and exercises. Appendixes provide a key to families of vascular plants and a glossary.

959    Webster, John. *Introduction to Fungi.* 2nd ed. New York: Cambridge University Press, 1980. 669 p. ISBN 0521228883; 0521296994 (paper).

Provides a detailed exploration of fungal taxa, with emphasis on easily obtainable specimens. The author discusses economic importance and ecology for each group as well as descriptions and taxonomy.

960    Woodland, Dennis W. *Contemporary Plant Systematics.* 3rd ed. Berrien Springs, MI: Andrews University Press, 2000. 569 p. plus CD-ROM. $64.99. ISBN 1883925258.

Like in Walters's *Vascular Plant Taxonomy,* above, Woodland provides an introductory text discussing both the practice of plant systematics and a survey of the plant kingdom. About one-third of the book consists of accounts of plant families, whereas the remainder covers the science and practice of systematics. There is a chapter on the literature of systematics that provides a list of major sources, but it is not as extensive as Radford's discussion in *Vascular Plant Systematics,* above. The text includes a copy of the CD-ROM *Photo Atlas of the Vascular Plants,* which is also available separately.

961    Zomlefer, Wendy B. *Guide to Flowering Plant Families.* Chapel Hill, NC: University of North Carolina Press, 1994. 430 p. $65.00; $34.95 (paper). ISBN 0807821608; 0807844705 (paper).

Includes descriptions and illustrations of 130 families of interesting or important plants. The descriptions include the number of genera and species, distribution, major genera, North American representatives, economic plants, comments, and references. Introductory material includes a discussion of taxonomy and information on observing and drawing flowering plants. Appendixes list the families according to Cronquist's system (Zomlefer uses Thorne's system), and there is a chart summarizing morphological features of each family.

# Associations

962   American Society of Plant Taxonomists (ASPT). c/o Dept. of Botany 3165, University of Wyoming, Laramie, WY 82071-3165. Phone: 307-766-2556. Fax: 307-766-2851. E-mail: aspt@uwyo.edu. URL: http://www.aspt.net/.

Botanists and others interested in all phases of plant taxonomy. Publishes *Systematic Botany*, *Systematic Botany Monographs*, newsletter.

963   International Association for Plant Taxonomy (IAPT). c/o Institute of Botany, University of Vienna, Rennweg 14, A-1030 Vienna, Austria. Phone: 43 1 427754098. Fax: 43 1 427754099. E-mail: office@iapt-taxon.org. URL: http://www.botanik.univie.ac.at/iapt/.

Coordinates work related to plant taxonomy and international codification of plant names. Formerly the Commission on the Nomenclature of Plants. Publishes *Regnum Vegetabile* and *Taxon*.

964   International Commission for the Nomenclature of Cultivated Plants (ICNCP). c/o Dr. C. D. Brickell, Chairman, The Camber, The Street, Nutbourne, Pulborough, West Sussex RH20 2HE, England, U. K. E-mail: brickell.camber@btinternet.com. URL: http://www.ishs.org/sci/icra.htm.

Cultivated plant taxonomists in 14 countries representing the fields of agriculture, forestry, and horticulture. Publishes *International Code of Nomenclature for Cultivated Plants*.

965   International Organization of Plant Biosystematists (IOPB). c/o Peter C. Hoch, Missouri Botanical Garden, P. O. Box 299, St. Louis, MO 63166-0299. Phone: 314-577-5175. Fax: 314-577-0820. E-mail: hoch@mobot.org. URL: http://www.iopb.org.

Scientists in 35 countries interested in promoting international cooperation in the study of biosystematics. Publishes *IOPB Newsletter*.

966   Missouri Botanical Garden. 4344 Shaw Boulevard, St. Louis, MO 63110. Phone: 314-577-9400 or 800-642-8842. URL: http://www.mobot.org/.

One of the world's top research botanical gardens and host to many of the taxonomic databases and floras mentioned in this chapter. Hosts annual systematics seminar. Publishes *Annals of the Missouri Botanical Gardens*; *Novon*; and many books on systematic botany.

967   New York Botanical Garden. 200th Street and Kazimiroff Boulevard. Bronx, NY 10458-5126. Phone: 718-817-8700. URL: http://www.nybg.org/.

One of the great research botanical gardens. Hosts annual systematics symposium. Publishes *Botanical Review*; *Brittonia*; and *Economic Botany*, as well as books on systematics, economic botany, and conservation.

968   Organization for Flora Neotropica (OFN). New York Botanical Garden, Bronx, NY 10458-5126. Phone: 718-817-8625. Fax: 718-220-6504. E-mail: wthomas@nybg.org. URL: http://www.nybg.org/bsci/ofn/ofn.html.

Established by the United Nations Educational, Scientific and Cultural Organization. Representatives from countries and organizations actively concerned with the taxonomy of neotropical flora, and interested individuals. Conducts research on plants of the New World. Publishes *Flora Neotropica Monographs*.

969   Royal Botanic Gardens, Kew. Richmond, Surrey, TW9 3AB, U. K. Phone: 44 020 8332 5655. Fax: 44 020 8332 5197. E-mail: info@kew.org. URL: http://www.rbgkew.org.uk.

One of the world's great research botanical gardens. Publishes *Kew Bulletin*; *Kew Journal*; *Kew Scientist*; and many bibliographies, catalogs, floras, databases, and reference works.

970   Willi Hennig Society. c/o Dr. William Presch, Treasurer, Department of Biological Science, California State University–Fullerton, Fullerton, California 92834. Phone: 714-278-3774-2215. Fax: 714-278-4289. E-mail: wpresch@fullerton.edu. URL: http://www.cladistics.org/.

An international association established to promote scientific exchange in the field of phylogeny. The society publishes *Cladistics* and sponsors an annual meeting. Its Web site contains educational material such as links to databases and explanations of cladistics, information on performing cladistic analyses, and society activities.

# References

Bramwell, David. 2002. How many plant species are there? *Plant Talk* 28:32–34. http://www.plant-talk.org/stories/28bramw.html.

Govaerts, Rafael. 2001. How many species of seed plants are there? *Taxon* 50(4):1085–1090.

Scotland, Robert W., and Alexandra H. Wortley. 2003. How many species of seed plants are there? *Taxon* 52(1):101–104.

# INDEX

Note: Reference and information sources are indicated by *italic* type.

# ABOUT THE AUTHORS

DIANE SCHMIDT is Biology Librarian and Associate Professor of Library Administration at the University of Illinois at Urbana-Champaign. She is a member of the Special Library Association and was awarded the SLA Biomedical and Life Science Division's Distinguished Member Award in 2004. She is also the author of more than ten articles and author or co-author of several bibliographic guides, including *Using the Biological Literature: A Practical Guide, Guide to Reference and Information Sources in the Zoological Sciences*, and *A Guide to Field Guides: Identifying.*

MELODY M. ALLISON is Assistant Biology Librarian and Assistant Professor of Library Administration at the University of Illinois at Urbana-Champaign. She has been active in the Medical Library Association Nursing and Allied Health Resources Section Task Force to Map the Literature of Nursing, and is the NAHRS Chair-Elect and Program Chair.

KATHLEEN A. CLARK is Biotechnology Librarian at the University of Illinois Urbana-Champaign since the Fall of 2001, where she is Associate Professor of Library Administration.

PAMELA F. JACOBS is Associate University Librarian for Collection Resources at Brock University, St. Catharines, Ontario. She is an active member of the Canadian and Ontario Library Associations and is co-author of *Using the Biological Literature: A Practical Guide.*

MARIA A. PORTA is Assistant Acquisitions Librarian and Associate Professor of Library Administration at the University of Illinois, Urbana-Champaign, and former Assistant Agriculture Librarian. She is the author of over ten articles and book chapters.